Dante's Gluttons

Dante's Gluttons

Food and Society from the Convivio to the Comedy

Danielle Callegari

LONDON AND NEW YORK

First published in 2022 by Amsterdam University Press Ltd.

Published 2025 by Routledge
4 Park Square, Milton Park, Abingdon, Oxon OX14 4RN
605 Third Avenue, New York, NY 10158

Routledge is an imprint of the Taylor & Francis Group, an informa business

ISBN: 9789463720427 (hbk)
ISBN: 9781041177920 (pbk)
ISBN: 9781003693666 (ebk)
NUR   684

Cover illustration: *Giotto's Wedding at Cana* (c. 1305, Scrovegni Chapel).

Cover design: Coördesign, Leiden

DOI   10.5117/9789463720427

For Product Safety Concerns and Information please contact our EU
representative: GPSR@taylorandfrancis.com
Taylor & Francis Verlag GmbH, Kaufingerstraße 24, 80331 München, Germany

For my sisters

Table of Contents

Acknowledgments

Finishing your first book is never easy, but a pandemic really puts a fine point on that statement. When I began this project I had many grand intentions; I hope to have fulfilled at least some of them. Whatever I have managed to do has been, like all worthy achievements, with the help of a rich network of caring and encouraging supporters.

This project came into being with the help of several institutions along the way, including multiple fellowships from Dartmouth College and New York University, and grants from the UCLA Center for Medieval and Renaissance Studies, the Scuola Normale Superiore di Pisa, and the University of California Middle Ages in the Wider World project. I also had the privilege of sharing my work in contexts that permitted me to receive invaluable feedback, notably the annual meeting of the Dante Society of America, the NYU-Columbia University Dante Project of New York, and "Three Days in Paradise" at UC Berkeley. Amsterdam University Press shepherded the book into existence with great care under the auspices of Erika Gaffney and Allen Grieco, both of whom have offered their careful attention and unwavering encouragement. Their exceptional enthusiasm for this project was the reason it came to fruition at all, and I am profoundly grateful for all the hard work they put into ensuring this volume was the best it could be.

En route to finishing this book I have had the pleasure of working alongside some of the finest scholars in literature, Italian or otherwise, beginning with my mentors and cohort at NYU, then my colleagues at UC Berkeley and UC Davis, and now my new colleagues at Dartmouth College. I owe a foundational debt of gratitude to my teacher, John Freccero, who first introduced me to Dante and who first convinced me that I might have something worth saying by being himself willing to listen to me—over a martini, naturally. Jane Tylus, who would eventually usher me all the way through my graduate studies and continue to support my work long beyond that, was a similarly pivotal point of reference at the outset of my studies. Alongside Jane and John, I had the privilege of gaining as an advisor Maria Luisa Ardizzone, whose intimate understanding of the medieval world continues to inspire me, and of working closely with Virginia Cox, who advocated for my work on medieval literature and food while furthermore finding ways for me to dabble in the early modern. While still at NYU, I met Fiona Griffiths, who became a mentor and confidant in addition to a source of incredible expertise. I spent many of these formative years in Florence, where the marvelous Bruce Edelstein took me under his wing and made it possible for me to approach research in my adopted country and adopted language, and also in Pisa, where Lina Bolzoni saw that I was fully immersed in Italian academic culture at the Scuola Normale.

At UC Berkeley, I was warmly received by Albert Ascoli, Steven Botterill, Mia Fuller, and Barbara Spackman, all of whom offered their support in various forms and ensured I never lost momentum in my research. Albert worked tirelessly to create opportunities in which I could share my work, and through which he could share his wisdom, and to have Steven read my writing was an unparalleled gift, felt even more keenly in his absence. Being part of the UC community gave me access to a network of medievalists who helped me to understand how this book could speak to a larger audience, beginning with Maureen Miller, whose Middle Ages in the Wider World project put me in touch with many generous colleagues, including Matthew Vernon, who was kind enough to read pieces of this manuscript in draft form and give insightful feedback.

Since arriving at Dartmouth, I have had the distinct pleasure of working closely with my co-Italianists Nancy Canepa and Graziella Parati, both of whom took pains to ensure I was well looked-after as I attempted to navigate a new institution while finishing this book. I was also lucky enough to have the Leslie Center for the Humanities sponsor a manuscript review, where I was completely overwhelmed by the generosity of my colleagues Nick Camerlenghi, Cecilia Gaposchkin, and Monika Otter, each of whom read my work closely and supplied incisive, thoughtful comments that gave me the motivation to push through my final revisions. They also—animated especially by Cecilia's incredible energy and that of my colleague in French and Italian Andrea Tarnowski—ensured that I was immediately welcomed into the Dartmouth Medieval Colloquium, where I shared my work and received feedback from the exceptional community of medievalists in the Upper Valley.

This book is, of course, first and foremost about Dante, and the scholars of Dante with whom I have had the honor of working deserve infinite thanks. Teodolinda Barolini was a champion of this project since I began it, and her conviction of its value often buoyed me in moments of discouragement. Alison Cornish more than once gifted me her fullest attention, including as a reader on my manuscript review committee at Dartmouth. Justin Steinberg consistently provided me with brilliant suggestions, often opening my eyes to possibilities I was unable to see myself. I have found a constant source of inspiration in conversations with the broader community of *dantisti*, many of whom offered their time without any expectation, including but not limited to Fabian Alfie, Ron Martinez, Kristina Olson, and Arielle Saiber. Akash Kumar has been equally valuable as a friend and an editor, reading my work, fielding my questions, and offering many virtual toasts in the dark days of revisions in lockdown. He, Beth Coggeshall, and Christiana Purdy Moudarres were especially crucial interlocutors as the manuscript was being completed, helping me to imagine how this work might become part of a new chapter in Dante studies.

To arrive at Dante's food I needed a great deal of help, and Allen Grieco's guidance was absolutely essential. Wandering around the reading rooms at Villa I Tatti, I also met David Rosenthal, who will someday be my co-author on a book about Last Suppers. While this book was still in its infancy, Laura Giannetti made herself available and shared some of the first stages of her own research into food and Italian literature which is now available in her new volume *Food Culture and Literary Imagination in Early Modern Italy: The Renaissance of Taste* (Amsterdam University Press). At the University of Minnesota I was treated to an array of exciting scholarship on Premodern Food Cultures, and while there met Paul Freedman, who has been an exceptionally generous point of reference, reading this manuscript in its entirety and giving me confidence in my steps forward. Along the way, Ken Albala has acted as an infinite font of information as energetic in our conversations as he is in his promotion of the field.

The list of those who answered my questions and offered me insight also includes many people who have not decided to dedicate their lives to Dante, but who have nonetheless been tremendously generous with their time, among them Catherine Flynn, Holly Flora (who helped me to select the cover image for this book), Amanda Gluibizzi, Abhishek Kaicker, Nicole Killian, Jonathan Mullins, Julia Nelsen, Elena Schneider, Stacey VanVleet, and Michael Wyatt. I'm especially grateful to Jessica Goethals, Shannon McHugh, Melissa Swain (who helped me to source the cover image for this book), and Anna Wainwright, who comprise the Women in Italian working group, and who read many, many versions of these chapters and gave careful criticism balanced with cheerful optimism. Joe Perna must also be singled out, for both his incredible friendship and his magnificent editorial skills. I am truly grateful to have availed myself of both often, not only but especially in the course of working on this book, where his exacting attention and sophisticated reflections were completely transformative. My assistant Adrian Russian was a godsend, helping to revise the manuscript and to build the index. To these invested colleagues I also add the voices of my students, so many of whom have inspired me to think more carefully or in a new way about the work I thought I knew so intimately.

Many of the people acknowledged here are both colleagues and dear friends, but there are also many dear friends and family members who have no professional investment and yet humor me still. I am grateful to Vanessa and Jim, who let me sleep on their couch innumerable nights while I commuted transcontinentally, watched me make their dining room table my desk, and kept me well fed when I was too tired to make my own dinner. My thanks also to Carmen Gomez and Katie Parla, both of whom have allowed and continue to allow me to color outside the lines of my academic work, enriching my passion for Italian food and beverage culture by taking me out of the library.

It goes without saying that I could not have done any of this without my big, loud, excessive family, who taught me about conviviality, especially my parents: Nestore, who welcomed me into his life *a braccia aperte*, and John and Kathleen and their companions Mary and Vic, who still "nonchalantly" place everything I've ever written on their coffee tables when guests arrive and shout to anyone who will listen about what a genius I am without ever hesitating to fact-check. I am acutely aware of how rare it is to have grown up with a mother and father who did not understand me but blindly supported all of my efforts, and how lucky I am that our ever-expanding nucleus has only provided me with more love as it has added members.

Diego, with his calming, centering presence and unaffected disposition, gave me the strength to finish this book. I write in the hope to impress him—anything more I accomplish is just icing on the cake.

And finally, I thank my sisters, because when we are at a table together I can look at the rest of the world and say, *la vostra miseria non mi tange*. This book is dedicated to them with the hope that we all die at an age too old to care, from laughing too hard with our mouths full of vintage Dom and Osetra.

Introduction

Ma vegna qua qualunque è per cura familiare o civile nella umana fame rimaso,
e ad una mensa colli altri simili impediti s'assetti; e alli loro piedi si pongano tutti
quelli che per pigrizia si sono stati, ché non sono degni di più alto sedere: e quelli e
questi prendano la mia vivanda col pane che la farà loro e gustare e patire.
Convivio 1.1.13[1]

Or ti riman, lettor, sovra 'l tuo banco,
dietro pensando a ciò che si preliba,
s'esser vuoi lieto assai prima che stanco.
Messo t'ho innanzi: omai per te ti ciba
Par. 10.22–25[2]

While innumerable readers have taken up the invitation to sit down and eat at the medieval poet Dante Alighieri's (1265–1321) banquet of knowledge in the seven hundred years since he first set himself to preparing it, very few of them seem to have asked why Dante insisted on setting a table and feeding his audience to begin with. From the very first dream of the *Vita nuova* in which the beloved feeds on the poet's heart, to the clearly pronounced table of the *Convivio*, to the encounter with Ugolino who chews on his enemy's head in *Inferno* 33, to the vision of salvation in *Paradiso* 24 described by Beatrice as the "gran cena / del benedetto Agnello" (great

---

1   "But let everyone come here whose truly human hunger remains unassuaged because of pressures of family or civic responsibilities; he is invited to take his place at table with all the others who have been similarly impeded. All whom laziness has held back may make a place for themselves at the others' feet, for they do not deserve a higher seat. And let each group take my food along with the bread provided, which will enable them both to taste and assimilate it." All citations from the *Convivio* are taken from Dante, *Convivio*, ed. Inglese, and Dante, *The Banquet*, ed. and trans. Ryan.
2   "Now stay there, reader, on your bench, thinking back on your foretaste here, if you wish to rejoice long before you tire; I have set before you, now feed yourself." All citations from the *Comedy* are taken from Dante, *La Commedia secondo l'antico vulgata*, ed. Petrocchi; translations are from Dante, *The Divine Comedy of Dante Alighieri*, ed. and trans. Durling and Martinez.

Callegari, D., *Dante's Gluttons: Food and Society from the Convivio to the Comedy.*
Taylor & Francis Group, 2022
DOI 10.5117/9789463720427_INTRO

feast of the blessed Lamb; *Par.* 24.1–2), many of the poet's best known verses rely on food or eating. *Dante's Gluttons: Food and Society from the* Convivio *to the* Comedy explores how Dante uses food to articulate and reinforce, criticize and condemn, and at times consciously manipulate the social, political, and cultural values of his time. Combining medieval history, food studies, and literary criticism, *Dante's Gluttons* historicizes food and eating in Dante, beginning with his earliest collected poetry and arriving at the end of his major work. By interrogating the contemporary cultural associations of "gluttons" and "gluttony"—the figures Dante characterizes by the foods they consume and how they consume them—this book establishes how one of the world's preeminent authors uses the intimacy and universality of food as a cultural touchstone, communicating through a gastronomic language rooted in the deeply human relationship with material sustenance. Using the language of food, Dante establishes our responsibility to create and sustain community through the act of nourishment and giving of the self.

While the absence of food has often been the focus of investigations into medieval literary culture, food was a very present, tangible, and accessible currency to all medieval people. Then as now, food was at once ceremonious and quotidian, occult and familiar. The range of ideas it continues to express is distinctively enhanced by its ability to go unnoticed, as it is an expected component of nearly every social interface and relevant to every human community. Food's power as a symbol, too, is rooted in its interaction with the body: to be alive one must eat, and by eating, one gives life. Because the relationship with food transcends chronologies and geographies—everyone must eat to live, in all places and all times—it offers a perfect basis for developing a language unbound by those limiting elements, one that can communicate a system of thought across cultures. Yet this same relationship with food also acquires specific terms in any given population, so even as the tensions Dante describes with respect to the appetite or the effects of consumption on the body remain universal and timeless, they take on value according to the community in which they are cultivated. Moreover, and of special importance to this book, the act of recording these values itself inscribes a value system, so that as Dante uses food to construct a vernacular and address the most pressing debates of his time, he affirms that the relationship with food and eating is the best means by which to do this, investing the act of expressing oneself through food as well as the food items themselves with meaning. Dante is an icon of the medieval in his status as its most famous product, but also because he infused its values and preoccupations into his works. Using diet and the struggle to find balance and satiation, Dante speaks to and for his time in the language that most accurately embodies it.

The abundance of research on food and foodways in the European Middle Ages now enables a thorough contextualization of food and eating practices in Dante's work. Food historians such as Ken Albala and Allen J. Grieco have provided substantial overviews of the intertwined relationships among food, class, and power in late medieval and early modern Europe.[3] Massimo Montanari has created an entire library of statistical and anecdotal accounts of the cultural values of food in medieval Italy, and Bruno Laurioux has reconstructed the rich network of culinary texts that circulated widely in the late thirteenth and early fourteenth centuries, especially on the Italian peninsula.[4] Paul Freedman has explored the spice trade, at once opening up a new branch of economic and social history and successfully undoing many of the primitivist myths surrounding medieval taste and choice.[5] Research on medieval medicine and its deep, nuanced connections with diet has been provided by historians of medieval medical culture, in particular in the important studies of Nancy Siraisi.[6] The vast body of work on gender, medieval theophilosophy, and food from Caroline Walker Bynum could alone prompt a reconsideration of all the literature produced in the period, not least the work of a poet deeply concerned with reaching a wide and diverse audience that explicitly included women, at least in the case of the *Convivio*.[7]

Approaching Dante through the material and cultural elements with which he engages has in fact already proven to be a fruitful path toward understanding the poet's ability to engage with such diverse audiences over centuries. In her examination of fashion in the *Comedy,* Kristina Olson has established that Dante uses clothing to articulate surprisingly complex and even revolutionary ideas, precisely because clothes signal social values through the quotidian. As she observes, "Dress forms an essential part of Dante's lexicon that is at once other-worldly and bound up in the things of

---

3   See Albala, *Eating Right in the Renaissance* and *A Cultural History of Food in the Renaissance;* Grieco, *Food, Social Politics and the Order of Nature in Renaissance Italy.*

4   For just a few examples particularly relevant to the present study, see Laurioux, "I libri di cucina italiani alla fine del Medioevo: un nuovo bilancio," pp. 33–58; Montanari, *L'alimentazione contadina nell'alto Medioevo, Alimentazione e cultura nel medioevo,* and *La fame e l'abbondanza.*

5   Freedman, *Out of the East,* and *Food: A History of Taste.*

6   Siraisi, *Taddeo Alderotti and his Pupils: Two Generations of Italian Medical Learning,* and *Medieval & Early Renaissance Medicine: An Introduction to Knowledge and Practice.*

7   See Bynum, *Holy Feast and Holy Fast,* and *The Resurrection of the Body in Western Christianity, 1200–1336.*

this world."[8] Olson distinguishes a crucial difference in Dante's perception of the corruption of his native city by reading the fashions he describes closely, demonstrating that Dante does not in fact see women as exclusively responsible for the immorality of contemporary Florence; instead, his writing provides a fuller view of all-gendered participation in the civic-cultural deterioration he witnessed. Also in a sartorial vein, Ronald Martinez has used textile mechanics and tailoring practice to identify a pattern against which Dante's poetic/political "weaving" can be viewed as a path toward the restoration of empire and human justice.[9] Looking carefully at legal culture, Justin Steinberg has shown that Dante's ability to create poetry—indeed, his very definition of art and self-expression—is strongly connected to his understanding of freedom, privilege, and sovereignty, concepts grounded in the active contemporary debates of the medieval justice system.[10] In his study of the musical structuring of the *Comedy,* Francesco Ciabattoni tracks a back-and-forth motion between the use of music in the poem and parallel progress in the musical culture of Dante's time, emphasizing how the poet was influenced by and became himself an influence in the textures of the medieval musical world.[11]

Using this rich body of critical work on Dante's dialogue with material culture alongside archival research on premodern Italian food and foodways, this book takes Dante's "gluttons" as its point of departure, arguing that no reading of Dante is complete without a firm understanding of the meaning of food in everyday life. By reconstructing the shared significance of foods and their perceived values, *Dante's Gluttons* establishes how Dante uses food and eating practices as a means to delineate the boundaries of his community—both a lived, political reality, with its associated civic duties and privileges, and a poetic one, tied together with a literary language that transcends boundaries of time and space by virtue of its ability to grow and change like the people who use it. Intertwining medieval literature, history, and gastronomy, the book confirms that food is an omnipresent communicator, and that it is the means by which Dante's work maintains its significance and accessibility today.

8   Olson, "Shoes, Gowns and Turncoats," p. 27. See also her study of sumptuary legislation and the use of the uncovered female body as a market of corruption, Olson, "Uncovering the Historical Body of Florence."

9   Martinez, "Dante 'buon sartore,'" pp. 22–61.

10   Steinberg, *Dante and the Limits of the Law.*

11   Ciabattoni, *Dante's Journey to Polyphony.* Alison Cornish has also explored this element of the poet's work specifically with respect to *Paradiso* 20, in "Music, Justice, and Violence in *Paradiso* 20," pp. 112–41.

Approaching Food in Dante

To suggest that food plays a pivotal role in the works of Dante is so obvious as to seem almost absurd. The author of the *Convivio* is hardly subtle in his reliance on the figure of the meal in his work, and the preponderance of food images and language has certainly not eluded the attention of scholars. Yet neither has it prompted any substantial or systematic study of their presence. In his classic study, Ernst Robert Curtius notably marked Dante as the foremost exponent of the type of metaphorics he branded "alimentary," though he opted not to explore their use nor the reasoning behind it further.[12] Marianne Shapiro observed that "on balance, hunger devours more of Dante's text than does lust, and its treatment is very little nuanced," and Pina Palma has underlined that it was Dante who first fully understood how food fused the human and the divine, a key reason for which food later became so important to Italian literature, if not all vernacular literature on the continent.[13] However, studies of food imagery in Dante have remained primarily focused on liturgical or biblical precedents, combing sources for visions of spiritual consumption and satiation.[14] The result is that even where the poet announces that the substance of his text will be like a material food, and that reading it will be akin to sitting at a table and enjoying a meal among companions, readers of Dante have not seriously or precisely considered what the poet might be offering through the use of these figures, nor the broader nutritional model itself.

The lack of attention to food in Dante may in part be due to a modern prejudice against the world of the Middle Ages. For most of the last century, sexuality and economics were far more studied by both medieval literary scholars and historians, perhaps because food did not and does not feel present to the modern imagination of the medieval.[15] The Renaissance, along with great art and grandiose architecture, evokes images of dance, music, and lively intellectual exchange accompanied by luxurious banqueting.

---

12   Curtius, *European Literature and the Latin Middle Ages*, p. 136.

13   Shapiro, *Dante and the Knot of Body and Soul*, p. 9; Palma, *Savoring Power, Consuming the Times*, pp. 27–31.

14   See Gibbons, "Alimentary Metaphors in Dante's *Paradiso*," pp. 693–706; O'Brien, "The 'Bread of Angels' in *Paradiso* II," pp. 97–106. The contributions by Purdy Moudarres, "Devouring Selves in the Circle of Gluttony," and Chiodo, "Tutti i frutti," in *Table Talk*, ed. Purdy Moudarres, offer two interpretations that open up the discussion by uniting theological concerns with medieval science and medicine.

15   See the complaint voiced in the mid-1980s by Bynum in "Fast, Feast, Flesh," pp. 1–25. If historians have increasingly turned to food in the intervening decades, studies of food in medieval literature remain limited, and rarer still in Italian literature.

The Middle Ages, on the other hand, recall asceticism, solitude, and lean times in cold palaces. This is not necessarily a misinterpretation of the contemporary reality—demographic, meteorologic, and technological pressures meant that most medieval European people lived under severe conditions—but it has frequently led to erroneous conclusions or extrapolations. The scarcity of food neither diminished its power to convey meaning nor its metaphoric omnipresence. When Jacques Le Goff termed the late medieval European continent a "universe of hunger," his purpose was to underscore the way in which food economies became a major factor in defining class, status, and the medieval self.[16] Ken Albala has illustrated how increased competition for food or impending famine in reality heightened its relational significance, and often led to an elaboration of the social and political values associated with foods.[17] Caroline Walker Bynum has repeatedly shown that food was the primary means of communicating courage, power, and virtue, precisely because of the more immediate threat of famine.[18]

The scholarly indifference to food in Dante in particular may also be due to a methodological bias against the use of material culture to read the poet's work. Despite the substantial increase in historical explorations of food on the peninsula over the last several decades, and in particular the depth of vision provided by historians of food and literature like Piero Camporesi and Bruno Laurioux, relatively few considerations of food in Italian literature have emerged.[19] Dantisti have traditionally responded with hesitance to the historical contextualization of the poet's work, and the placement of food at the bottom of the hierarchy of material culture studies in the literature of the canon makes it an unlikely place from which to test that position. Like Curtius, who first acknowledged but then dismissed Dante's alimentary metaphors in order to favor the more ancient and austere nautical ones, scholars of Dante have felt a certain distaste in giving too much attention to food-based figurative language in the work of their author.

The tendency to simultaneously accept Dante's heavy reliance on this tool (and even attribute its ubiquity in later literature to its development under his auspices) but resist the need to further nuance its presence has limited modern readers' understanding of Dante. It is certain that food was

16   Le Goff, *La civilisation de l'occident médiéval*, p. 290.
17   Albala, *Eating Right in the Renaissance*, pp. 186–87.
18   Bynum, "Fast, Feast, Flesh."
19   See Camporesi, *The Magic Harvest*, trans. Hall; Laurioux, *Le moyen âge à table* and *Scrivere il Medioevo: lo spazio, la santità, il cibo, un libro dedicato ad Odile Redon*. For exceptions, see Palma, *Savoring Power, Consuming the Times* and Purdy Moudarres, *Table Talk*.

not trivial to medieval people, and it is certain that Dante would not have turned to it unthinkingly. Teodolinda Barolini has voiced the need to address this critical lacuna and the dismissal of the "very real and material forms of life and culture" Dante uses as the basis for his metaphors, including food, proposing that new scholars of Dante "Only Historicize!"[20] Robert Durling significantly argued that investigating food imagery in the *Comedy* would almost certainly lead us closer to "some of the fundamental issues of [Dante's] poetics," and followed the thread from its explicit beginnings in the *Convivio* through to the complications and preoccupations it conveys in the *Comedy*.[21] Imagining the finished poem as a healthy body and contrasting it with the diseased organs of lower Hell, Durling moved back and forth between the consumption and digestion that leads to physical growth in the individual and the analogous intellectual process that grows a mind, a parallel that is fully delineated in the poet's major work. Durling's approach not only demonstrates the richness of a reading that takes food and physiology as points of departure for interpreting intellectual expression and the produc-tion of literature, it establishes the integral role of a nutritional-generational model in Dante's poetry. If knowledge is food, its digestion and assimilation will set the reproductive process in motion, but it is up to Dante to determine a way to serve it without creating the dyspepsia that plagues the residents of the infernal city.

Durling's emphasis on the "usefulness of the body" in the *Comedy* in particular is part of a substantial tradition that probes medieval scientific patrimony for Dante's sources, most notably through the work of Bruno Nardi.[22] The groundwork laid by Nardi prompted a number of closer analyses of Dante's scientific culture, especially the way in which texts on anatomy and physiology newly available to Dante and his contemporaries informed the poet's understanding of the interaction between the mind and body.[23] Patrizia Bertini Malgarini's extensive account of medical and anatomical language confirmed that the Galenic concepts of humors and complexions fully permeate all of Dante's works, and that biological (pre)conditions are perceived and reported in his descriptions of himself and the individuals he

---

20   Barolini, "'Only Historicize': History, Material Culture and the Future of Dante Studies," p. 39.

21   Durling, "Deceit and Digestion in the Belly of Hell," p. 62.

22   For this term and a further elaboration of the body as a structural principal in the *Comedy*, see Durling, "Body," in *The Dante Encyclopedia*, ed. Lansing, p. 116; and Durling, "The Body and the Flesh in the *Purgatorio*" in *Dante for the New Millennium*, ed. Barolini and Storey, pp. 183–191.

23   Many of Nardi's publications are relevant here but perhaps most important is *Dante e la cultura medievale: nuovi saggi di filosofia dantesca*.

encounters.[24] Employing these sources to read more closely, Patrick Boyde made numerous suggestive connections between the medieval science of the body and the production of visions and dreams in Dante's poetry, reflecting on the verisimilitude created in the hazy recollections of the *Vita nuova* by indications of complexion changes.[25] The concepts of *complessione* and physical ability or impairment are readily addressed as important concerns to the philosopher of the *Convivio*, as Luca Bianchi has highlighted, for without a healthy body, there is no chance to engage the mind.[26]

In a similar vein but with focused attention on the major work, scholars like Vivian Nutton and Simon Gilson have shed light on the influence of dietary and medical tracts on Dante's development of the *contrapasso* and the bodily images which feel punishment in Hell.[27] In the first canticle of the poem, humoral theory and dietary disorder beset the damned; corporeal descriptions are provided for the pilgrim, the shades, and the very design of lower Hell which the reader can follow like an anatomical map. More than this, as Christiana Purdy Moudarres has shown, Dante's depiction of the sin of gluttony (and its correction) engages directly with contemporary debates on the effects of consumption not just on the body but also on one's identity and soul.[28] Manuele Gragnolati, too, has reiterated that physical signs must be read in the central canticle as well, as it is the space where the spirit and the flesh are reconciled rather than severed.[29]

Exploring the substantial circulation of illuminated texts like the *Tacuinum sanitatis* and other medical-nutritional pamphlets, Simon Gilson has proposed that these sources be understood as a "common intellectual patrimony that was diffused in a wide range of medical textbooks and other writings that condensed their teachings," one that Dante and his contemporaries had absorbed into their milieux.[30] The same can be said for the gastronomic texts of the period, the prevalence of which testify to a shared awareness of

24 Malgarini, "Il linguaggio medico e anatomico nelle opere di Dante," pp. 1–108.

25 Boyde, *Perception and Passion in Dante's Comedy*.

26 Bianchi, "*Noli comedere panem philosophorum inutiliter*," pp. 335–55.

27 Nutton, "Dante, Medicine and the Invisible Body," and Gilson, "The Anatomy and Physiology of the Human Body in the *Commedia*," in *Dante and the Human Body*, ed. Barnes and Petrie, pp. 11–42 and pp. 43–60.

28 See Purdy Moudarres, "Devouring Selves in the Circle of Gluttony," and Purdy Moudarres, "Bodily Starvation and the Ravaging of the Will," pp. 205–28. Purdy Moudarres's forthcoming book, *Dante Poet of the Future: Faith, Science and the Immanence of the Age to Come* promises to make a major contribution to this argument.

29 Gragnolati, *Experiencing the Afterlife*.

30 See Gilson, "The Anatomy and Physiology of the Human Body in the *Commedia*," p. 17, and Malgarini, "Il linguaggio medico e anatomico nelle opere di Dante."

culinary culture and a desire to acquire and exchange knowledge about food preparation and presentation. As the careful philological reconstructions of Jean-Louis Flandrin and Odile Redon have demonstrated, there were numerous texts in both Latin and the vernacular dedicated to ingredients, recipes, and the staging of a meal alongside more scientifically or medically inclined dietary treatises.[31] Anna Martellotti's extensive study of the *Liber de coquina*, which locates its initial production at Frederick II's court in Palermo circa 1230, confirms that attention to the socio-political values of food was a crucial part of a complete intellectual identity at this time, as relevant as the work Frederick commissioned on mathematics, poetry, and law.[32] Indeed, Bruno Laurioux describes the *Liber* and its progeny—for it spawned many further culinary copies—as a "thoroughly diffused network" that began to proliferate in the thirteenth century and that became particularly rich on the Italian peninsula, just as Dante began composing in earnest.[33]

Approaches to Medieval Gluttony

In *An Alphabet for Gourmets*, M. F. K. Fisher provided perhaps the most insightful modern reflection on gluttony, observing that it was the trait that ties all humans together:

> It is a curious fact that no man likes to call himself a glutton, and yet each of us has in him a trace of gluttony, potential or actual. I cannot believe that there exists a single coherent human being who will not confess, at least to himself, that once or twice he has stuffed himself to the bursting point, on anything from quail financière to flapjacks, for no other reason than the beastlike satisfaction of his belly. In fact I pity anyone who has not permitted himself this sensual experience, if only to determine what his own private limitations are, and where, for himself alone, gourmandism ends and gluttony begins.[34]

Her statement might be amended to read "I cannot believe that there exists *or has existed*," since gluttony is a preoccupation that, like the need for food

---

31   See especially Flandrin and Redon, "Les livres de cuisine italiens des XIVe et et XVe siècles," pp. 393–408.
32   Martellotti, *I ricettari di Federico II: Dal* Meriodionale *al* Liber de coquina.
33   Laurioux, "I libri di cucina italiani alla fine del Medioevo," p. 35.
34   Fisher, *An Alphabet for Gourmets*, p. 47.

itself, transcends both space and time. Our relationship with food and the line between eating and overeating—"where gourmandism ends and gluttony begins"—has always been troubling, in large part because that line is flexible and only determined "for [one]self alone." Spanning secular and sacred traditions from antiquity to the present, the excessive desire for food has always been seen as the most likely and thus the most damaging of human proclivities. In contrast to other consumption practices that might be utterly prohibited, from drugs to sex to violence, eating stubbornly refuses to be eliminated as a daily practice. The inability to set immovable boundaries and the multiplicity of poles—between extreme asceticism and unfettered consumption and between hoarding and prodigal hospitality—creates a zone of perennial tension that is constantly challenged by the inadequacy of established social parameters. As any interpretation can demonstrate, be it biological, historical, or anthropological, no human being can survive without eating at least a little bit and occasionally; no community can grow without developing convivial and culinary practices; no state can thrive without effectively provisioning its population. At the same time, too much eating, or even too much thinking about food, is almost universally abhorred, dangerous to society and soul alike.

In the late Middle Ages, widespread famine converged with a growing population and shifting class structures to pose gluttony and food itself as questions of both quantity and quality, with secular and spiritual implications in equal measure. Food consumption (whether in excess or in abstention) and foodstuffs were part of a thoroughly elaborated "socio-gastronomic" value system that was deeply imprinted on the premodern consciousness. This culinary code was woven into medieval literary production, as authors relied upon a collective sensitivity to the significance of food and dietary habits to construct their texts and articulate their arguments. As an author attempting to construct the most ambitious and significant literary work to date using the vernacular, Dante saw food as the omnipresent communicator, and as an exile after his banishment from Florence in 1302 as a result of political turmoil, he suffered from the true threat of possible starvation, recognizing the absolute value of food as sustenance during an itinerant existence that lasted until his death in 1321.

In the nutritional themes the poet makes use of and the broader digestive body of his work, Dante establishes that gluttony is an interaction with food that undermines the social contract: it is a rejection of civic duty that prompts a disintegration of the ties that hold a community together. The corruption of the body provoked by gluttony also leads to a corruption of the soul, not simply by means of turning one's attention away from God or allowing the intellect to wander, but by diluting the essential elements of human identity and adulterating the physical processes through which food leads to reproductivity, both sexual and intellectual. By asking us to reflect on the meaning of overeating, with respect to both food itself as well as the practices relating to the production and consumption of food, Dante's gluttons become an interpretive key, unlocking a reading of his work that has not yet been appreciated by critics but that in fact points to the durability and accessibility of it, reaching through the universally familiar feeling of hunger to touch audiences hundreds of years after the poet finished writing.

Dante's Gluttons demonstrates that for Dante, gluttony is an individual devastation *and* a public tragedy. It begins by bloating and discomposing the body as a result of excess food, then continues to destabilize the core of one's identity and cloud the intellect. It attacks from both sides, inasmuch as it can be the result of a disordered will and its cause, and it attacks the many even as it appears to afflict only the individual. As the encounters with Dante's gluttons show, the danger of the excessive, indiscriminate consumer is found in their own self-sabotage as well as in the domino effect that soon radiates outward, the undermining of healthy exchange and the fissure that opens up in the foundation of the human community. Dante's work strives to root out gluttony through an investigation of its many insidious iterations, which he contrasts with the natural desire and conscious consumption that grow and give back, that acknowledge responsibility and propagate good health. In doing so, he creates a template that functions across all the levels of human contributive potential, wherein there exists a gluttonous personhood, politics, and poetics set against a temperate productivity that binds us all together.

Structure of the Book

With this critical apparatus in place, *Dante's Gluttons* begins with a first chapter that contextualizes and historicizes the idea of gluttony and appropriate eating practices in the medieval world. This chapter confirms Dante's historical moment as a time when the meaning of food was particularly charged, especially in the growing cities of the central Italian peninsula, as populations surged and social ordering and governing techniques alike were increasingly tied to food and foodways. It further considers the peculiar tension created by the highly personal and relativized meanings of gluttony, which developed according to a range of influences, and which were informed by sources Dante would have referenced but that have not been recognized as part of his library, especially the *Liber de coquina* and other culinary texts, that in fact would have been very familiar in Dante's circles. By identifying these crucial influences and elaborating the contemporary context, this chapter lays the foundation for the dialogue between Dante's representations of food and eating and the rich gastronomic culture of his time. It demonstrates that for Dante, gluttony is an interaction with food that assaults a person's body and soul equally, while on a larger scale it undermines the social contract and leads to a break down of community. Gluttony emerges as a primary preoccupation for Dante in that, as a literally senseless, self-defeating process, it stands in perfect opposition to his goal of creating a united community.

The second chapter begins with Dante's youthful poetry and his first "glutton," Dante's friend and poetic rival Forese Donati, whom the poet playfully berates first for his partridge eating and then for his love of mutton. Attending to the hierarchical distinctions expressed by food and foodways in the European Middle Ages, this chapter focuses on social structuring and self-fashioning through food. Mutton and partridge are shown to be examples of figures in a classification that records and reiterates a system of community organization, and they permit Dante to comment in his verses on an established hierarchy and the roles he and his fellow poets play therein. Though superficially the poet calls Donati a "glutton," it is not his over-indulgence in food that is truly targeted, but rather his inability to recognize his responsibility to those around him as demonstrated by his dietary choices. This chapter then reconsiders Dante's use of bread in his philosophical treatise, the *Convivio*, where he positions himself as a distributor of bread to the hungry. Though scholars have often commented on the metaphoric meaning of food and hunger in the treatise, they have not explored the material values that informed the poet's use of this specific food item. Considering the social hierarchy and the social stakes of food, this chapter shows that Dante's metaphoric distribution of bread to the hungry and his condemnation of grain hoarding are in fact a realpolitik explanation of how to maintain power (and how it may be abused). Taking up mutton, partridge, and bread, Dante is not only communicating the more complicated wrongs his interlocutor commits against the community, he also enacts the method by which these shared understandings can be used to form communal bonds. The limitations of the *Convivio* dictate that it is ultimately not the space where Dante will explore this possibility fully, but these first exercises give shape to the concept of gluttony that will be articulated in the *Comedy*, where Dante will follow food through the human body into questions of identity, intellect, and soul, passing from the individual to the collective.

The third chapter addresses the sinners in Dante's *Comedy* who are designated as gluttons in Hell. The most explicit gluttons in Dante's work present perhaps the most complicated vision of an (in)appropriate relationship with food, not least because they do not appear to be directly associated with food at all. Indeed, the primary spokesman for the infernal gluttons, Ciacco, is an anonymous figure with no known history of gluttony who delivers a political prophecy. By offering an "official" introduction to infernal gluttony with Ciacco—who explains how the city of Florence will buckle under its useless, gluttonous leaders—and extending the thread to the bottom of Hell, where the pilgrim encounters the trifecta of insatiable consumers in Count Ugolino, Fra' Alberigo, and Lucifer, the poet constructs a counter-image of the social harmony effected through feeding. These unchecked appetites demonstrate the multifold and profound consequences of gluttonous behavior on the health of the human city, but they also begin the work of extending those anticipated outcomes to the physiological model used for the production of new bodies—the paradigm of reproduction that Dante delineates for humans and their creative impulses, whether flesh or art. The belly of Hell is, like a human belly, the first organ in a reproductive process that results in new bodies and new spirits. Using an analogy rooted in dietary science, Dante shows his reader how the act of overstuffing the stomach jeopardizes the body's natural functions: first by diluting its essence and degrading the will, and then by inhibiting its ability to procreate, creating an indigestion that will poison not just this generation but also the next.

The fourth chapter turns to gluttony's correction on the terraces of Purgatory. The terrace designed to purge this sin sees Dante reunited with his old friend Forese Donati, who delivers a historiography of the lyric tradition and baptizes the "dolce stil novo," before giving way to the famous, challenging discourse on embryology provided by the Roman poet Statius. The long path to understanding the process that leads from consumption to creation, whether of humans or art, is mapped across an equally long portion of the poem. Statius's discourse on embryology, which finally provides the pilgrim with an explanation—albeit a perplexing one—of the generation of shade bodies and human bodies, only arrives in *Purgatorio* 25, when the poem is closer to its end than its beginning. In the purgatorial space where the fraught debate over the connection between body and soul is constantly present, Dante embraces a position somewhere in between the hylomorphic and the separated model, imagining the body as always and inexorably linked to the soul but also distinct from it, while on the journey through this life and the next.[35] After *Inferno* reveals the fate of gluttons who either suffer from a stunted peristalsis that causes them to lose what makes them human, or go on consuming until they eat even the flesh of their loins, condemning both themselves and their progeny, *Purgatorio* models both how gluttony can be corrected and the growth and continuity that results from a healthful relationship with food. Coding the poetry of his former cohort as the consequence of overeating, Dante contrasts their now-obsolete poetic production with his own successful composition, the product of a judicious appetite. Turning once more to the question of production, but now in the form of bodies and souls, Dante emphatically confirms the connection between consuming and creating, insisting that anyone who knows how to eat can contribute to the formation of a lasting human community, be it through poetry, politics, or procreation.

The final chapter begins by examining the rejuvenation of the physical body that the pilgrim experiences in his passage from the purgatorial mountain to the realm of Heaven; it then confirms Dante's lasting emphasis on the perfection of the human need for material sustenance that compels us to construct community. *Paradiso* necessarily turns away from the appetites for food that have appeared so far in the poem, yet it is also where Dante affirms definitively how good provisioning and convivial consumption strengthen the bonds of community. This occurs most crucially in the prophecy of his exile through a food-based metaphor, delivered by the poet's ancestor Cacciaguida, but also in the presentation of Dante's body as it shrinks in the face of a lean diet. Pouring himself into his work, the last self-portrait Dante paints in the *Comedy* is of a man who finds himself finally beyond the reach of gluttony. Through his poem, he has found the means for a fruitful fast: a way of channeling his appetite into work that produces for the community, and of sharing what he has so that what he does not consume might be left to feed others.

Dante's Gluttons thus sets out to respond to a recent drive in Dante studies: a push to historicize and apply material culture studies in an effort to open up traditional models of literary criticism. It addresses the increasing call in medieval studies to identify the larger phenomena that characterized the

---

35   Gragnolati distills Dante's position in this way: "Dante's *Comedy* settles for neither a fully dualistic nor a fully hylomorphic view of the body: it is precisely by endorsing the potential of the tension between these views that his Comedy succeeds in expressing a sense of the body as being tightly connected to the soul without being reducible to it." See Gragnolati, "Gluttony and the Anthropology of Pain in Dante's *Inferno* and *Purgatorio*," p. 250. For more on the subject and a thorough summary of relevant bibliography, see Gragnolati, *Experiencing the Afterlife*, as well as the fourth chapter of this book.

experience of producing and receiving culture. It confirms the importance, in particular, of a monograph-length study that engages these scholarly trends while promoting the study of literature through and with food as a means of connecting the European literary canon to a larger canon of global cultural exchange. These goals are achieved by reading the work of Dante, but also by responding to the call of the poet himself. As an author dedicated to the pursuit of salvation and self-knowledge, Dante finds in the relationship with food an opportunity not just to restrain the self but to improve the self, and through this process find contributive potential. Everyone eats, and thus everyone understands the language of food; more than this, everyone is poised to be able to employ the language of food. In this sense, close attention to the human relationship with food and Dante's use of it reveals the effect he had on those who came later, through the poet's use of these shared terms and his belief that they could form the basis for a successful literary language. Dante's gluttons are not just a through line or a persistent presence, but indeed a hermeneutic unto themselves—a means by which to access Dante's work in the comprehensive and transcendent way he intended.

Works Cited

Albala, Ken. *Eating Right in the Renaissance*. Berkeley: University of California Press, 2002.

Albala, Ken. *A Cultural History of Food in the Renaissance*. London: Bloomsbury, 2014.

Alighieri, Dante. *Convivio*. Edited by Giorgio Inglese. Milan: Biblioteca Universale Rizzoli, 1993.

Alighieri, Dante. *The Banquet*. Edited and translated by Christopher Ryan. Saratoga, CA: Anma, 1989.

Alighieri, Dante. *La Commedia secondo l'antico vulgata*. Edited by Giorgio Petrocchi. 4 vols. Milan: Mondadori, 1966–67.

Alighieri, Dante. *De vulgari eloquentia*. Edited and translated by Steven Botterill. Cambridge: Cambridge University Press, 2009.

Alighieri, Dante. *The Divine Comedy of Dante Alighieri*. Edited and translated by Robert M. Durling, with introduction and notes by Ronald L. Martinez and Robert M. Durling. 3 vols. New York: Oxford University Press, 1996–2003.

Barolini, Teodolinda. "'Only Historicize': History, Material Culture and the Future of Dante Studies." *Dante Studies* 127 (2009): 37–54.

Bianchi, Luca. *"Noli comedere panem philosophorum inutiliter*: Dante Alighieri and John of Jandun on Philosophical 'Bread.'" *Tijdschrift voor Filosofie* 75 (2013): 335–355.

Boyde, Patrick. *Perception and Passion in Dante's Comedy*. Cambridge: Cambridge University Press, 1993.

Bynum, Caroline Walker. "Fast, Feast, and Flesh: The Religious Significance of Food to Medieval Women." *Representations* 11 (1985): 1–25.

Bynum, Caroline Walker. *Holy Feast and Holy Fast: The Religious Significance of Food to Medieval Women*. Berkeley: University of California Press, 1987.

Bynum, Caroline Walker. *The Resurrection of the Body in Western Christianity, 200–1336*. New York: Columbia University Press, 1995.

Camporesi, Piero. *The Magic Harvest: Food, Folklore and Society*. Translated by Joan K. Hall. Cambridge: Polity Press, 1993.

Chiodo, Carol. "Tutti i frutti: The Fruits of Treachery and the Roots of the Soul in *Inferno* 33." In *Table Talk: Perspectives on Food in Medieval Italian Literature*, edited by Christiana Purdy Moudarres, 97–110. Cambridge: Cambridge Scholars Press, 2010.

Ciabattoni, Francesco. *Dante's Journey to Polyphony*. Toronto: University of Toronto Press, 2010.

Cornish, Alison. "Music, Justice, and Violence in *Paradiso* 20." *Dante Studies* 134 (2016): 112–141.

Curtius, Ernst Robert, *European Literature and the Latin Middle Ages*. Translated by Willard R. Trask. Princeton, NJ: Princeton University Press, 1953.

Durling, Robert. "Deceit and Digestion in the Belly of Hell." In *Allegory and Representation: Selected Papers from the English Institute, 1979–1980,* edited by Stephen Greenblatt, 61–93. Baltimore: Johns Hopkins University Press, 1981.

Durling, Robert. "Body." In *The Dante Encyclopedia*, edited by Richard Lansing, 115–118. New York: Garland, 2000.

Durling, Robert. "The Body and the Flesh in the *Purgatorio*." In *Dante for the New Millennium*, edited by Teodolina Barolini and H. Wayne Storey, 183–191. Fordham: Fordham University Press, 2003.

Fisher, M. F. K. *An Alphabet for Gourmets*. New York: North Point Press, 1949.

Flandrin, Jean-Louis, and Odile Redon. "Les livres de cuisine italiens des XIVe et et XVe siècles." *Archeologia medievale* 8 (1981): 393–408

Freedman, Paul. *Out of the East: Spices and the Medieval Imagination*. New Haven: Yale University Press, 2008.

Freedman, Paul, ed. *Food: A History of Taste*. Berkeley: University of California Press, 2007.

Gibbons, David. "Alimentary Metaphors in Dante's *Paradiso*." *The Modern Language Review* 96, no. 3 (2001): 693–706.

Gilson, Simon. "The Anatomy and Physiology of the Human Body in the *Commedia*." In *Dante and the Human Body: Eight Essays,* edited by John C. Barnes and Jennifer Petrie, 43–60. Dublin: Four Courts Press, 2007.

Grangnolati, Manuele. *Experiencing the Afterlife: Soul and Body in Dante and Medieval Culture*. South Bend: University of Notre Dame Press, 2005.

Grangnolati, Manuele. "Gluttony and the Anthropology of Pain in Dante's *Inferno* and *Purgatorio*." In *History in the Comic Mode: Medieval Communities and the Matter of Person*, edited by Rachel Fulton Brown and Bruce Holsinger, 238–250. New York: Columbia University Press, 2015.

Grieco, Allen J. *Food, Social Politics and the Order of Nature in Renaissance Italy*. Cambridge, Mass.: Harvard University Press, 2019.

Laurioux, Bruno. *Le moyen âge à table*. Paris: Biro, 1989.

Laurioux, Bruno. "I libri di cucina italiani alla fine del Medioevo: un nuovo bilancio." *Archivio Storico Italiano* 154, no. 1 (Jan-March 1996): 33–58.

Laurioux, Bruno, ed. *Scrivere il Medioevo: lo spazio, la santità, il cibo, un libro dedicato ad Odile Redon*. Rome: Viella, 2001.

Le Goff, Jacques. *La civilisation de l'occident médiéval*. Paris: Arthaud, 1964.

Malgarini, Patrizia Bertini. "Il linguaggio medico e anatomico nelle opere di Dante." *Studi Danteschi* 61 (1989): 1–108.

Martellotti, Anna. *I ricettari di Federico II. Dal* Meridionale *al* Liber de coquina. Florence: Olschki, 2005.

Martinez, Ronald L. "Dante 'buon sartore' (*Paradiso* 32.140): Textile Arts, Rhetoric, and Metapoetics at the End of the Commedia." *Dante Studies* 136 (2018): 22–61.

Montanari, Massimo. *L'alimentazione contadina nell'alto Medioevo*. Naples: Liguori, 1979.

Montanari, Massimo. *Alimentazione e cultura nel medioevo*. Rome: Laterza, 1988.

Montanari, Massino. *La fame e l'abbondanza*. Rome: Laterza, 2006.

Nardi, Bruno. *Dante e la cultura medievale: nuovi saggi di filosofia dantesca*. Rome: Laterza, 1949.

Nutton, Vivian. "Dante, Medicine and the Invisible Body." In *Dante and the Human Body: Eight Essays,* edited by John C. Barnes and Jennifer Petrie, 11–42. Dublin: Four Courts Press, 2007.

O'Brien, William J. "The 'Bread of Angels' in *Paradiso* II: A Liturgical Note." *Dante Studies* 97 (1979): 97–106.

Olson, Kristina. "Uncovering the Historical Body of Florence: Dante, Forese Donati, and Sumptuary Legislation." *Italian Culture* 33, no. 1 (March 2015): 1–15.

Olson, Kristina. "Shoes, Gowns and Turncoats: Reconsidering Cacciguida's History of Florentine Fashion and Politics." *Dante Studies* 134 (2016): 26–47.

Palma, Pina. *Savoring Power, Consuming the Times: The Metaphors of Food in Medieval and Renaissance Italian Literature*. South Bend, IN: University of Notre Dame Press, 2013.

Purdy Moudarres, Christiana. "Devouring Selves in the Circle of Gluttony: A Gloss on the Contrapasso of *Inferno* 6." In *Table Talk: Perspectives on Food in Medieval*

Italian Literature. Edited by Christiana Purdy Moudarres, 3–18. Newcastle upon Tyne: Cambridge Scholars Publishing, 2010.

Purdy Moudarres, Christiana. *Table Talk: Perspectives on Food in Medieval Italian Literature.* Newcastle upon Tyne: Cambridge Scholars Publishing, 2010.

Purdy Moudarres, Christiana. "Bodily Starvation and the Ravaging of the Will: A Reading of *Inferno* 32–33." *Viator* 47, no. 1 (2016): 205–228.

Siraisi, Nancy. *Taddeo Alderotti and his Pupils: Two Generations of Italian Medical Learning.* Princeton: Princeton University Press, 1981.

Siraisi, Nancy. *Medieval & Early Renaissance Medicine: An Introduction to Knowledge and Practice.* Chicago: University of Chicago Press, 1990.

Shapiro, Marianne. *Dante and the Knot of Body and Soul.* New York: St. Martin's Press, 1998.

Steinberg, Justin. *Dante and the Limits of the Law.* Chicago: University of Chicago Press, 2013.

1. Dante's Gluttony

Abstract

This chapter defines gluttony in the medieval European context, reviewing the many spheres that influenced its interpretation: cultural, medical, social, and theological. It establishes that gluttony in Dante is an interaction with food that undermines the social contract and breaks down community. In this way, gluttony becomes a kind of anti-poetry for Dante: in contrast to the *stil novo* or "new style" that sought to inspire, unite, and create understanding at human and divine levels, gluttony is consumption that takes from others, stunts growth, and makes expression more difficult. Dante's gluttons thus become an interpretive key, unlocking a reading of his poetry that has not yet been appreciated by modern critics.

Keywords: abstinence, diet, digestion, gluttony, self-regulation

"City is gluttony." —Amiri Baraka/LeRoi Jones[1]

While the persistence of the human relationship with food may transcend boundaries of time and place, the terms of this relationship are dictated by many factors: geography, climate, faith, politics, and technology. Food continues to enjoy the same universal recognizability and presence in everyday life, and it continues to exercise the same intimacy with the individual while acting as a tool for binding individuals into groups, both spiritual and secular. The terms of our interaction with food are connected to technologies and mores, however. In medieval Italy, people spent more time and labor to access and consume food. The ways in which food punctuated the day were more decisive and specific, and the expectation that the governing body was a literal provider of food was more deeply rooted. For Dante, so thoroughly a product of his culture, gluttony was nuanced

---

1   Baraka, *The System of Dante's Hell*, p. 33.

Callegari, D., *Dante's Gluttons: Food and Society from the* Convivio *to the* Comedy.
Taylor & Francis Group, 2022
DOI 10.5117/9789463720427_CH01

by these parameters, and in dialogue with the chief preoccupations of the late Middle Ages. If in the modern, developed world a fat body is the first and most evocative marker of the glutton, the premodern world was significantly less focused on the changes in physique that resulted from gluttony than on its causes and far-reaching consequences.[2] Dante and his contemporaries understood gluttony as a complex equation of many qualitative decisions.[3] Reading Dante's gluttons thus presents an opportunity to become better readers of Dante's poetry, to see what Dante took from and gave to food. By discussing food and eating practices, the poet infused them with meaning, and demonstrated the efficacy in expressing meaning through these figures. The act of infusing that significance in turn affected how those foods and practices were received after him. In placing the meanings of abstaining and overeating in context, it becomes clear that the poet saw food not just as one heuristic among many, but—at least to some extent—as *the* heuristic. Consuming food is the means by which earthly existence is sustained; it is the literal means for growth but also a metaphor for intellectual and spiritual maturity; most crucially for Dante, it is at once the real and metaphysical way humans may encounter God. If Dante's goal is to create literature that can, like Scripture, be read anagogically and create community, he must rely on a similarly layered approach to material food and food imagery, using the fight with appetite as a template for the human journey.

That gluttony was a threat to the individual in a spiritual sense—as the turning away of one's attention from communion with God and higher knowledge—was clearly a grave concern. But crucially, and more deeply troubling still in a moment where the connection between body and soul was the crux of a major theological dispute, gluttony's corruption of the body was believed to potentially lead through a physiological process to the corruption of identity and the soul. The question of where the body ended and the intangible elements of human essence began was hotly debated just before and during Dante's time. Theologians deliberated at length over the potential influence a physical disturbance could have over the essence of individual identity and the rational soul, which controlled intellect and will (the two elements that distinguished humans from non-human sentient

2   Susan Hill provides a thorough introduction to the contrasting interpretations of fatness and gluttony over time in *Eating to Excess: The Meaning of Gluttony and the Fat Body in the Ancient World*, pp. 1–21.
3   A comprehensive general introduction to gluttony in the Middle Ages is provided in Casagrande and Vecchio, *I sette vizi capitali: storia dei peccati nel medioevo*, pp. 124–148.

beings).[4] If incorporation of food, as the term implies, changed the body, then disordered eating could adulterate the physical processes by which food leads to sexual and intellectual reproductivity, and perhaps even broach the threshold where the flesh gave way to human essence and soul. In this way, gluttony becomes a kind of anti-poetry, a consumption that denatures one's identity and makes self-expression impossible as it stunts growth and inhibits contributive potential. It stands in contrast to the new style Dante sought to use to inspire, unite, and create understanding at human and divine levels.

In the nutritional themes the poet develops and in the way in which the body of his work often mimics the human body, Dante expands the individual experience of gluttony to the collective: he proposes it as a large-scale interaction with food that undermines the social contract and breaks down community. As his transposition of the Latin *convivio* into an Italian vernacular context succinctly confirms, living together means eating together, and eating together means living together. The poet's well-documented personal desire for citizenship and engagement in civic life, fueled by his expulsion from his native city and subsequent itinerancy, is thus either underpinned by the exchange of nourishment or undermined by the refusal to participate.[5] Gluttony can be a specific rejection of civic duty that leads to logistical challenges (like hoarding or wasting), or a habitual tendency to ignore the needs of others (overfilling one's own belly even as a neighbor is hungry), but it is always more pernicious than the literal act of overeating: it resonates as a broader gesture of bad faith, and it prompts a disintegration of the ties that hold people together. For Dante, the sharing of food in the city of man was meant to imitate and presage the great banquet in the city of God, and its perversion inevitably leads to the fall of the former and inability to access the latter.

---

4   This will be discussed at length in Chapter 3 regarding the *contrapasso* of the gluttons and Count Ugolino, and in Chapter 4 with respect to the parallel production of human and poetic life. See Gragnolati, *Experiencing the Afterlife,* and Purdy Moudarres, "Bodily Starvation and the Ravaging of the Will," pp. 205–228.

5   In her dedicated study that also provides an essential bibliography, Catherine Keen notes that beyond being the space that set the terms for Dante's political thinking more broadly, the city is also where Dante locates the development of individual identity, which is necessarily grounded in the civic: "The city appears in the *Comedy* as a polity where such interests (i.e. personal and social) can find full expression—though for bad as well as for good—in a forum neither so large that institutions overwhelm individuals, nor so small that individuals can retreat into self-sufficiency, but rather where civic and individual needs can, and ideally do, coincide in all manner of ways." *Dante and the City,* p. 12.

Gluttony in the Universe of Hunger

For the late medieval European, living in what Jacques Le Goff evocatively termed the "universe of hunger," the relationship with food was especially fraught.[6] While Le Goff's description has been re-evaluated and tempered in recent years, the nutritional resources on the continent were indeed under strain during the late thirteenth and early fourteenth centuries.[7] The "Medieval Warm Period" that had provided the European continent with nearly three centuries of mild weather and fine harvests ended abruptly somewhere around 1250, reverting to a cold so bitter that cultivation was not only limited but sometimes halted.[8] The population nonetheless continued to grow, and in fact would not be significantly thinned (even by famine) until the plague of 1348.[9] By the latter half of the thirteenth century, however, the precarious balance between the growing population and agricultural production was faltering, giving way even more firmly to Le Goff's desolate universe of hunger. Though a fear of starving had never quite left the medieval consciousness, the general prosperity of the previous decades had permitted a cautious respite from the persistent anxiety of earlier centuries. In the years following Dante's birth in 1265, hunger returned to loom ominously over late thirteenth and early fourteenth century life.[10]

Between the years 1150 and 1300, the population of Florence grew no less than ten times from approximately 10,000 inhabitants to 100,000 over the course of a century and a half, metamorphosing from a small and politically insignificant interior village to a major urban center. Even as the population surged across Europe, Florence stood out, with a number of inhabitants comparable to that of London and Venice at the time; recent

6   Le Goff, *La civilisation de l'occident médiéval*, p. 290.
7   For a comprehensive overview of the factors that charged and complicated the relationship with food in the late Middle Ages in Europe, see Flandrin and Montanari, eds., *Storia dell'alimentazione*.
8   See Hoffman, *An Environmental History of Medieval Europe*, pp. 318–374.
9   Among the sources that have pieced together an overview of the boom in population across Europe that peaked around 1300, see Herlihy, "Medieval Demography" in *Dictionary of the Middle Ages*, pp. 136–148 and Bartlett, *The Making of Europe: Conquest, Colonization, and Cultural Change, 950–1350*. More precise studies are available for specific geographic areas, including those listed below for central Italy.
10   Massimo Montanari usefully summarizes the reversal of trends: "All'incirca a iniziare dal 1270…il precario equilibrio fra aumento demografico e crescita produttiva si sta spezzando: è quello che J. Le Goff ha chiamato il 'ritorno della fame' Non che questa avesse mai cessato di affliggere le popolazioni urbane e rurali; ma…ora ridiventa protagonista assoluta." In Montanari, *La fame e l'abbondanza,* pp. 87–88.

historical scholarship has thoroughly reconstructed the growth and shift of
populations and the necessarily changing tactics in provisioning during the
century leading up to the plague of 1348 with specific attention to the Tuscan
city-states, and especially Dante's Florence.[11] The growing economy and
vast infrastructural expansion of the city both encouraged and permitted
the arrival of people from the surrounding countryside, and the new walls
of the city—particularly the 1284 enlargement—absorbed the developing
suburbs and their population.[12] This movement also created an exponential
imbalance in the provisioning structure, as the number of people providing
the labor for food production to supply the city dwindled and the number of
people requiring food within the city grew. As Florence slowly consolidated
power over the century by negotiating truces with the neighboring cities
of Pisa and Lucca and warding off the Tuscan counts, it also took on the
responsibility of sustaining an ever larger number of citizens.

This increase in population was prompted in part by greater sophistica-
tion in food supplying techniques, but it placed heavy demands on the
provisioning apparatus of the city. As George Dameron has suggested,
Florence likely owes its special surge in political and economic prominence
from 1300 forward to its ability to provision better than other Tuscan centers,
particularly with regard to grain: "[Florence's] exploitation of food resources
in southern Italy, Sicily, and Sardinia to supplement its own domestic food
supply and its ability to control the flow of grain to its rivals helped catapult
it into a position of regional supremacy by the early fourteenth century."[13]
The successful 1174 attack against the Guidi counts in Poggibonsi—a critical
market for grain in Tuscany—marks an early chapter in this process; the
establishment of the public grain market at Orsanmichele in the center
of Florence in 1290 offers a culminating visible manifestation of the city's
ability to guarantee a stable source of food for all citizens.[14] This persistent
attention to civic provisioning reveals deep anxieties as much as it represents
successful efforts. As more people crowded into urban spaces and were

11   See Herlihy, *Medieval Households*, pp. 79–111, and *Pisa in the Early Renaissance: A Study
in Urban Growth*, pp. 109–13, for notes on population statistics; Cherubini, *Le città europee del
medioevo*, and Cherubini, *Città comunali di Toscana*, pp. 11–24.
12   Day, "Economy," pp. 30–32.
13   Dameron, "Feeding the Medieval Italian City-State: Grain, War, and Political Legitimacy in
Tuscany, c. 1150–c. 1350," pp. 982–983. George Dameron was kind enough to provide me with a
copy of this article even before it was published; it represents an invaluable contribution to the
study of food and politics in the Tuscan communes from the twelfth to the fourteenth centuries.
14   Day discusses the battle over Poggibonsi and the references in the *Comedy* to the local
figures who succeeded in securing a peace between Florence and the Guidi counts in "Economy,"
pp. 35–38.

removed from environments in which micro-agricultural practices could provide nutritional support, the city's food stores increasingly felt the strain.

Food's status as a weapon made it a prize for the power hungry as much as for the physically hungry. A constant supply was crucial for obvious reasons of self-defense and community stability, which made it a prominent target of any military offensive, the primary culprit for any unrest, and a constant temptation for those in control of it. These political realities gave gluttony a special valence: the gluttonous were not only those who consumed in excess or enjoyed food too zealously, but also those who jeopardized its availability through mismanagement or corruption. Maintaining a secure, constant source of food required the careful development of policy and savvy political maneuvering. It also required a mindful, farsighted governing body or individual leader, prepared to make sacrifices and put the good of the whole before the interests of the few. If successful, that effort would be recognized and rewarded with stability in the commune and trust from the citizens. But the increased value of food in times of scarcity inevitably tempted administrators to hoard for themselves, to allow prices to spiral out of control, and to exploit a dearth of resources to keep the population desperate. Indulgence in food thus marked the selfish, but especially the shortsighted, as gluttony in the individual body risked weighing down the entire community.

Gourmand or Glutton?

The image of medieval Europe as a "universe of hunger" is helpful to the extent that it captures the urgency and charged meaning that surrounded the food supply, but it is also part of a larger scheme of flawed interpretations of the medieval as primitive and abject.[15] The value of food was not simply determined by the threat of its absence. Even as its availability grew less certain, medieval Europeans witnessed food become more diversified and more rarified at once. People delighted in eating, and they paid close attention to the cultivation of taste, using dietary choices and pantry purchases to define themselves. The emerging elite classes reformulated the space of excess into one for fussiness and the gourmand was born (à la

---

15   For a discussion of the tendency to connect the medieval with the primitive, and recent attempts to detach "medieval" from its pejorative connotations, see Goodson, Symes and Lester, *Cities, Texts and Social Networks, 400–1500: Experiences and Perceptions of Medieval Urban Space*, pp. 14–44; forthcoming work from participants in The University of California: Middle Ages in the Wider World Project is also focused on this issue.

M. F. K. Fisher's later observation). With this sharpened contrast between indiscriminate consumption habits and exacting ones, gluttony began to more clearly incorporate a measure of quality alongside quantity.[16] Larger urban centers and greater concentrations of wealth enabled a richer exchange of knowledge of foods which allowed these definitions of quality to be appreciated; the various arts of preparing food were likewise honed as shops and taverns arose to serve expanding urban populations, supported by newly formed guilds.[17] The expansion of trade routes and subsequent growth of the maritime republics of Venice and Genoa brought vast arrays of rare and remarkable goods to the Italian peninsula and the rest of the continent. A variety of non-indigenous foods were made available to an increasing population with disposable income and with these foods—in particular, spices and sugar—the possibility to create finer distinctions among the classes of people consuming them. Hierarchical distinction was in fact a defining characteristic of food and foodways in this period, and both consumed and consumer became part of a carefully elaborated system of classification that determined and confirmed the social value of each one.[18] This interchange between human types and food types gave rise to a distinctive taxonomy. The strict codification of edible plants and animals according to their intrinsic virtues began to structure the diets of people of correlated status, and in turn, diets and palates shifted to symmetrically reflect status in the community.[19] The desire for the delicate became in itself another potential pitfall, however, and it would eventually become associated with a kind of emasculation that threatened the community in another way. Gluttony was often associated with a feminine tendency toward excessive consumption due to unbridled passions as a misogynist

16   See the discussion on negative and positive semantic fields around terms associated with gluttony across Romance languages in Quellier, *Gola: Storia di un peccato capitale*, pp. 7–10.

17   The example of butchers has been given considerable scholarly attention, for example: while butchers were still relegated to the periphery of the city, the wealth they accumulated in this period granted them a significant improvement in social status and political participation. On the late medieval maturation of the art of butchery in general, see Toussaint-Samat, *A History of Food*, pp. 95–102; for the central Italian context specifically, see Pinto, *Toscana medievale: paesaggi e realtà sociali*, pp. 101–105 and pp. 208–210.

18   See Grieco, *Food, Social Politics, and the Order of Nature in Renaissance Italy*; Grieco, "Alimentazione e classi sociali nel tardo Medioevo e nel Rinascimento in Italia," pp. 371–880; Grieco, "The Social Politics of Pre-Linnaean Botanical Classification," pp. 131–149; Laurioux, "Table et hiérarchie sociale à la fin du moyen âge," pp. 87–108; Montanari, *Alimentazione e cultura nel medioevo*, pp. 13–22.

19   Commenting on the rigidity of this social-culinary structure, Grieco has observed that the link between social order and food could sometimes constitute a "quasi-symbiotic relationship." See Grieco, "The Social Politics of Pre-Linnaean Botanical Classification," p. 132.

tradition held (and still holds) that women were naturally weak of will, and thus were more likely to give in to whims.[20]

Gender was only one means by which gluttony was defined, both unto itself and for each individual. The process by which types of people were slowly aligned with types of food can be traced back to the *scala naturae* first proposed by Aristotle, though it found its most significant elaboration in the late Middle Ages. In his thirteenth-century treatise on plant life, *De vegetabilibus libri VII*, Albertus Magnus set forth a double classification of plants according to morphology and the inherent virtues they were understood to possess. Following the pseudo-Aristotelian *De plantis* and the work of Aristotle's student Theophrastus, Magnus's text had a long and profound influence on the value and significance of food items.[21] All of God's creations, equally good but nonetheless different, could be placed on the great chain of being; there, they occupied a position above a less complex essence and below the next more complex one. Following this intricate design, corresponding positions in the human hierarchy could be easily assigned what they might properly consume according to their status.[22] Men, whose humoral dispositions ostensibly made them hot and dry, could and should eat many things that women, naturally cold and damp, should not. Class added yet another layer: foods of great nobility were meant for men of great nobility, just as humble men were drawn to humble foods. Moreover, eating something inappropriate to your station became a form of gluttony all its own, whereby not just the quantity or quality of the food, but also its precise hierarchical standing could suggest a degenerate indulgence.

While many characteristics were taken into account in determining the social-nutritional hierarchy, taste and accessibility strongly influenced the desirability of many items. Spices and botanicals were particularly charged in this sense, and Dante takes advantage of their ability to socially

20 Olson points out how misogyny has obscured scholarship on material culture more generally, noting with regard to medieval fashion that scholars' "unwillingness to see male protagonists in this fashion history stems from a combination of empirical observations contemporary to their times together with a rhetorical tradition, both classical and scriptural, that identifies women as the protagonists in the landscape of consumption." In Olson, "Shoes, Gowns and Turncoats," p. 32.

21 On Albert's botany and his influences, see Grafton, Most, and Settis, eds., *The Classical Tradition*, p. 622; Weisheipl, ed., *Albertus Magnus and the Sciences: Commemorative Essays 1980*, and Reeds, "Albert on the Natural Philosophy of Plant Life," pp. 341–354.

22 Beyond the section on the Middle Ages in Lovejoy's classic study, *The Great Chain of Being*, pp. 67–98, Grieco has more recently provided helpful visual representations in *Food, Social Politics, and the Order of Nature in Renaissance Italy*, p. 111 (fig. 1), p. 130 (fig. 2), and plate 35. See also Montanari, "Contadini, guerrieri, sacerdoti," pp. 229–232.

influence, memorably in *Inferno 29* when the pilgrim hears the group of young decadent Sienese nobles known as the "brigata spendereccia" enjoyed cloves, which were rare and expensive, prompting them to become a recognizable marker of status in their city: "e Niccolò che la costuma ricca / del garofano prima discoverse" (and Nicholas who first discovered the rich custom of cloves; *Inf.* 29.127–128).[23] On the other hand, a spice too readily available or too ordinary quickly lost its appeal when it could no longer mark a clear difference between the haves and have-nots. As Paul Freedman has demonstrated, a once-exotic item like pepper had already become so common in the late Middle Ages as to be considered declassé, and indeed Dante uses the peppercorn as a point of comparison for the grotesque black bellies of the thieves in *Inferno 25*, described as "livido e nero come gran di pepe" (livid and black like a grain of pepper; *Inf.* 25.18).[24] The general aversion to water in the Middle Ages provides an even more remarkable example. Premodern hydrophobia has long been attributed to the dangers associated with untreated bacterial content and waste runoff; the 1442 quarantining of the butchers onto the Ponte Vecchio in Florence so that they could immediately dump their rotting carcasses into the river is all one requires to believe this commonplace. Already suspicious for its cold and damp nature, water may have thus become a real source of disease and death to its consumers. Yet as A. Lynn Martin has underlined, the true "Dark Ages" for water in Europe were the decades following the Industrial Revolution, when intense urbanization and ignorance of hygienic dangers created conditions that favored the flourishing of dangerous bacteria in water and repeated cholera pandemics.[25] Paolo Squatriti observes further that the assumption that medieval water must have necessarily been worse than modern water ignores the surprisingly high medieval European standards for public water access and quality. Moreover, he has established that by the high Middle Ages, distaste for water was primarily a means of expressing social distinction—"plain water was the drink of commoners, of boors, and of poor folk, and to drink it implied too little separation from them"—so that water

---

23   In her study of *brigate* in the works of Dante and his contemporaries, Barolini refers to this moment in *Inferno,* noting it confirms Dante's view of excess consumption as "a social and economic ill that is given immediate ethical focus"; see Barolini, "Sociology of the Brigata," pp. 10–11.

24   Freedman, "Spices and Late-Medieval European Ideas of Scarcity and Value," pp. 1209–227. Freedman's comprehensive study on spices in the Middle Ages is also a crucial point of reference for understanding the social-political value of food more generally; see Freedman, *Out of the East.*

25   Martin, "The Baptism of Wine," p. 22.

drinking was rarely mentioned in historical and literary documentation precisely because of its banality.[26]

The appearance of the first books of recipes that could codify entire cuisines in these years helped to elaborate this status-sensitive understanding of consumption. Taking advantage of the foundation laid by Jean-Louis Flandrin and Odile Redon, Bruno Laurioux has established that culinary texts proliferated and circulated widely on the Italian peninsula in the late thirteenth and early fourteenth centuries, a fact confirmed by the diversity of texts that were in circulation and the existence of a few key texts that were frequently copied or translated into other vernaculars.[27] In particular, the commissioning of the *Liber de coquina*, or Book of Cooking, around 1230 marked a turning point as the first collection of recipes recognizable as a cookbook became available to the literate public on the peninsula. While suggestions for food preparations had circulated in other forms (particularly within medical treatises), the early thirteenth century saw the birth of the first written text dedicated to eating that was not framed by medicinal or theological concerns, but focused principally on the preparation and service of fine foods. As Anna Martellotti has noted in her work linking the text to the courtly milieu of Emperor Frederick II in Palermo, the *Liber de coquina* is defined by a series of exceptional characteristics. It is a text produced in a distinctive, highly cultured environment, where it was possible to compose recipes in the vernacular and have them simultaneously translated into Latin by someone equally fluent in French and Arabic, who was accompanied by a cadre of expert cooks up-to-date on the most important dietary trends of the Mediterranean. More importantly still, the *Liber* was promoted and encouraged by a single, inspired mind with an ambitious plan to lift the dispersive practice of vernacular recipe collecting into the high sciences through a uniform structure and with a clear philosophy.[28]

With its imperial pedigree and easily replicable format, the *Liber de coquina* became the urtext for many later culinary works on the Italian peninsula and across the continent.[29] It made its way through courts and

---

26 Squatriti, *Water and Society in Early Medieval Italy*, pp. 40–41.

27 Laurioux, "I libri di cucina italiani alla fine del Medioevo: un nuovo bilancio," pp. 33–58.

28 As also noted in the introduction, the *Liber de coquina* is typically called the "first cookbook" in that it is likely the first text to collect ingredients and instructions in a format that is clearly for practical use and without the trappings of a philosophical or medical treatise. See Martellotti, *I ricettari di Federico II: Dal "Meriodionale" al "Liber de coquina,"* for evidence on its commissioning at the court of Frederick II of Hohenstaufen and its place as the first in a genealogy of directly copied or imitative manuscripts that circulated across Europe in the following centuries.

29 Laurioux describes the *Liber* and its progeny as a network that was "diffusissima"; see Laurioux, "I libri di cucina italiani," p. 35, and the introduction to this book.

elite households in several Latin copies and vernacular translations, including a Tuscan redaction that was likely commissioned by Ubaldino della Pila, remembered by Dante among the gluttons in *Purgatorio* 24.[30] Their presence points to a shared consciousness surrounding food culture in the late Middle Ages, analogous but also intrinsic to the medical-scientific knowledge that Dante and his contemporaries enjoyed. The *Liber* and its progeny brought to life a means of interacting with food that celebrated carefully researched ingredients, painstaking preparation techniques, and aesthetically inclined presentations. In turn, these culinary texts codified the food of the high-born and contributed a foundational component to the hierarchy of food, through which the terms of abstinence and indulgence could vary according to the role an individual played in a given community. By showing how food could be appreciated for its aesthetics (and could become even more desirable when unnecessary) as well as its politics (in that it demonstrated that knowledge of food was part of the means by which power could be acquired and performed), the *Liber* contributed to the work of lifting food into the realm of art.

Spiritual Gluttony

While the intervals between the high-born and low-born and their corresponding diets multiplied, the space between the glutton and the ascetic was more simply defined in the late medieval paradigm of gluttony. The demonization of the hoarder or the excessive eater was thoroughly rooted in teachings of the Christian faith, beginning with the early Church doctors, who saw a lack of self-control in the face of food as a haunting reminder of the original sin that condemned mankind to its unfortunate state—Eve's first bite of the apple. It was food that had prompted the shift from the prelapsarian world where God's omnipresent bounty met all human needs, and as the Old Testament recorded, an irrational desire for food continued to plague humanity ever since, from the plate of lentils for which Esau abandoned his birthright (Gen. 25) to the disdain the Israelites show to the manna God has sent down to them (Num. 11).[31] Eve and other examples

---

30   Tracing the various branches of the textual genealogy, Martellotti connects the manuscript known as the *Anonimo Toscano*, a Tuscan translation of an early copy of the *Liber*, to Ubaldino, and confirms the connection through the recipe for "frittelle ubaldine," a typical way of "signing" the commission of a cookbook; see Martellotti, *I ricettari di Federico II*, pp. 87–88.

31   Quellier provides a comprehensive overview of the Biblical precedents for especially nonsensical or non-urgent but adamant desires for food that demonstrate human failing in

were reminders of the fact that gluttony was not simply a surrender to animal instinct; in shedding the reasoning capacity that defined a human as something more than animal, the gluttonous rendered themselves unfit to participate in human community.

Though the place gluttony held in the hierarchy of sins would be frequently debated, the fourth-century Greek ascetic monk Evagrius of Pontus laid the groundwork for gluttony's classification as the worst of sins early on when discussing the *logismoi*, or patterns of temptation, that structure many of his works. Evagrius placed gluttony at the top of his ladder of evil thoughts that would eventually lead to the damnation of the soul, believing that a loose grip on this first and most essential of appetites would open the floodgates to other, more visibly harmful excesses.[32] His student John Cassian cemented this perception of gluttony as the most treacherous of all the mortal sins, calling it "the first struggle." Cassian was especially concerned with how challenging it was to find a rule regarding gluttony that suited everyone equally. In his fifth Conference, he noted that different body types, genders, and ages required different amounts of food in different times and different ways:

> And so on the manner of fasting a uniform rule cannot easily be observed, because everybody has not the same strength; nor is it like the rest of the virtues, acquired by steadfastness of mind alone. And therefore, because it does not depend only on mental firmness, since it has to do with the possibilities of the body, we have received this explanation concerning it which has been handed down to us, viz.: that there is a difference of time, manner, and quality of the refreshment in proportion to the difference of condition of the body, the age, and sex: but that there is one and the same rule of restraint to everybody as regards continence of mind, and the virtue of the spirit.[33]

Cassian's trouble in arriving upon a simple dictate for all points to the underlying reason for which gluttony inspired fear in the hearts of even the most pious: eating "too much" was not clearly defined. Worse yet, as Gregory the Great elaborated further in the *Moralia* while revising these lists

---

Gola, pp. 18–23. Many of the themes in this section are also summarized in Grumett and Muers, *Theology on the Menu*, pp. 9–11.

32   Shaw explains Evagrius's position, as well as those of John Chrysostom and Cassian, in *The Burden of the Flesh*, pp. 139–159.

33   Cassian, *Conferences* 5.5.

into the format that would become recognizable as the "seven deadly sins," excess with eating could come in no less than five different forms.[34] Thomas Aquinas later distilled these into a simple mnemonic device, reminding the faithful they could commit gluttony by desiring food "too soon, too expensively, too much, too eagerly, too daintily."[35]

The constant threat of gluttony was commented upon frequently by scriptural exegetes across the Middle Ages. With the sins of violence, there was a distinction between participation and rejection (no amount of murder is acceptable, at any age or for any gender), and with the other sin of the flesh, activity could be avoided altogether (to ensure one is not adulterous or lascivious, one can choose to never engage in sex). Accidentally being a little gluttonous, on the other hand, seemed entirely too plausible, since in order to live, everyone must eat. Getting closer to his fully converted self, Augustine lamented in terms that recall Cassian's first struggle:

> In the midst of these temptations I struggle daily against greed for food and drink. This is not an evil which I can decide once and for all to repudiate and never to embrace again, as I was able to do in the case of fornication. I must therefore hold back my appetite with neither too firm nor too slack a rein.[36]

Even the bishop of Hippo, better known for his struggle to reach chastity, was overwhelmed by his fear of food and the persistent menace of gluttony due to its slippery nature. The very inappropriateness of eliminating food altogether was gluttony's fundamental complication. True conversion included the recognition of eating as an essential component of human life, imposed by God on man, and the acknowledgment that gluttony's opposite is neither total abstinence nor a clearly punctuated middle ground. Rather, it is a sliding scale, a vast grey area between too much and not enough, determined by and for each individual, in consultation with God and one's own conscience.

Thomas Aquinas also recognized this, and in the objections to his articles verifying gluttony as a mortal sin, he voiced the one that could not be avoided: "The first movement in taking food is not a sin, otherwise hunger and thirst

---

34 Gregory the Great, *Moralia* 30.8.

35 "Praepropere laute nimis ardenter studiose," in Aquinas, *Summa* 2a 2ae q.148 a.4 ad.1.

36 "In his ergo temptationibus positus, certo cotidie adversus concupiscentiam manducandi et bibendi: non enim est quod semel praecidere et ulterius non attingere decernam, sicut de concubitu potui. itaque freni gutturis temperata relaxatione et constrictione tenendi sunt." Augustine, *Confessions* 10.31.

would be sinful. Therefore gluttony is not a sin."[37] He responded to himself by acknowledging a crucial distinction: the nutritive soul's desire for food, the biological need, could not be sinful.[38] Emphasizing that while the substance of food and even the precise quantity might change according to the individual and the circumstance, he noted there was a signal determining factor: "Gluttony denotes, not any desire of eating and drinking, but an inordinate desire. Now desire is said to be inordinate through leaving the order of *reason* [...] It is a case of gluttony only when a man *knowingly* exceeds the measure in eating, from a desire for the pleasures of the palate."[39] For Aquinas, reason—which he tellingly acknowledges as "dulled" by too much food, but avoids directly addressing the possible interaction between food and the rational soul—and self-awareness were decisive: in knowingly, consciously allowing oneself to damage the body in search of pleasure, gluttony damaged the soul, affecting reason, physical appetite, speech, and action:

> First, as regards the reason, whose keenness is dulled by immoderate meat and drink, and in this respect we reckon as a daughter of gluttony, "dullness of sense in the understanding," on account of the fumes of food disturbing the brain [...] Secondly, as regards the appetite, which is disordered in many ways by immoderation in eating and drinking, as though reason were fast asleep at the helm [...] Thirdly, as regards inordinate words, and thus we have "loquaciousness" [...] Fourthly, as regards inordinate action, and in this way we have "scurrility," i.e. a kind of levity resulting from lack of reason, which is unable not only to bridle the speech, but also to restrain outward behavior.[40]

37 "Praeterea, in quolibet genere peccati primus motus est peccatum. Sed primus motus sumendi cibum non est peccatum, alioquin fames et sitis essent peccata. Ergo gula non est peccatum." Aquinas, *Summa* 2a 2ae, q.148 a.1 ad.3.

38 In *De anima* 3.12.434a22–434b18, Aristotle had defined the different types of souls available to living organisms as nutritive, sensitive, and intellectual. All living things have a nutritive or vegetative soul, nonhuman animals also have a sensitive or perceptual soul, and humans, who can reason, also have an intellectual soul.

39 "Respondeo dicendum quod gula non nominat quemlibet appetitum edendi et bibendi, sed inordinatum. Dicitur autem appetitus inordinatus ex eo quod recedit ab ordine rationis, in quo bonum virtutis moralis consistit. Ex hoc autem dicitur aliquid esse peccatum quod virtuti contrariatur. Unde manifestum est quod gula est peccatum." *Summa* 2a 2ae q.148 a.1 ad.1 (emphasis mine).

40 "Primo quidem, quantum ad rationem, cuius acies hebetatur ex immoderantia cibi et potus. Et quantum ad hoc, ponitur filia gulae hebetudo sensus circa intelligentiam, propter fumositates ciborum perturbantes caput. Sicut et e contrario abstinentia confert ad sapientiae perceptionem, secundum illud Eccle. II, cogitavi in corde meo abstrahere a vino carnem meam, ut animum meum transferrem ad sapientiam. Secundo, quantum ad appetitum, qui multipliciter

Aquinas's closing arguments on gluttony would seem to confirm that even if it was not the most grievous of the mortal sins, the broad and perpetual threat it constituted made it the most menacing, and a severe lifestyle was the only clear response. Yet even Aquinas did not conclude by suggesting that asceticism was the answer; rather, he encouraged the practice of *mediocritas*, a sustained attempt to achieve balance.

As Aquinas's thought attests, it is important to avoid the tendency to assume food was a kind of spiritual enemy for medieval Christians, or that one's relationship to it was determined by fear and lack. On the contrary, the intensity with which food and eating were scrutinized in doctrine was a reflection of their profoundly intimate and compelling nature. Food occupied a spiritually rich place where warmth and strength could be found and through which community bonds were formed. In response to the long-standing critical emphasis on money and sex in studies of medieval spirituality, Caroline Walker Bynum has confirmed that food was not just a fundamental material concern to medieval people, but that extreme asceticism became the preferred method for medieval self-fashioning as a result of the central role food played in both secular and religious culture. Hunger and eating were so overwhelmingly the focus of medieval life that they became the expression of other preoccupations and interests: "When we look at what medieval people themselves wrote, we find that they often spoke of gluttony as the major form of lust and of fasting as the most painful renunciation," but also, crucially, "of eating as the most basic and literal way of encountering God."[41] As David Grumet and Rachel Muers point out, one of the first reasons that early Christian ascetics attempted to eliminate eating from their lives was "because of the wider nexus of desires and social commitments which that act signifies."[42] For those who believed earthly life was to be lived out in quiet contemplation—avoiding engagement with the city of man at all costs in anticipation of their arrival in the city of

deordinatur per immoderantiam cibi et potus, quasi sopito gubernaculo rationis. Et quantum ad hoc, ponitur inepta laetitia, quia omnes aliae inordinatae passiones ad laetitiam et tristitiam ordinantur, ut dicitur in II Ethic. Et hoc est quod dicitur III Esdrae III, quod vinum omnem mentem convertit in securitatem et iucunditatem. Tertio, quantum ad inordinatum verbum. Et sic ponitur multiloquium, quia, ut Gregorius dicit, in pastorali, nisi gulae deditos immoderata loquacitas raperet, dives ille qui epulatus quotidie splendide dicitur, in lingua gravius non arderet. Quarto, quantum ad inordinatum actum. Et sic ponitur scurrilitas, idest iocularitas quaedam proveniens ex defectu rationis, quae, sicut non potest cohibere verba, ita non potest cohibere exteriores gestus." *Summa* 2a 2ae q.148 a.6 ad.6.

41 Bynum, "Fast, Feast, Flesh: The Religious Significance of Food to Medieval Women," pp. 138–139.

42 Grumett and Muers, *Theology on the Menu*, p. 11.

God—food represented the ultimate temptation as a symbol of civic duty and communal exchange.

When Augustine pondered the relationship with food that had vexed him precisely for its ability to be good and bad at once, for body and soul alike, he also contemplated how a balance might be struck. He underlined that the defect of human nature is not the practice of consuming generally, which is a necessity that sustains our bodies and allows us to imitate in the city of man the great feast to be enjoyed in the city of God. Food was not meant to be eliminated; fasting was a tool, and a diet that injured or threatened to destroy the body bestowed by God was a sinful one. This was a problem encountered frequently by the women mystics of the late Middle Ages, who were often rebuked for eating too little and purposely doing harm to themselves. Catherine of Siena, Dante's near-contemporary, reminded other women to use fasting as an "instrument," meant to "kill the will, not the body," while fighting her own tendency toward violent asceticism. Unfolding this belief, Bynum observes that for the medieval mystics, "insatiable, devouring hunger is evil, desire run out of control [...] But if human hunger is controlled, it will be met with the bread of heaven, new flesh to redeem the flesh of Adam."[43] The error Augustine finally identified was that indulging the craving for food too frequently or too extravagantly comes all too often at the expense of others—for one person to eat richly meant another must eat little, or not at all. Not severe abstinence but a frugal lifestyle, Augustine determined, ensures one does not engage in gluttony, and the leftover food will be stored for the hungry Christ in heaven.[44] In this way, the act of consuming could hold the double value of energizing the body that it might be ready to serve the community while also leaving adequate provisions aside for one's fellow citizens.

Physical Gluttony

Aquinas's scholastic discussion of gluttony also signals, somewhat unexpectedly, how closely the development of the spiritual paradigm surrounding gluttony was in dialogue with medieval medical learning. Indeed, even as the prevailing theology of the later Middle Ages moved toward a different hierarchical structure of sins, medical knowledge seemed to reinforce the

---

43 Bynum points out that religious men also frequently rebuked their female counterparts for "unbecoming" or "unsuitable" fasting. See Bynum, *Holy Feast and Holy Fast*, pp. 73–112.
44 Augustine, *Sermons* 210.

earlier perception of gluttony as a "gateway" to all further indiscretion, most evident in the straight line from consuming food to producing sexual desire. By the thirteenth century, this idea had found significant support, and was widely diffused through the work of the Arabic philosopher Avicenna via his careful tracing of the Galenic model of digestion from food to sperm. In his commentary on Aristotle's *De generatione animalium* (most likely transmitted to Dante and his contemporaries through Albertus Magnus), Avicenna had drawn a line that stretched from the consumption of food through three subsequent digestions into blood which served to administer the body and its organs, into a fourth digestion that resulted in the essential reproductive material.[45] This important theory of the body thus bound eating to sexual reproduction, and in turn overeating with lustful behavior.

As Aline Rousselle has established, Church fathers such as Jerome and Cassian relied expressly on earlier versions of this medical theory to argue that overeating leads to the overproduction of seminal fluid and the successive desire to use it.[46] As Cassian writes in his second Conference, "that which has once been collected inside because of abundance of food is necessarily discharged, and it is expelled by a law of nature itself, which does not allow an abundance of any superfluous humor whatsoever to reside in it, as this is harmful and injurious."[47] Gregory the Great noted that the disposition of the human body makes this plain, since the genitals appear below the belly.[48] By indulging the stomach beyond measure, the genitals necessarily became aroused in preparation to use the material that resulted from the digestion process, leading to a sexual act that had no reproductive purpose and was thus impure. When Thomas Aquinas reiterated gluttony's place as a capital sin in *De Malo*, he went so far as to explicitly describe the possibility

45 "Sperma est superfluitas digestionis quartae que fit cum dispartitur cibus in membris resudando a venis: tertia digestione iam expleta: et est de summa humiditatis proxime coagulationi ex qua nutriuntur membra dura ut pote vene et arterie et similia eius." Avicenna, *Canon* III, fen 19, tr.1, c.3. For the Aristotelians, both men and women had "sperm," thus the process resulted in the same ultimate product, and was gendered according to the biological sex of the body producing it. Nancy Siraisi provides a more comprehensive overview of the digestion process as conceived of by Galen and reiterated by Avicenna in *Medieval & Early Renaissance Medicine: An Introduction to Knowledge and Practice*, pp. 105–106.

46 Rousselle, "Abstinence et continence dans les monastères de Gaule méridionale," pp. 239–254. In fact, Jerome seems to have relied often on Galen, as did several other early Christian writers; see Pease, "Medical Allusions in the Works of St. Jerome"; Courcelle, *Late Latin Writers and their Greek Sources*, pp. 86–87.

47 "Nam quod semel per escarum abundantiam concretum fuerit in medullis, necesse est egeri atque ab ipsa naturae lege propelli, quae exuberantiam cuislibet umoris superflui velut noxiam sibi atque contrariam in semet ipsa residere non patitur." Cassian, *Collationes* 2.

48 Gregory the Great, *Moralia* 31.89.

of triggering ejaculation by overeating (in addition to its familiar derivation from animal desire for sexual pleasure):

> Emission of semen can result from a cause related to the animal nature of human beings, for example, from the desire for a perceived sense pleasure, and such belongs chiefly to sexual lust. Or emission of semen can result from an internal bodily cause, namely, from surplus fluid abounding within the body, surplus fluid that causes a man to have an emission of semen, and we accordingly designate sexual impurity a daughter of gluttony.[49]

This process by which the premodern world could "alimentarize lust," as William Ian Miller has described it—following the intuitive line from belly to genitals, in contrast to the modern tendency to sexualize food—brought the emphasis firmly back to the food consumed as opposed to the sexual act.[50] Teresa Shaw has observed that scriptural exegetes specifically used the causal relationship they discerned between "the *amount and type* of food consumed and the level of sexual humors and desire generated in the body" when they discussed how best to avoid gluttony and maintain a pure body and soul.[51] In fact, though these discussions were ultimately using medicine to understand a process that threatened the soul, the suggested means for controlling gluttony were also medical. Not prayer or communion with God but rather Galen's suggestion of a diet comprised of cool foods is what Jerome endorses as a response, following Galen's indication that cold foods promote healthy digestion and offer a preemptive attack against rising sexual heat.[52] Rather than constant abstinence, food should be avoided in response to encroaching feelings of carnal desire in the same way that diet was manipulated in reaction to the sensation of an oncoming illness. Even when sinfulness was not the concern, lust was often blamed on diet and corrected with medical intervention; this was precisely the advice Dante received when he first circulated his sonnet, "A ciascun'alma presa e gentil core." Soliciting his friends for their readings of his dream in which Love

---

49   "Ad tertium dicendum, quod pollutio corporis potest provenire ex causa animali, puta ex concupiscentia delectationis apprehensae; et hoc principaliter pertinet ad luxuriam: vel ex causa corporali et intrinseca, scilicet ex superfluo humore interius abundante, ex quo stimulatur homo ad corporis pollutionem; et secundum hoc immunditia ponitur filia gulae." Aquinas, *De Malo* q. 14 art. 4 ad. 3.
50   Miller, "Gluttony," p. 95.
51   Shaw, *The Burden of the Flesh*, p. 24, emphasis mine; see also pp. 79–128.
52   Jerome, *Epistulae* 54.9.

displays Dante's beloved and feeds her the poet's heart, Dante da Maiano concluded his friend Alighieri must have allowed his body to overproduce sexual heat from eating. Replying to the poet, da Maiano suggested washing the genitals generously in cold water to cool both the hot vapors and Dante's overheated body: "lavi la tua coglia largamente / a ciò che stinga e passi lo vapore."[53]

Keeping the body healthy and energized was entirely dependent on a carefully calibrated relationship with food, since food was often the best and only means of maintaining or restoring health. While the most important of the dietary treatises that circulated around Dante, the eleventh-century Arabic medical treatise known to the West as the *Tacuinum sanitatis*, lists six "non-natural" causes of sickness, it dedicates a full three-quarters of its discussion to food, an expression of the firm conviction that an unbalanced diet was the most common cause of disease and an improved equilibrium its most effective treatment. As Marilyn Nicoud has observed, the hundreds of health regimens that appeared across the European continent beginning in the thirteenth century are at times better described as "dictionaries of food," given how much greater emphasis was placed on food and drink than on the so-called non-naturals.[54] Nicoud in fact proposes that the *ars medica* of the Middle Ages was understood in its own time as a kind of cooking, one that allowed human civilization to progress by replacing the poverty of knowledge surrounding food and its preparation with a highly specialized expertise that saved lives and souls alike.[55] To be sure, Dante's contemporaries and compatriots Taddeo Alderotti and Dino del Garbo both spoke about dietary choices at length in their works, and Alderotti's specificity and attention to spices renders the line between the culinary and the medical nearly indistinguishable, as Nancy Siraisi has commented.[56]

The human body thrived when its humors were balanced, a precarious science that demanded constant attention to avert the tendency towards an excess or lack of heat and moisture. Avicenna's *Liber Canonis Medicinae* and its careful delineation of Galenic humoral principles was again the point of reference for understanding the complicated arithmetic that could strike a balance of humors in the body. Maintaining the proper levels of heat and cold and moisture and dryness required attention first to one's

53 "Give your testicles a good wash, so that the vapours...be extinguished and dispersed." Dante da Maiano, "Di ciò che stato sei dimandatore," vv. 7–8.

54 Nicoud, "Food Consumption, a Health Risk? Norms and Medical Practice in the Middle Ages" p. 7.

55 Marilyn Nicoud, "Nutrirsi secondo i medici nell'età antica e medievale," p. 43.

56 Nancy Siraisi, *Taddeo Alderotti and his Pupils,* p. 293.

own disposition—a natural tendency derived from gender, birth place, and time—and then to the features of foreign substances introduced into or surrounding the body. Diet was both prevention and cure; it should respond to shifts in physical needs according to seasons, age, and illness.[57] Matching the needs of certain body types was an integral part of determining diet, and every individual was responsible for knowing their own constitution and responding to it.

Gluttony was a major threat to this careful balance, unsurprisingly, but here too it occupied a nebulous place. Following the science of humors, it could be gluttonous to indulge in too many cold foods normally, but on a hot day when the body naturally requires ingredients identified as cold it would not be just permitted but most appropriate to consume them in large quantities. It was essential to combine conscientious attention to changing external and internal factors with discretion and constant vigilance to ensure that eating habits were salutary. Like the spiritual fast, the medical maintenance of the body's stability incorporated flexible but rigorous dietary rules based on self-knowledge. It insisted on the need for an intimate relationship with food, an intellectual engagement that took account of the broader consequences of food consumption practices, and the pursuit of moderation rather than extremes. This equilibrium was critical not simply because it maintained the well-being of the individual body (and in turn the soul), but also because a balanced diet crucially sustained a natural sexual appetite for healthy sexual reproduction, ensuring the continuity of the community through the next generation.

Literary Gluttony

The human proclivity for overeating was also associated with a stunting of creative capability, perhaps most famously outlined in Plato's *Timaeus*:

> Those who formed our race were aware that we should be intemperate in eating and drinking, and that through madness we should use far more than is either necessary or moderate. For fear then of rapid destruction induced by disease, and lest our mortal race should perish without fulfilling

---

57   On the inextricable tie between diet and medicine and the careful attention to humoral science in the Middle Ages, see Nicoud's comprehensive *Les régimes de santé au Moyen Âge*; Siraisi, *Medieval and Early Renaissance Medicine*, pp. 115–152; and Scully, *The Art of Cookery in the Middle Ages*, pp. 28–65.

its end—to provide against this, the gods formed for the reception of the superfluous food a receptacle beneath, called *a belly*, and formed in it the convolutions of the intestines to prevent the food from passing so quickly as to require fresh and rapid supplies of nutriment for the body, and so by insatiable gluttony making our whole race unphilosophical and unmusical, insubordinate to the most godlike part of our composition.[58]

The tendency to eat too much or too richly was both a real and a metaphoric difficulty, and just as in the physical process of eating and digestion, so too in the metaphoric process the domino effect was of primary concern. Eating well allowed food to take its course, enriching the body with its fruits and then permitting waste to pass naturally—Mary Carruthers even notes the monastic trope of prayer as "spiritual flatulence," the Latin *flatus* permitting a convenient double-entendre.[59] Like Ezekiel, John of Revelation is able to eat the text, but it turns bitter when it reaches his stomach (*Rev.* 10:10). As Proverbs had cautioned with regard to the Bible, even those who were prepared for the sweetness of the word of God could lack restraint, and stuff themselves to the point of immediate regurgitation: "You have found honey: eat what is sufficient for you, lest perchance when you have eaten your fill you vomit it up." (*Prov.* 25.16)[60] Augustine mocked the misguided elite Manicheans, who claimed that after ingesting figs they belched forth angels, and Petrarch would later complain that while many men who wished to be poets tasted the Pieran honeycomb, almost no one managed to properly digest it.[61]

By the thirteenth century, a curated "eating practice" was the basis for a profitable engagement with a text, the activity that separated the thinking from the unthinking. As Mary Carruthers points out, while "there is no questioning the fact that written material came increasingly into use from the eleventh century on," she emphasizes that this seems to have made little difference with respect to how one interacted with the text, whether it was received visually or aurally, spoken aloud or copied down while transcribing.[62] The first step was to taste the word on the tongue—whether

---

58 Plato, *Timaeus 73a.*
59 Carruthers, *The Book of Memory*, pp. 207–208.
60 "Mel invenisti: comede quod sufficit tibi, ne forte satiatus evomas illud."
61 See Augustine, *Confessions* 3.10; Petrarch, *Familiares* 13.7.
62 See Carruthers's now classic examination of the digestion-reading analogy in *The Book of Memory*, pp. 195–234. Carruthers erodes the prevailing theory that the rise of textuality and literacy following the eleventh century weakened the ancient models for reading, creating memory, and composing, and gives several examples of graphic realizations of textual peristalsis in the late Middle Ages.

repeating it quietly to oneself while reading, pronouncing it aloud to an audience, or receiving it silently by eye or ear—and then to begin moving it through the body. The necessity for this derived directly from organic principles: as Remi Brague puts it in his study of medieval modes of learning, "inclusion is an artificial procedure, digestion is a natural process; it is even among the most elementary mechanisms of life."[63] Like ingesting and incorporating food into the body, reading and comprehending were acts that began with the mouth, an exercise that was literalized in the practice of *ruminatio*. For reading to be effective, it was expected that one see the mouth moving, chewing each word and tasting it on the tongue.

As the final conflation among grasping, reading, and changing in his own conversion scene would suggest, Augustine saw a need to interact intimately and at length with a text to experience its full effect. He himself prescribed first chewing and then a further "rumination" as a method in itself of demonstrating a natural predisposition for the text: "When you hear [the Bread, i.e., the Word of God], when you read it, you are eating it; when you meditate on it afterwards, you are ruminating, that you might prove you are a clean animal, not an unclean one."[64] This activity had been codified in the Benedictine Rule, which drew upon the comprehensive description provided by Cassian in his *Conferences*. Cassian surmised that by feeding upon the text, one could expel useless erudition from the mind and replace it with nourishing spiritual knowledge:

> Of necessity, your mind will be taken up by those poems (which you learned in childhood) for as long as it fails [...] to give birth to matters spiritual and divine in place of those unfruitful and earthly things. If it manages to conceive these deeply and profoundly, *if it feeds upon* them, either previous texts will be pushed out one at a time or they will be erased altogether [...] And so it will happen that not only your memory's concentrated meditations but all its wanderings and strayings will turn into a holy, *unceasing rumination* of the Law of the Lord.[65]

---

63 Brague, *The Legend of the Middle Ages*, p. 147.

64 "Quando [panem] audis, aut quando legis, manducas; quando inde cogitas, ruminas, ut sis animal mundum, non immundum." See Augustine, *Enarrationes en Psalmos* 36.3.5.

65 "Necesse est enim mentem tuam tamdiu illis carminibus occupari, quamdiu [...] pro illis infructuosis atque terrenis ac divina parturiat. Quae cum profonde alteque conceperit atque *in illis fuerit enutrita*, vel expelli priores sensim poterunt vel penitus aboleri [...] Atque ita fiet ut non solum omnis directio ac meditatio cordis tui, uerum etiam cunctae evagationes atque discursus cogitationum tuarum sint tibi divinae legis sancta et *incessabilis ruminatio*." Cassian, *Conferences* 14.2; trans. Carruthers, in *The Craft of Thought*, p. 90–91 (italics mine).

As Carruthers observes, Cassian is deliberate in his emphasis on the physiology of this process, as he proceeds to note that by truly feeding upon the texts the useless ideas will be "expelled" from the body in the way some authors feared; however, new ideas will "flow forth" simultaneously. To his mind, then, while some texts were inevitably eliminated from the body as waste, the nourishing ones went on to set the generation of fresh ideas in motion. Cassian is, perhaps not coincidentally, also considered the first to lay out the fourfold method of reading, a layered approach to engaging with Scripture. Later, in the preface to his twelfth-century *De tribus maximis circumstantiis gestorum*, Hugh of St. Victor fully outlined a reading process that followed a continuous, four-part action, progressing from the literal to the anagogical. The fourfold interpretation of Scripture advanced by medieval exegetes—which also corresponded to Avicenna's description of Galenic digestion from food to perfect blood—was described by Hugh more precisely as three plus one. Upon arriving at the third level, readers could turn the word into their own, growing themselves and then inspiring others:

> Tropology is when in that action which we hear was done, we recognize what we should be doing. Whence it rightly receives the name "tropology," that is, converted speech or replicated discourse, for without a doubt we turn the word of a story about others to our own instruction when, having read the deeds of others, we conform our living to their example.[66]

In this passage, Hugh expands upon the chewing and digesting of the text described by his contemporaries, demonstrating that textual ingestion was in reality the beginning of a longer process leading from nourishment to growth. Jerome had been still more explicit on this point. He returned to a fundamental passage from Seneca to explain that digestion is best understood as the first step toward composition. As Seneca had said in *Ad Lucilium epistolae morales* 84:

> What in our own bodies we see Nature do without any conscious effort of ours (for the foods that we take in are a burden as long as they keep their own qualities and swim solid in the stomach, but once they have

---

66 "Tropologia est cum in eo quod factum audimus, quid nobis sit faciendum agnoscimus. Unde etiam recte tropologia, id est, sermo conversus sive locutio replicata, nomen accepit, quia nimirum alienae narrationis sermonem ad nostram tunc eruditionem convertimus, cum facta aliorum legendo ea nobis ad exemplum vivendi conformamus." Hugh of St. Victor, *De Tribus Maximis Circumstantiis Gestorum*, p. 491. Carruthers notes the relationship and provides the translation in *The Book of Memory*, p. 343 (Appendix A).

been changed from what they were, then they go over into strength and blood), we must perform on those things that nourish the mind, so that whatever we swallow we do not permit to remain unchanged, lest it be foreign. Let us digest it; otherwise it goes into the memory, not into the wit. Let us faithfully give books our assent and make them our own, that we may put together one thing out of many.[67]

Jerome in turn complemented this by calling up the proto-Eucharistic moment in Ezekiel 3.3: "'Son of man, your belly shall eat, and your bowels shall be filled with this book, which I give you,' and I ate it, and it was sweet as honey in my mouth." This should be done with the Bible, Jerome indicates, to make of it "originales libri": an ancestor or father to future textual progeny.[68]

While condemning preachers who dared to climb to the pulpit after having wasted their contact with books, Dante's contemporary the bishop and famed bibliophile Richard de Bury praises those who rightly appreciate and commit to memory—which is to say, consume and digest—the texts to which they have access. Those who model this activity are able to disseminate the knowledge they have gathered, but in doing so also render the books themselves [re]productive:

> First it behooves you to eat the book with Ezekiel, such that the belly of your memory may be internally sweetened. Thus in the way of the perfumed panther, to whose breath men, beasts, and cattle draw near that they might inhale it, the sweet scent of your aromatic understandings will be perceived externally. Thus our nature works secretly within our familiars, and the happy listeners run to surround you as the magnet draws the willing iron. What an infinite power of books lies in Paris or Athens, and yet resounds at the same time in Britain and Rome! While they lie quietly they are moved, while holding their very places they are carried about to the minds of listeners.[69]

---

67 "Quod in corpore nostro videmus sine ullo opere nostra facere naturam (alimenta quae accepimus, quamdiu in sua qualitate perdurant et solida innatant stomacho, onera sunt; at cum ex eo quod erant mutata sunt, tunc demum in vires et sanguinem transeunt), idem in his quibus aluntur ingenia praestemus, ut quaecumque hausimus non patiamur integra esse, ne aliena sit. Concocquamus illa; alioqui in memoriam ibunt, non in ingenium. Adsentiamur illis fideliter ac nostra faciamus, ut unum quiddam fiat ex multis." Seneca, *Epistolae morales ad Lucilium*, vol. 4, pp. 278–281.

68 "Fili hominis, venter tuus comedet, et viscera tua complebuntur volumine isto quod ego do tibi. Et comedi illud, et factum est in ore meo sicut mel dulce." See also Carruthers, *The Book of Memory*, 236–238.

69 "Primum oportet volumen cum Ezechiele comedere, quo venter memoriae dulcesat intrinsecus et sic more patherae refectae redoleat extrinsecus conceptorum aromatum odor suavis,

De Bury notably puts little weight on the distance between oral and textual propagation on the reproductive end, describing it as a kind of inhalation and exhalation. The key is that the reader engage properly with the text, eating and digesting with care; a community will then form around the reader and the text by force of nature, like iron filings to a magnet.

In the late Middle Ages, cycles of feast and famine, growing urban populations, and an increased attention to physiology and the connections between mind and body came together to create an atmosphere in which food and its consumption had vast potential for significance, one that permitted a wide and diverse audience to use it as a way to understand the world. Defining an appropriate relationship with food—locating gluttony and its opposite, and everything in between—was a synecdochic process that stood in for defining identity and participation in community. To decode and recode the values of his historical moment, Dante naturally turns to the visceral, charged relationship with food to understand himself and his community. Intimacy with food is precisely the feeling that the reader absorbs through an engagement with Dante's text—the sense of an author who speaks through food because he and his audience are equally comfortable and familiar with this language. Gluttony becomes a thread that carries the poet from his early exercises in poetic rivalry to his philosophical banquet, up through and including each canticle of his *Comedy*.

As Dante's work both reflects and reinforces, the interaction among food, body, and soul was part of a shared cultural consciousness that understood gluttony as existing on a spectrum. The focus on quality (or at least specificity) over quantity decentralizes the issue of eating too much, and requires instead an evaluation of a much broader set of factors that give an unexpected shape to the sense of what is too much, too extreme, or too far. Dante's interpretation of gluttony is clearly influenced by all of these contexts—religious, political, economic—but also elaborated according to his personal preoccupations. Spending most of his life in exile, the poet had firsthand experience with the real terror of starvation, and with the cruel torture of being excluded from the community and its communion. His near-obsession with the construction of citizenship and the individual duty

ad cuius anhelitum coanhelent accedere omnes bestiae et iumenta. Sic nostra natura in nostris familiaribus operante latenter, auditores auccurrunt benevoli, sicut adamas trahit ferrum neququam invite. O virtus infinita librorum iacent Parisius vel Athenis simulque resonant in Britannia et in Roma! Quiescentes quippe moventur, dum ipsis loca sua tenentibus, auditorum intellectibus circumquaque feruntur." Richard de Bury, *Philobiblon* 4.58.29–30.

to serve the greater whole leads him to find a very important and precise meaning in gluttony. Dante's interpretation of this sinful tendency sees it as an act that takes from others to give to the self, and that in so doing, untethers the self from its essence and leads to the breakdown of the bonds that hold together the human community.

Works Cited

Aristotle. *De anima*. Edited by Christopher John Shields. Oxford: Oxford University Press, 2020.

Aquinas, Thomas. *Summa Theologiae*. Translated by Fathers of the English Dominican Province. 3 vols. New York: Benziger, 1948.

Aquinas, Thomas. *On Evil*. Edited and introduction by Brian Davies. Translated by Richard Regan. Oxford: Oxford University Press, 2003.

Augustine. *Confessions*. Translated by R. S. Pine-Coffin. New York: Penguin, 1961.

Augustine. *Sermons*. Translated by Edmund Hill, O.P. Hyde Park, NY: New City Press, 1990.

Augustine. *Enarrationes en Psalmos*. 3 vols. Turnhout: Brepols, 1956.

Baraka, Amiri. *The System of Dante's Hell*. New York: Grove Press, 1963.

Barolini, Teodolinda. "Sociology of the *Brigata*: Gendered Groups in Dante, Forese, Folgore, Boccaccio—From 'Guido, i' vorrei' to Grisela." *Italian Studies* 67, no. 1 (2012): 4–22.

Bartlett, Robert. *The Making of Europe: Conquest, Colonization, and Cultural Change, 950–1350*. Princeton, NJ: Princeton University Press, 1994.

Brague Remi. *The Legend of the Middle Ages: Philosophical Explorations of Medieval Christianity, Judaism, and Islam*. Translated by Lydia G. Cochrane. Chicago: University of Chicago Press, 2009.

Bynum, Caroline Walker. *Holy Feast and Holy Fast: The Religious Significance of Food to Medieval Women*. Berkeley: University of California Press, 1987.

Bynum, Caroline Walker. "Fast, Feast, Flesh: The Religious Significance of Food to Medieval Women." In *Food and Culture: A Reader*, edited by Carole Counihan and Penny Van Esterik, 138–158. New York: Routledge, 2008.

Carruthers, Mary. *The Book of Memory*. Cambridge: Cambridge University Press, 1990.

Carruthers, Mary. *The Craft of Thought: Meditation Rhetoric, and the Making of Images 400-1200*. Cambridge: Cambridge University Press, 1998.

Cassian, John. *Conferences*. Edited and translated by Boniface Ramsey. Mahwah, NJ: Paulist Press, 1997.

Cherubini, Giovanni. *Città comunali di Toscana*. Bologna: CLUEB, 2003.

Cherubini, Giovanni. *Le città europee del medioevo*. Milan: Mondadori, 2009.

Courcelle, Pierre. *Late Latin Writers and their Greek Sources*. Translated by Harry E. Wedeck. Cambridge: Harvard University Press, 1969.

Day, William. "Economy." In *Dante in Context*, edited by Zygmunt G. Baranski and Lino Pertile, 30–46. Cambridge: Cambridge University Press, 2015.

de Bury, Richard. *Philobiblon*. New York: P.C. Duschnes, 1945.

Dameron, George. "Feeding the Medieval Italian City-State: Grain, War, and Political Legitimacy in Tuscany, c. 1150–c. 1350." *Speculum* 92, no. 4 (October 2017): 976–1019.

Flandrin, Jean-Louis and Massimo Montanari, eds. *Storia dell'alimentazione*. Rome: Laterza, 1996.

Freedman, Paul. "Spices and Late-Medieval European Ideas of Scarcity and Value." *Speculum* 80, no. 4 (Oct. 2005): 1209–227.

Freedman, Paul. *Out of the East: Spices and the Medieval Imagination*. New Haven: Yale University Press, 2008.

Goodson, Caroline, Carol Symes, and Anne Lester, eds. *Cities, Texts and Social Networks, 400–1500: Experiences and Perceptions of Medieval Urban Space*. New York: Routledge, 2010.

Grafton, Anthony, Glenn W. Most, and Salvatore Settis, eds. *The Classical Tradition*. Cambridge: Harvard University Press, 2010.

Gregory the Great. *Morals on the Book of Job*. 3 vols. Translated by James Bliss. London: J.G.F. and J. Rivington, 1844.

Grangnolati, Manuele. *Experiencing the Afterlife: Soul and Body in Dante and Medieval Culture*. South Bend: University of Notre Dame Press, 2005.

Grieco, Allen J. "The Social Politics of Pre-Linnaean Botanical Classification." *I Tatti Studies: Essays in the Renaissance* 4 (1991): 131–149.

Grieco, Allen J. "Alimentazione e classi sociali nel tardo Medioevo e nel Rinascimento in Italia." In *Storia dell'alimentazione*, edited by Jean-Louis Flandrin and Massimo Montanari, 371–380. Rome: Laterza, 1996.

Grieco, Allen J. *Food, Social Politics and the Order of Nature in Renaissance Italy*. Cambridge, Mass.: Harvard University Press, 2019.

Grumett, David and Rachel Muers. *Theology on the Menu: Asceticism, Meat and Christian Diet*. London: Routledge, 2010.

Hill, Susan. *Eating to Excess: The Meaning of Gluttony and the Fat Body in the Ancient World*. Oxford: Praegar, 2011.

Herlihy, David. *Pisa in the Early Renaissance: A Study in Urban Growth*. New Haven: Yale University Press, 1958.

Herlihy, David. *Medieval Households*. Cambridge, Mass.: Harvard University Press, 1985.

Herlihy, David. "Medieval Demography." In *Dictionary of the Middle Ages*, vol. 4, edited by Joseph R. Strayer, 136–148. New York: Scribner, 1989.

Hoffman, Richard C. *An Environmental History of Medieval Europe.* Cambridge: Cambridge University Press, 2014.

Hugh of St. Victor. *De Tribus Maximis Circumstantiis Gestorum.* Edited by William M. Green. *Speculum* 18, no. 4 (1943): 484–493.

Jerome. *Select Letters.* Translated by F. A. Wright. Cambridge, Mass.: Harvard University Press, 1933.

Keen, Catherine. *Dante and the City.* Gloucestershire: Tempus, 2003.

Laurioux, Bruno. "Table et hiérarchie social à la fin du moyen âge." In *Du manuscrit à la table: essais sur la cuisine au moyen âge et répertoire des manuscrits médiévaux contenant des recettes culinaries*, edited by Carole Lambert, 87–108. Montreal: Université de Montréal, 1992.

Laurioux, Bruno. "I libri di cucina italiani alla fine del Medioevo: un nuovo bilancio." *Archivio Storico Italiano* 154, no. 1 (567) (1996): 33–58.

LeGoff, Jacques. *La civilisation de l'occident médiéval.* Paris: Arthaud, 1964.

Lovejoy, Arthur O. *The Great Chain of Being.* Cambridge: Harvard University Press, 1936.

Martellotti, Anna. *I ricettari di Federico II: Dal "Meriodionale" al "Liber de coquina."* Florence: Olschki, 2005.

Martin, A. Lynn. "The Baptism of Wine." *Gastronomica* 3, no. 4 (Fall 2003): 21–30.

Miller, William Ian. "Gluttony." *Representations* 60 (Autumn 1997): 92–112.

Montanari, Massimo. *Alimentazione e cultura nel medioevo.* Rome: Laterza, 1992.

Montanari, Massimo. "Contadini, guerrieri, sacerdoti." In *Storia dell'alimentazione*, edited by Jean-Louis Flandrin and Massimo Montanari, 229–232. Rome: Laterza, 1996.

Nicoud, Marilyn. *Les régimes de santé au Moyen Âge: Naissance et diffusion d'une écriture médicale*, 2 vols. Rome: Ecole française de Rome, 2007.

Nicoud, Marilyn. "Food Consumption, a Health Risk? Norms and Medical Practice in the Middle Ages." *Appetite* 51 (July 2008): 7–9.

Nicoud, Marilyn. "Nutrirsi secondo i medici nell'età antica e medievale." In *Nutrire il corpo, nutrire l'anima nel Medioevo*, edited by Chiara Crisciana and Onorato Grassi, 41–68. Pisa: Edizioni ETS, 2017.

Olson, Kristina. "Shoes, Gowns and Turncoats: Reconsidering Cacciguida's History of Florentine Fashion and Politics." *Dante Studies* 134 (2016): 26–47.

Pease, Arthur Stanley. "Medical Allusions in the Works of St. Jerome." *Harvard Studies in Classical Philology* 25 (1914): 73–86.

Pertile, Lino. "Ciacco, Brunetto and the Voice of God." In *Legato con amore: Essay in Honor of John A. Scott*, 157–174. Florence: L.S. Olschki, 2013.

Pinto, Giuliano. *Toscana medievale: paesaggi e realtà sociali.* Florence: Le Lettere, 1993.

Plato. *Timaeus, Critias, Cleitophon, Menexenus, Epistles*, edited and translated by R. G. Bury. Cambridge, Mass.: Loeb Classical Library, 1960.

Purdy Moudarres, Christiana. "Bodily Starvation and the Ravaging of the Will: A Reading of *Inferno* 32–33." *Viator* 47, no. 1 (2016): 205–228.

Quellier, Florent. *Gola: Storia di un peccato capitale.* Translated by Vito Carrassi. Bari: Edizioni Dedalo, 2012.

Reeds, Karen. "Albert on the Natural Philosophy of Plant Life." In *Albertus Magnus and the Sciences: Commemorative Essays 1980,* edited by James Weisheipl, 341–354. Toronto: Pontifical Institute of Medieval Studies, 1980.

Rousselle, Aline. "Abstinence et continence dans les monastères de Gaule méridionale à la fin de l'antiquité et au dèbut du moyen âge: Etude d'un regime alimentaire et da sa fonction." In *Hommages à André Dupont (1897–1972): Etudes médiévale languedociennes par ses anciens collègues, élèves et ami,* 239–254. Montpellier: Fédération Historique du Languedoc Mediterranéen et du Rousillon, Université Paul-Valery, 1974.

Scully, Terrence. *The Art of Cookery in the Middle Ages.* Woodbridge, UK: Boydell, 1995.

Seneca. *Epistolae morales ad Lucilium.* Translated by Richard M. Gummere. 10 vols. Cambridge, Mass.: Loeb Classical Library, 1920.

Shaw, Teresa M. *The Burden of the Flesh: Fasting and Sexuality in Early Christianity.* Minneapolis: Augsburg Fortress, 1998.

Siraisi, Nancy. *Taddeo Alderotti and his Pupils: Two Generations of Italian Medical Learning.* Princeton: Princeton University Press, 1981.

Siraisi, Nancy. *Medieval and Early Renaissance Medicine: An Introduction to Knowledge and Practice.* Chicago: University of Chicago Press, 2009.

Squatriti, Paolo. *Water and Society in Early Medieval Italy.* Cambridge: Cambridge University Press, 1998.

Toussaint-Samat, Maguelonne. *A History of Food.* Translated by Anthea Bell. London: Wiley-Blackell, 2009.

Weisheipl, James. ed. *Albertus Magnus and the Sciences: Commemorative Essays 1980.* Toronto: Pontifical Institute of Medieval Studies, 1980.

2. Convivial Gluttony

Abstract

This chapter examines representations of gluttony in Dante's early lyric poetry and in his philosophical treatise *Convivio*. While the early poetry begins to play with the value systems food can express and reinforce, the treatise-as-banquet is where food's many layers of significance become apparent. By taking up food and the human relationship with eating, Dante is able to express his values through each item or practice; more than this, he performs how the act of expression itself can be used to develop communal bonds. Though the treatise would ultimately be abandoned, the scaffolding of the *Convivio* becomes the through line of the *Comedy*, enabling Dante to use the everyday realities of food consumption to comment on the means of forming human community and the supernatural mystery of union with God.

Keywords: civic duty, community, hierarchy, identity, power, social values

If Dante's engagement with food has been explored relatively infrequently, his preoccupation with power and station has instead garnered extensive critical attention. There is, however, a popular posthumous anecdote that brings these two themes together, and it suggests that Dante's sensitivity to the way food could be used to wield power and express status was recognized by his contemporary audience. In his late fourteenth-century *Novelliere*, Giovanni Sercambi recounts an apocryphal tale of a dinner hosted by King Roberto of Naples to which Dante was invited at the king's behest. The poet, arriving in a state of dress unbecoming of the royal court, is seated last and at the least important table, thoroughly ignored by the king. When King Roberto finally bothers to inquire where the great poet might be, Dante has already departed, and a messenger must be sent after him to request his audience once again. This time, Dante returns dressed richly, and he is promptly seated next to the king at the head of the first table. Yet upon being served, the poet splashes his food and wine into his lap, soiling his

Callegari, D., *Dante's Gluttons: Food and Society from the* Convivio *to the* Comedy.
Taylor & Francis Group, 2022
DOI 10.5117/9789463720427_CH02

beautiful clothes while the court looks on in confusion and distaste. The moral unfolds as follows:

> The king, who had seen everything, turned to Dante and said, "What's this I saw you do? I understood you to be most wise, and yet you behave in such an unseemly way!" And Dante, who apprehended what the king wished to know, said: "Your highness, I know that you have afforded this great honor to my clothes, and for that reason I wanted my clothes to enjoy the food offered here [...] since I was seated at the end of the table because I was badly dressed [...] while when I was well dressed you allowed me to sit at the head."[1]

Though the story is an invention, it cannily captures the way in which Dante was understood to use the social values of material goods to express his disdain for certain behaviors and to suggest correctives. As Kristina Olson has demonstrated in her examination of Dante's use of fashion in the *Comedy*, "the adornment of the body becomes a fulcrum for discussing the political and social issues associated with the material realities of consumption and display," confirming that the poet saw excess in sartorial display as a political issue as well as a moral one.[2] In the Sercambi anecdote, the king's misjudgment of the poet serves as an opportunity to portray Dante setting himself at odds with the adage later made famous by Erasmus, *vestis virum facit*. More importantly, it shows Dante reminding his host that attention to clothing and attention to duty are not one and the same. The poet's shifting seats and the act of "feeding" his clothes present Dante as one intimately familiar with the roles played out at the dinner table, while highlighting the king's impoverished interpretation of hospitality. It is a reminder of how Dante's use of food as a communicator of boundaries and duties in his own work influenced those who came after him, creating a lasting gastronomic language that could be employed by authors wishing to comment in their own way on class, status, and obligation.

In the late Middle Ages, the space in which food was consumed, as well as the food itself, expressed ordering principles, so that social structures

---

1   "Lo re, che ha veduto tutto, rivoltòsi a Dante dicendoli:—Dante, che è quello che io v'ho veduto fare? Tenendovi tanto savio, come avete uzato tanta bruttura?—Dante, che ode quello desiderava, dice:—Santa corona, io cognosco che questo grande onore ch'è ora fatto, lo avete fatto a' panni; e pertanto io ho voluto che i panni godano le vivande aparecchiate. E che sia vero, vi dico che io non ho ora meno di senno che ci avea poi che in coda di taula fui asettato, e questo fue perch'io era mal vestito. E ora con quel senno avea son ritornato ben vestito e m'avete fatto stare in capo di taula." Sercambi, *Il novelliere*, vol. 2, pp. 63–64.

2   Olson, "Shoes, Gowns and Turncoats," pp. 36–37.

and power systems were communicated through these gastronomic gestures. As Jack Goody has noted in his study of the food practices that tie human communities of different times and places together, Chaucer's characters—particularly the gourmand Franklin and the well-mannered Physician—offer "a picture of medieval food-ways that is marked by hierarchical distinction and is most unlikely to be purely 'literary.'"[3] Like the The Canterbury Tales and other late medieval texts, Dante's works played with many aspects of food culture, but perhaps none could as succinctly and successfully transmit a wide array of ideas as did the hierarchy established around the table—and on it. Indeed, though most readers have perceived only biting insults in Dante's first indictment of a glutton in the *tenzone* with his friend Forese Donati, a closer look at these early poetic exchanges shows that the food in which his friend is accused of indulging speaks far more to the role he is meant to play in his community than to his excessive calorie intake. Describing eating habits, whether good or bad, becomes a tool for Dante to set forth a hierarchy of his own—one that establishes how diet affects the physical health and intellect of an individual as well as the peace and health of the community at large.

Examining the poet's youthful work provides a crucial foundation for understanding the elaborate distinctions he lays out in his philosophical "banquet," the *Convivio*. There, Dante plays the part of one who distributes food in appropriate types and amounts, guarding against gluttons. Both the *tenzone* and the *Convivio* establish Dante's intention to employ the language of food to reach a wide readership and use familiar terms to express ideas about self-governance and community governance; when he then uses the metaphor of setting a table and serving food in the *Convivio*, Dante anchors his work in a gesture of nourishment and confirms the glutton as a looming threat to its success. The philosophical treatise as banquet is where the richness and potential of food's many layers of significance become apparent: the real struggle with appetite and the concrete use of food as a tool for political and social order; the more nebulous space between the physical and the spiritual that food can speak to as it moves through body, intellect, and soul; and the metaphoric representation of knowledge as food consumed and made a part of the self, shared in turn with others as it inspires reproduction. Though the treatise would ultimately be abandoned, the scaffolding of the *Convivio* becomes the through line of the *Comedy*, enabling Dante to use the everyday realities of food consumption to bring

3   Goody, *Cooking, Cuisine and Class*, p. 134.

together the means of forming human community with the supernatural mystery of union with God.

The Great Chain of Eating, and Dante's First Glutton

As Goody suggests, it is unlikely that a medieval author could have ignored the collective consciousness surrounding food and its hierarchical values, and no mention of food or eating habits in medieval literature can be properly understood without a full vision of the social hierarchy of food. As traced in the previous chapter, the *scala naturae* put forth by Albertus Magnus in the mid-thirteenth century had paved the way for a detailed ladder of where edible plants and animals stood relative to one another. The organization that this hierarchy of consumers and consumed provided was exceptionally appealing to those on the Italian peninsula in the late Middle Ages, as the population grew unwieldy and the boundaries of social stratification were tested by the growth and circulation of wealth. In fact, the relationship between diet and status has been shown to have become a major means of enforcing those divisions during periods of population growth, particularly when they coincided with the emergence of new social classes. In his studies of Renaissance cuisine and food culture in Europe, Ken Albala has identified the decades around the turn of the fourteenth century—just before the plague of 1348 decimated the population—as the moment in which food was cemented as the primary means by which men judged themselves and others. The anxieties of the elite, felt acutely in the often precariously maintained Italian city-states, were thus assuaged with an extraordinarily specific and fiercely implemented dietary code.[4]

Beginning with his earliest work, Dante took full advantage of this shared and profound social consciousness of food and the nuance it brought to perceptions of indulgence. This is particularly visible in the poems that fall into the "other genre" of Italian vernacular love poetry, dedicated to, as Kenelm Foster and Patrick Boyde have summarized, "anti-idealist themes [that] make free use of local words and forms, concrete, particular, often vulgar in diction, seeking a colloquial pungency, but nevertheless in their own way, stylized and 'institutionalized.'"[5] The *tenzone* with Forese

---

4   Albala, *Eating Right in the Renaissance*, pp. 186–187. On overpopulation and problems in food production at this time, see also the brief but essential overview in Cherubini, *Agricoltura e società nel medioevo*, pp. 28–31.

5   Foster and Boyde, *Dante's Lyric Poetry*, vol. 2, p. 243.

Donati—Dante's most conspicuous exercise in the "other genre"—long troubled scholars, not only because they found its style unbecoming of the great poet, but also due to the difficulty in deciphering the many allusions to contemporary cultural context packed within it.[6] However, this "colloquial pungency" has since revealed itself to be a useful approach to reading this early exchange of poetic jabs between the two young men, as readers have demonstrated by considering late medieval Tuscan economics, law, and politics to provide glosses for its obscurities.[7] Teodolinda Barolini has further remarked on how Dante shines in the *tenzone*, getting in a barrage of insults in a quarter of the space Forese requires for just one.[8] In fact, Dante's insults are not only more frequent and more successful, they elevate the peacocking of the two poets into a debate over civic duty and community construction.

A conspicuous example is found in Dante's response to Forese's provocation, "Chi udisse tossir la malfatata," where Dante imagines Donati's mother-in-law lamenting the unjust marriage contract she was forced to accept on behalf of her daughter:

La tosse, 'l freddo e l'altra mala voglia
    noll'adovien per omor' ch'abbia vecchi,
    ma per difetto ch'ella sente al nido.
Piange la madre, c'ha più d'una doglia,
    dicendo: "Lassa, che per fichi secchi
    messa l'avre'n casa del conte Guido!"[9]

(The coughing and cold and other troubles—these don't come to her from ageing humours, but from the gap she feels in the nest. Her mother, who

---

6   As Foster and Boyde recall, "the many obscure personal references and allusions to contemporary places and events in these sonnets used to pose enormous problems for the commentator." *Dante's Lyric Poetry*, vol. 2, p. 244. On more recent efforts to discredit the attribution to Dante due to the "almost incomprehensible" nature of the poems in the known Dantean context, see Noakes, "Virility, Nobility, and Banking," p. 241.

7   See Alfie, *Dante's* Tenzone *with Forese Donati*, which dedicates an entire chapter to possible readings of the exchange in full historical context, demonstrating that even the mention of "conte Guido" might be understood as a multivalent reference to contemporary politics (whereby Dante implies Nella's betrayal of Forese's family), pp. 33–59. Noakes gives attention to the socioeconomic and legal context and proposes new translations, though she holds off on proposing new readings, in "Virility, Nobility, and Banking," pp. 241–258.

8   Barolini, *Dante and the Origins of Italian Literary Culture*, pp. 39–40; see also Barolini, "From Editorial History to Hermeneutic Failure," pp. 3–28.

9   Text and translations from Foster and Boyde, *Dante's Lyric Poetry*, pp. 148–149.

has more than one affliction, weeps saying: "Alas, for dried figs I could
have married her to Count Guido!")

The intention of the verses is clear, with or without further context, and
even a modern reader can quickly discern that Dante is calling Forese
an impotent husband. Nella's coldness is nonetheless a telling point of
departure, if only as a confirmation that medicine, and specifically Galenic
humoral theory, is at play here. Forese's wife finds herself cold even in
the summer months, but this is not, Dante emphasizes, caused by the
anticipated cooling of the humors that accompanies old age.[10] Putting aside
the physiological reasons that are to be expected, Dante turns to a different
preoccupation and confirms it is instead the "gap" Nella feels in her "nest"
that leaves her so frigid. This internal imbalance that causes external
physical symptoms points to a dietary connection, and the metaphor
can allude to both the wife's body and the hearth of the home. Forese's
impotence in maintaining his household is seen not only in the marital
bed he leaves cold, but also in the pantry he leaves empty. The "dried figs"
that Forese's mother-in-law could have substituted for a dowry, saving
her own finances while saving her daughter from misery, might simply
point to their place among the most common conservable food items at
the time.[11] In this case, the implication would be that once Forese had
unscrupulously and foolishly run through all of Nella's dowry—on fresh
foods that might have kept his wife in good health—dried fruit was all
that remained in his larder. More pointedly, figs also inevitably recall
female sexual organs, which allows Dante to elaborate on the "difetto"
he identified in her nest.[12] The double meaning of the figs can actually
provide a slightly different reading of the passage: if Nella's mother had
known that her daughter's genitals (*fichi*) would be left to dry up (*secchi*),
she would have done just as well to save her money and give Nella to an
impotent old man.

10   As discussed in the introduction to this book, a number of studies have now considered the
familiarity of the Galenic corpus and humoral theory in Dante's milieu, demonstrating that at
least the medical-nutritional values of food were firmly understood even at the popular level,
thanks to the wide circulation of illuminated texts like the *Tacuinum sanitatis* and other less
famous but commonly available pamphlets. See Gilson, "The Anatomy and Physiology of the
Human Body in the *Commedia*," p. 17, and Patrizia Bertini Malgarini, "Il linguaggio medico e
anatomico nelle opere di Dante."
11   Cherubini, "The Peasant and Agriculture," p. 117.
12   The slang remains in common use at present; for its etymology, see Boggioni and Casalengo,
"Fico," in *Dizionario storico del lessico erotico italiano,* p. 213. Dante himself memorably describes
Vanni Fucci's hand gesture that plays on the vulgar second meaning of figs in *Inf.* 25.2.

Dante's following response, "Ben ti faranno il nodo Salamone," is more manifestly gastronomic, as the poet reinforces the gross incontinence Forese shows in the face of rich fare:

Ben ti faranno il nodo Salamone
    Bicci novello, e' petti de le starne,
    ma peggio fia la lonza del castrone,
    ché 'l cuoio farà vendetta de la carne.
tal che starai più presso a San Simone,
    se tu non ti procacci de l'andarne:
    e 'ntendi che 'l fuggire el mal boccone
    sarebbe oramai tardi a ricomprarne.[13]

(Partridge breasts, young Bicci, will truss you in Solomon's knot all right! But loins of mutton will be still worse for you, for the skin will take revenge for the flesh! So much so that you'll live a bit nearer San Simone, if you don't hurry and get away. And by now, mind, it's too late to redeem your debts by giving up guzzling.)

Targeting Forese's gluttony might seem as likely as any step to take following an effective attack on his wealth and sexual prowess. Yet Dante is intensely specific when he relates what his friend gorges himself on, suggesting that a random choice will not do when a careful selection can show Forese's indulgences go far beyond the table. In naming "petti de le starne" and "lonza del castrone," Dante exhibits his talent for using the familiarity of food to express a multiplicity of meanings in a single image. Just as the "nodo Salamone" to which Dante refers here invokes subjugation and commitment, as Fabian Alfie's careful dissection has determined, so the edible items contain a more subtle message.[14] Like all men and all foods, partridge and mutton had their place on the great chain of eating, and by using these foods Dante connects gluttony to the social hierarchy and, critically, to the civic duty that is vital to community participation.

The "lonza del castrone," or loin of wether (castrated male sheep), might seem to vaguely indicate a rich meat at first, but its "social identity" was

---

13   Foster and Boyde, *Dante's Lyric Poetry,* pp. 150–151.
14   Alfie, *Dante's* Tenzone *with Forese Donati,* pp. 40–43. Alfie summarizes a part of the vast critical tradition on the "nodo," which incidentally demonstrates the lack of attention to the food items in comparison, though Alfie himself gives space to the nuances of gluttony in the secular medieval context.

rigorously nuanced by its age, accessibility, and appropriateness.[15] Like most meat, the *castrato* or *castrone* was generally precious in the late Middle Ages: it was a product that required substantial investment in its preparation for human consumption, it spoiled easily, it was expensive, and its availability was limited.[16] The High Middle Ages had marked a shift towards appreciating meat on the Italian peninsula, as Carolingian culture became the primary point of reference; meat was for warriors and thus the ruling classes, even as they slowly became less likely to act as warriors themselves. The late thirteenth century saw the privatization of land and the exclusion of most of the population from hunting rights across much of Europe, creating a correlation between land-holding and meat-eating. Though the grain-centric medieval Mediterranean diet did not likely suffer notably due to meat shortage, and conditions could vary widely according to the local government, the clear move to consolidate and control the food that could be gleaned from the land had powerful social effects if not nutritional ones.[17] Even birding, a right as commonly exercised in cities as in the countryside, was slowly restricted in another step toward reigning in common goods and appropriating them to the "most noble," or the highest bidder. Crucially, what was considered "the forest" and more specifically "hunting territory" often extended far beyond the obvious borders of visibly uncultivated or wooded land, encompassing huge swaths of property previously understood as a part of a shared outdoor space.[18]

Castrone was, in particular, a meat associated with high tables and fine dining. Price schemes from the time demonstrate that castrated mutton

---

15   Foster and Boyde point out that Barbi first gave a definition of the "castrone" as the common contemporary term for "montone castrato," in *Dante's Lyric Poetry*, vol. 2, p. 249. See also Baldelli, "Castrone," p. 871.

16   In addition to Cherubini, "The Peasant and Agriculture," and Flandrin and Montanari, *Storia dell'alimentazione,* see Maria Giagnacovo, *Mercanti a tavola,* pp. 163–167, which gives an overview of the progress toward the aristocratization of meat on the Italian peninsula from the High to the late Middle Ages.

17   Montanari, *Campagne medievali,* pp. 149–173, and "Strutture di produzione e sistemi alimentari nell'alto Medioevo," p. 220. On the movement of hunting from "common good" in the High Middle Ages to "privilege" in the late Middle Ages, see Tucci, "La caccia, da bene comune a privilegio," pp. 424–425. Tucci notes that these newly introduced prohibitions did not, at least at first, actually seem to stop people from hunting entirely, but likely had a more symbolic value, laying the groundwork for associating hunting with the highest classes. See also Capatti and Montanari, *La cucina italiana,* pp. 76–77, which points out that nobles were less likely to be warriors and more likely to be standard-bearers of taste.

18   See Le Goff, ed., *Dizionario dell'occidente medievale,* pp. 119–131, where Alain Guerreau surveys research demonstrating the tendency for the boundaries of hunting territories to reflect social status and desired delimitations rather than visibly uncultivated land, leading eventually to a de facto prohibition of hunting for the local rural populations.

commanded higher prices than not only the oft-maligned pork but also beef, suggesting that *castrone* was more highly prized than other options.[19] Its castrated state was a key factor contributing to its value, as castrating was often described in dietary treatises as a way of trapping nutritive substances in the body and ensuring that meat remained humorally balanced in terms of its moisture (neither too damp nor too dry) and its temperature (neither too hot nor too cold).[20] More than merely healthful, *castrone* had become part of the diet of the elite, as witnessed by multiple recipes for the meat prepared in complex and delicate ways included in the *Liber de coquina* and, more pertinently, the Tuscan redaction of that text known as the *Anonimo toscano*—including spinach leaves stuffed with *castrone* (no. 5) and stuffed rolled shoulder of *castrone* (no. 111).[21] By indulging leisurely in such foods, Forese Donati betrays his indecorous aspirations to higher status while neglecting his duty to his wife, who sits cold and suffering at home.

The example of the *starne*, grey partridges, offers still more depth to Dante's accusation of Forese as a glutton. Beloved as one of the tastiest game birds, its lightness, quickness, and ability to fly unequivocally marked the grey partridge as a food for the "highest" of consumers. Occupying a rarefied place at the top of the food hierarchy, birds were volatile and suited to few consumers. Their allure for most men came from a desire to hover similarly above others. Women, always more susceptible to humoral imbalance, were especially threatened by bird-eating. Indeed, the female proclivity toward wanton sexual behavior required that women be strongly discouraged from eating them at all.[22] Galen had classified fowl as exceedingly hot in his *De sanitate tuenda*, and popular dietary treatises and *tacuina* of the late Middle Ages reiterated this; they emphasized that the innate heat of a flying bird

19 A pricing scheme for meat in medieval Tuscany is provided by Pinto, *Toscano medievale*, p. 101; see also the note on most prized meats in later *trecento* Tuscany in Giagnacovo, "Due 'alimentazioni' del basso Medioevo," p. 825.

20 See Scully, *The Art of Cookery in the Middle Ages*, pp. 47–48, and Toussaint-Samat, *A History of Food*, pp. 305–12. Everyone from Gentile da Foligno (in *Consilium contra pestilentiam*, "De quadrupedibus") to the anonymous author of the thirteenth-century Salernitan dietary treatise *De flore dietarum* insist that meat from castrated animals is most healthful and especially more easily digested. The Romans had long ago demonstrated the efficacy of castration in the pursuit of a fatter animal, so it is likely that the insistence on the healthfulness of the process was also influenced by a question of taste; the Romans are thought to have invented the capon, or castrated rooster, in response to the 162 BC declaration of the Lex Faunia that prohibited the use of grain to fatten chickens.

21 Martellotti furnishes transcriptions from the original manuscripts with recipe numbers for clarity in Martellotti, *I ricettari di Federico II*, pp. 199–280.

22 Grieco emphasizes this point in "Alimentazione e classi sociali nel tardo Medioevo e nel Rinascimento in Italia," p. 374.

gave rise to its insatiable sexual appetite, and its flesh could translate that heat to its consumer, leading the body to generate excess semen and the impulse to use it.[23] This double meaning evoked by a bird, both noble and erotic, was played upon frequently in literature. In a famous example, the falcon that Federigo degli Alberighi serves his beloved in Boccaccio's *novella* from the fifth day of the *Decameron* acts as a symbol of the lady's great virtue: a bird noble enough to be a companion in life acts as a meal for an impenetrable woman. But while Alberighi apparently cooks the falcon out of desperation, he simultaneously manages to harness its potential heat, as it is after ingesting the falcon that his lady abandons her abstinence and finally marries him.[24]

The pretensions to dominance represented by partridge, whether in terms of sexual or broader social conquest, were easily recognizable as they were closely associated with the kitchens and diets of the powerful. Partridge in particular appears repeatedly in culinary texts of the period, including the *Liber de coquina*; as Anna Martellotti has demonstrated in her careful examination of culinary texts from the thirteenth century, birds in general were heavily featured in presentations of *alta cucina*, and partridge was commonly listed in these written records of what and how the high born ate—appearing no less than seven times in one fragment.[25] Later examples show that partridge so effectively communicated the intention to exercise power that careful men were wary of being seen to indulge in it. The biographer of Filippo Maria Visconti, the duke of Milan, recalls that the duke ate "pernice, fagiano o coturnice" (partridge, pheasant or rock partridge) only when he wished to indulge in "gola" (gluttony).[26] In a letter frequently studied by food historians, the notary Lapo Mazzei vehemently declined an invitation to eat grey partridge with the Pratese merchant Francesco di Marco Datini, surprised that his friend would dare to offer something so inappropriate for him:

> Please let me alone with your grey partridges, and other things God knows
> I do not look upon willingly: for their cost, which it hardly pleases me to

---

23 Grieco incorporates a very useful overview of birds in the late medieval and early Renaissance Italian diet into his study of bird imagery and sexuality in "From Roosters to Cocks," pp. 112–113.
24 Boccaccio, *Decameron*, 5.9. Grieco also points out the necessity of understanding the falcon's place in the "great chain of being" to appreciate Boccaccio's story, though he reads it as a symbol of the lady's virtue and a device for evoking *pathos* rather than an instrument of sexual power. See "Alimentazione e classi sociali nel tardo Medioevo e nel Rinascimento in Italia," p. 378.
25 Martellotti, *I ricettari di Federico II*, p. 47
26 Capatti and Montanari, *La cucina italiana*, p. 78.

spend in one go, and neither does it please me to send them to those who enjoy them, nor would selling them soothe my conscience.[27]

Importantly, in his letter Mazzei goes on to underline that there was a time in his life when he would have been capable of ingesting such a dish—that is, during his time as a prior in the Florentine government: "S'io fussi nelle servitudi delle genti, come già fui, sarebbono stato pasto mio" (If I were in the service of the people, as I once was, they would be an appropriate meal for me).[28] Service to the people would have been precisely the reason for which indulgence in such a food type might have been appropriate—an act of giving oneself to the community that justly required refreshment of the body, and during which the desire to exercise power over others was in line with duty. Grieco has looked to the meticulous records kept of the daily provisions for the *mensa dei priori* to demonstrate that the priors "were, in fact, required to eat great quantities of partridge and fowl in general, since this was seen as an outward sign of the civic and political power they wielded, as well as a physical necessity given the grueling work of governance."[29] In one particularly notable example, the twelve priors and their few guests consumed about 65 partridges per day in December 1398, going through 1,300 birds over the course of the month.[30]

Like Federigo degli Alberighi's falcon in Boccaccio's novella, the partridge in Dante's poem might be read simply as a symbol of wealth and status, and more generally as a taunt about Forese's unrestrained appetite. Yet the association between the partridge and power—one that eventually led to the priors' table itself—suggests that the evocation of this bird brought more to the medieval mind than general intemperance or even nobility. The correlation between the highest class of men and the highest class

27 "Voi non mi lasciate stare con vostre starne, e cose che Dio sa io non veggio volentieri, e per lo costo, ché non mi diletto tanto a struggere a un tratto, e à goditori non mi contento mandarle, e vendelle non me lo patisce l'animo." The letter is discussed by Grieco in "Menu, Banchetti e Tavole Imbandite in Toscana," p. 375, and in "From Roosters to Cocks," pp. 114–116; selections from the same exchanges are highlighted in Origo, *The Merchant of Prato: Francesco di Marco Datini, 1335–1410*.

28 Grieco, "Menu, Banchetti e Tavole Imbandite in Toscana," p. 375.

29 Grieco, "From Roosters to Cocks," pp. 114–116.

30 For a comprehensive consideration and reproduction of several folios of *Ashburnham* 1216, held at the Biblioteca Medicea Laurenziana, see Frosini, *Il cibo e i signori*. The codex contains a thorough list of the food purchased and prepared for the Florentine priors at various intervals ranging from 1344 to 1428. These accounts are not limited to itemization, but also extend occasionally to recipes and recognition of what specific individuals ate as a result of necessary dietary changes (due to illness, for example).

of animals belies a more intricate design. By choosing to call Forese a glutton in these terms, Dante is remarking more on Forese's role in their community and his self-awareness than on his eating habits. Believing he should digest the viands of great men and pose as a leader of his city, Forese engages in both a distasteful endeavor to be someone he is not and an immoral rejection of his responsibility toward the common good. In the *tenzone*, Forese is not accused of consuming uncouth amounts, he is indicted for consuming indiscriminately. Knowing his friend would gladly indulge in these foods, Dante reminds him not only that he can't afford them, but that he isn't fit for them. The pairing of the mutton and the partridge—the one a reminder of a good taken away from the public, and the other a prize for the men engaged in a public good—rigorously conveys this message.

Gluttons for Grain

The lines exchanged with Forese Donati are hardly Dante's last experiment with food, and the poet will have much more to say about hierarchy and community through eating habits. In fact, as pre-announced by its title, in the *Convivio* Dante approaches the question in a still more explicit fashion. He presents a philosophical discourse as a banquet, the contents of which are distinguished by the type, quality, and order of food served. He states that in the course of his work, he will depend on the nuance of meaning permitted by distinctions in both the foods themselves and the ways in which they are consumed to communicate with his audience. Given the obviously metaphoric quality of the food served in the *Convivio*, the gastronomic paradigm is often taken for granted as a useful but peripheral device in the work, important as the structural girding of the text but irrelevant in terms of its own content. To be clear, Dante's textual meal is hardly meant to be read as a recipe, and its symbolic substance is where its "meat" is to be found. Yet the care and attention with which the poet selects his ingredients are a reminder that even metaphoric food must draw upon tangible realities with which the audience is familiar in order to be effective. Moreover, it is the space that food occupies between the literal and the metaphoric, between the physical and the spiritual, that makes it such a valuable tool for the poet.

The *Convivio*'s difficult opening paragraphs make this point immediately, as they require a sensitive understanding of the meaning of food to unravel Dante's intentions. These lines show the poet employing the many valences of food and its consumption, from medical learning to civic duty, doctrine, and moral code:

> I now intend to respond to their want by providing a full-scale banquet of the food I displayed before their eyes, by supplying also the bread that must accompany such food, without which they would find the food too rich. This banquet, which demands that bread, has food of such quality that I have no intention of seeing it served in vain. So let no one take a seat who is incapacitated from eating properly because he lacks teeth or tongue or palate, nor anyone given to vice, for his stomach is full of poisonous fluids incompatible with my food which would prevent him keeping it down. But let everyone come here whose truly human hunger remains unassuaged because of pressures of family or civic responsibilities; he is invited to take his place at table with all the others who have been similarly impeded. All whom laziness has held back may make a place for themselves at the others' feet, for they do not deserve a higher seat. And let each group take my food along with the bread provided, which will enable them both to taste and assimilate it (*Conv.* 1.1.11-13).[31]

In laying out his treatise, Dante is explicit and highly specific in the terms he employs to "apparecchiare" (set) his proverbial table (1.1.11). He explains that the ultimate goal is to consume the "pane degli angeli" (bread of angels), though humans can only hope to enjoy "quello che da loro cade" (that which falls) from that table, sitting beneath it and collecting crumbs (1.1.7; 1.1.10). He reveals his prose commentary will also be like a bread, but hardly leaving it to the imagination, Dante further confirms that this will be a rustic "pane di biado" (bread of mixed grain; or, animal fodder) rather than "frumento" (wheat), and thus a "pane orzato" (bread of mostly barley), but that he will slice off the outer crust so that "ogni macula" (every impurity) will be eliminated before it is set before the diners (1.5.1; 1.13.12; 1.2.1). This barley

---

31 "Per che ora volendo loro apparecchiare, intendo fare un generale convivio di ciò ch'i' ho loro mostrato, e di quello pane ch'è mestiere a così fatta vivanda, sanza lo quale da loro non potrebbe essere mangiata. Ed ha questo convivio di quello pane degno co[n] tale vivanda qual io intendo indarno [non] essere ministrata. E però ad esso non s'assetti alcuno male de' suoi organi disposto, però che né denti né lingua ha né palato; né alcuno assettatore de' vizii, perché lo stomaco suo è pieno d'omori venenosi contrarii, sì che mai vivanda non terrebbe. Ma vegna qua qualunque è [per cura] familiare o civile nella umana fame rimaso, e ad una mensa colli altri simili impediti s'assetti; e alli loro piedi si pongano tutti quelli che per pigrizia si sono stati, che non sono degni di più alto sedere: e quelli e questi prendano la mia vivanda col pane che la farà loro e gustare e patire." All citations from the *Convivio* are taken from Dante, *Convivio*, ed. Inglese, and Dante, *The Banquet*, ed. and trans. Ryan.

bread will ultimately serve to absorb the "vivanda" (main dish) represented by the fourteen courses of *canzoni* (1.1.14). Those invited to consume the meal are similarly identified through precise diet-related characteristics, and men or women who have "male de' suoi organi disposto" (their bodily organs ill-disposed) or who are "assettatore de' vizii" (inclined toward vice) are excluded (1.1.12-13).

Lamenting the scarce glossing the *Convivio*'s introductory passage has received in Dante scholarship, Luca Bianchi has insisted that the distinctions made through the images of food and the body in these lines are of vital importance.[32] The poet's philosophical banquet table is unusually large and exceptionally inclusive, leaving space for men who are illiterate in Latin, men deprived of formal study, and even women. At the same time, it is also true that Dante does not seat diners arbitrarily, nor does he see the sustenance of his text as appropriate for all palates. There are clear statements from the author outlining limitations to his guest list: those who are disabled by nature or wickedly prone to vice will be either excused or vituperated, and in either case, will not be invited to participate in the meal. The men or women who have "male de' suoi organi disposto" or those who are "assettatore de' vizii" (1.1.12-13) are excluded from the table specifically because they consume indiscriminately or intemperately, as he reiterates later in the text:

> Here it should be explained that there are certain vices in man to which he is naturally inclined—some men, for instance, are inclined to anger through having a choleric disposition; vices of this kind are innate, that is, connatural. Other vices are habitual, blame for which lies not with a person's disposition but with his habits—for instance, intemperance, especially as regards wine; these vices are avoided and overcome by good habits (*Conv.* 3.8.17).[33]

Recalling both the Galenic humors ("choleric disposition") and the qualitative connotations of intemperance ("wine") here, Dante points again to his

---

32 Bianchi, "*Noli comedere panem philosophorum inutiliter*," pp. 340–341. Albert Ascoli has further examined this passage with regard to inclusion/exclusion in his discussion of the tension between prose and poetry in Dante's works, *Convivio* and beyond, in "Ponete mente almeno come io son bella," pp. 115–143.

33 "E qui è da sapere che certi vizii sono nell'uomo, alli quali naturalmente elli è disposto—sì come certi per complessione collerica sono ad ira disposti—e questi cotali vizii sono innati, cioè connaturali. Altri sono vizii consuetudinarii, alli quali non ha colpa la complessione ma la consuetudine, sì come la intemperanza, e massimamente del vino: e questi vizii si fuggono e si vincono per buona consuetudine."

more nuanced interpretation of gluttonous behavior, emphasizing to his reader that his concern is for those who know their proclivities and those who strive to control them. Dante excuses the men and women who are made by nature in such a way that they cannot maintain a healthful diet or cannot nourish themselves properly; he has no sympathy, however, for those who simply eat and drink thoughtlessly and inordinately. For Dante, it is crucial that his reader acknowledge the relationship among reason, will, and diet, both because intemperance with food and beverage may be the sign of a weakened or weakening will, and because the act of disordered eating could itself be the *cause* of a weak will and the loss of reason.[34] That said, whatever the relation of cause to effect, the result of intemperance in the face of food was that some would have more than they required, while others, who show restraint, would find themselves part of a group that "di questo cibo vivono sempre affamati" (pass their entire lives starved of this food) (*Conv.* 1.1.6). While the contents of a philosophical treatise might never mitigate the risk of actual starvation, Dante uses the parallel to demonstrate the value of his gesture of nourishment and the behavior of one who wishes to participate in community, whether intellectual or spiritual, in contrast with the exclusion and deterioration that would come from taking more than one's fair share.

Despite these references to earthly food habits, critics have long wondered if Dante did not intend for his bread to be exactly the material to which the exegetical tradition referred—which is to say, theology. Though Etienne Gilson firmly established that Dante's invocation of Lady Philosophy and her cult confirms the poet's intention to treat secular knowledge in the *Convivio*, theological texts have remained the primary point of reference for deciphering the bread that forms the basis of his philosophical discussion.[35] Yet just as Paul had explained his offer of milk in place of solid food for the young Christians in 1 Corinthians 3:2, so many scholastic philosophers saw that certain men were still *lactantes parvuli* while others were prepared to receive the *solidus cibus*. Indeed, as Bianchi points out, the presentation of higher knowledge as solid food or bread in contrast to the milk of basic knowledge became a frequent topos in secular milieux, and even before Dante it was used in at least one notable example to refer to the acquisition of non-theological knowledge.[36] In his commentary on the *Consolation of*

---

34 See Purdy Moudarres, "Bodily Starvation and the Ravaging of the Will."

35 Gilson, *Dante et la philosophie*. Gilson's edition of reference, in which editor Giorgio Inglese sends the reader to *Psalm* 77:25 (p. 42, n. 7), is one of many examples.

36 Bianchi, "*Noli comedere panem philosophorum inutiliter*," pp. 345–347.

Philosophy, William of Conches had explained: "Philosophy is like milk, and it is the lesser material the untrained and youths learn; it also contains solid food with which those advanced in knowledge nourish themselves: thus milk nurses infants, bread feeds adults."[37] The purpose of making this distinction was to define the distance between the new student and the advanced intellectual. In the case of the Church, this usually indicated the gap between the layman, desirous of hearing God's word but incapable of understanding the allegory of theologians, and the cleric, trained and prepared to break the outer shell of the letter to arrive at the spirit within. Lacking a codified hierarchy, philosophical study did not always provide a clear-cut titular boundary between the neophyte and the master; transposing the biblical model onto secular learning allowed for this model to project a layering of possible intellectual "nourishments" even in the world of philosophy.[38]

Though Bianchi is concerned with the question of Dante's philosophical intentions, his emphasis on the multiplicity of traditions, and particularly secular concerns, draws attention to the oft-overlooked complexity of the text's gastronomic indications. The "pane orzato" that Dante insists is the analogue to his prose commentary—emphasizing that it is wholly unlike *either* bread of angels *or* wheaten bread—has been overlooked too quickly by scholars who know it to descend from the five loaves of John 6:1–15, and who do not stop to trouble the expressly non-theological context or even the implications of such a comparison. While the "panes hordacei" form a crucial element of Dante's analogy, it is not the most essential one. That the breads are five (the basis of their interpretation as the Pentateuch in the Biblical passage) is of less interest to Dante than the fact that they are the iconic symbol of nourishment, and especially that they are made of barley, the rough grain that feeds the multitudes. That is, Dante is employing these "loaves" in the same way they were used originally in Scripture: to provide a familiar point of reference when explaining a complex idea, and to attempt to have his text function on multiple levels, from the literal to the anagogical. Like Scripture, then, Dante can also effect an inscription on the items, so that something that already held value—in this case, bread, a dietary cornerstone representing vital nutriment—is now also imbued with the value granted it by the poet.

The question of feeding the many was no doubt *literally* present in Dante's mind as he wrote the *Convivio*, looking back from exile on his brief time as a

---

37 "Philosophia habet lac, id est minores sententias quibus rudes et nouellos imbuit, habet alimenta quibus prouectos in scientia nutrit, secundum illud: Lacte rigans paruos, pane cibans ualidos." William of Conches, *Glossae super Boethium* 1.2.61.

38 Bianchi, "*Noli comedere panem philosophorum inutiliter*," p. 345.

Florentine prior and composing a treatise that affirmed the need to provision liberally in order to sustain the community. As discussed in Chapter 1, the period between 1270 and the plague of 1348 witnessed a perfect storm of food shortage and demographic growth that assailed late medieval Tuscany in a most unforgiving fashion. The volatile political climate meant that cities were often under siege, blocked from trade, or simply unable to obtain provisions. Local governments understood that ensuring the constant flow of food into their respective cities was not simply a moral obligation but perhaps their only means of survival. Food was attentively, even maniacally, controlled and distributed, with the intent of ensuring the population was always well fed. Hostilities and wars among the emergent communes were focused strongly on food: maintaining it for oneself and denying access to or destroying the food supplies of one's enemy.[39] As George Dameron has affirmed, the political and economic climate in the central Italian communes of the thirteenth and early-fourteenth centuries dictated that "access to a steady and dependable supply of food was absolutely essential for growth, stability, survivability, and political legitimacy."[40]

At the local level, the relative cost of grain and the central place of bread in the diet further reinforced this political truth, as the average peasant would likely spend between forty-five and fifty percent of monthly income just on flour for bread. Even a member of the merchant class could expect to put aside nearly thirty-five percent of one's earnings for bread flour, making the primary ingredient for bread both the most costly item in a household budget and the most likely to suffer in times of need.[41] To combat this in a practical and at the same time visible way, grain was given special attention in its public accumulation and storage. The establishment of a central granary in most Tuscan cities, like that of Orsanmichele in Florence, reflected an attempt to exhibit both the government's constant dedication to the principal food source as well as its real commitment to fighting impropriety in the distribution of the collective supply. As citizens walked through the center of their city, they could directly observe the presence of

39 See Pinto, *Il libro del biadaiolo*, for a study of Domenico Lenzi's recollection of food shortages and local hostilities.

40 Dameron, "Feeding the Medieval Italian City-State," p. 985. As Dameron points out, "an attention to food security, however, was a consistent, constitutive, essential element in the governance of the medieval commune in times of prosperity and dearth," pp. 980–981.

41 On the relative value of bread in the budgets of the communes and individual households, see Pinto, *Toscana medievale*, and La Roncière, *Prix et salaires à Florence au XIVe siècle (1280–1380)*; see also La Roncière, *Florence: centre economique regional au XIVe siecle*, in which the author confirms that provisioning was seen as a "sacred duty," vol. 2, p. 601.

abundant grain and the work being done to protect this critical resource.[42] Most communes also enacted temporary laws in times of strain or famine, restricting or eliminating grain exports and trade and setting up grain-specific magistracies. In addition, they purchased or simply requisitioned grain from private individuals and pressured the Church to donate to the shared supply, actively favoring the poor with special grain subsidies and occasional free allocations.[43] Nonetheless, during moments of real severity and true famine, these actions did not always guarantee that food would be provided, not least because productivity did not necessarily correspond to availability.[44] It also meant that a savvy, unscrupulous maneuverer could exploit the grey area between actual lack and perceived lack, keeping the population scared and beholden, as in the case of the newly installed local leader in Florence who in 1390 encouraged his colleagues to "keep the *popolo* hungry for bread" if they wanted to maintain control.[45]

Bread was thus not only the primary component of most meals, but the first and last concern of the head of household, the principal function of the governing body, and the gauge of a city's stability as a whole.[46] When Dante offers bread at his banquet of knowledge, his food is not an abstract metaphor, empty of true sustenance. It is instead a gesture signifying very clearly his intention to provide for his new literary community as a good leader should, capitalizing on the real relationship with food—the individual struggle to control appetite, agricultural and political vicissitudes that undermined provisioning, the intimacy of the act of nourishment—just as

42   On the importance of Orsanmichele in particular, and its role in stabilizing and advancing Florence as a successful city in this moment, see D'Aguanno Ito, "Orsanmichele – The Florentine Grain Market."

43   As John Henderson points out, Florentine governments of the early *Trecento* worked hard to distribute grain at a "highly subsidized rate," if only to prevent food riots. See Henderson, *Piety and Charity in Late Medieval Florence*, pp. 242–243.

44   As John Najemy writes, "despite the productivity of the contado...and the ample supplies imported from southern Italy, it was impossible to prevent periods of short-term scarcity and skyrocketing prices." See *A History of Florence, 1200–1575*, p. 109. Dameron also points out that when, in the *Libro del biadaiolo*, Domenico Lenzi states that Florence could only feed itself five months of the year during these decades, he is likely discussing the amount of "domestically grown grain that was capable of making its way into the city, not the total amount of grain available in the contado." See "Feeding the Medieval Italian City-State," p. 986.

45   Najemy cites this observation from an anonymous fourteenth-century chronicler as an example of the approaches to dealing with the unwieldy middle- and lower-class populations in *A History of Florence*, p. 177.

46   Piero Camporesi underlines that even in the most dire conditions, the impoverished and starving would find a method to produce bread before anything else, sometimes resorting to nuts, weeds, and brambles as a basis for flour. See *The Magic Harvest*, pp. 20–21.

the Bible did, and for the same reasons. The audience of his *Convivio* was all too familiar with grain shortages caused by weather and war, as well as those caused by partisan politics, mismanagement, and unchecked greed. Dante knew his readers would recognize what it meant to be invited to a table where all were welcome and where they could safely enjoy their bread without fear of it being torn from their hands by an intemperate fellow diner, and beyond that, what it meant to commune with others over a meal meant to sustain body and mind.

Dante's insistence on the type of grain is furthermore indicative of his intentions. While all nutritional items bore a value and could be generally associated with an upper- or lower-class citizen, bread held a special place. As Ken Albala has underlined, "the most interesting and subtly malleable food prejudices always have and still do center around bread. As the staple, bread preferences are almost always an encapsulation of more complex food prejudices."[47] In some ways the most elaborate example in the great hierarchy of food, the quantity, purity, and milling of each type of grain dictated a value to be associated with the final product. Like the game birds and meat Dante used to brand his first glutton Forese Donati, fully wheaten bread sat high on the chain, and it was a food appropriate to the divine or the earthly elite; bread of mixed grains was suitable for humble palates. Dameron observes that unlike the rest of Europe, "in Tuscany both the urban and the rural populations in most of the region [...] preferred white bread made of *frumentum* [...] to black bread made of the lesser grains."[48] This cultural taste in turn had a complementary economic effect: wheat grew on the best soils, and the best soils were in the possession of the rich. The constant reiteration of wheat as the "best" kind of bread thus allowed the landed aristocracy to enjoy the privilege of consuming only the best, while also collecting the highest returns for their crops. *Frumento* was food for the highborn and an international trade commodity, while *biade*—any of the ten varieties of grain grown in the Tuscan countryside in addition to wheat—was food for peasants and animals.

Against this background there existed an interpretive tradition that relied upon a cultural prejudice toward the rough bread which peasants were able to eat. While the earliest exegetes sometimes refer to the teachings of the New Testament as grain in contrast to the straw of the ancient Hebrew text, the comparison soon became that of two different qualities of grain: *hordeum* versus *triticum*, or barley versus wheat. Citing Bede and Ambrose,

47   Albala, *Eating Right in the Renaissance*, p. 196.
48   Dameron, "Feeding the Medieval Italian City-State," p. 986.

Henri de Lubac summarized the shift, noting that while the five barley loaves of the Pentateuch were first considered "a healthful food," "those that the Lord now invites to the wedding feast in the Church are no longer delighted 'in the rough bread and country food of the letter'; the sons are no longer nourished except 'on the grain of wheat.'"[49] Thomas Aquinas took the evaluation of the purity of bread quite literally and set a corresponding standard for the production of Eucharistic wafers. The bread which will become the flesh of the Lord, he determined, should always be made from wheat, or where wheat was lacking and a mixture was required, the quantity of wheat must always be greater than that of any other grain.[50] The pure white bread made from wheat was sometimes even outside of the Church referred to as *paindemain*, from *panis dominicus*, or the Lord's bread.[51]

Le Goff's "universe of hunger" was certainly at times plagued by the need for bread, but the interest in wheaten bread is more distinctive.[52] The cultural preference and resulting economic demand for wheat bread in Florence gave rise to food instability that did not exist elsewhere, and—it would seem to Dante's mind, at least—need not have existed.[53] Dante's demand for one type of bread is equally emphatic, and yet it is not the expected kind. Dante's bread is made of mixed grain, a mostly barley bread, from which he removes "ogni macula," implying that it was furthermore cooked in ashes rather than a proper oven, as it would be in a lower-class household. With it, he completes his self-portrait as a provider, chastising the wasteful community that allows some to starve while others gluttonously reject imperfect bread. He is himself storming the granaries and delivering bread—be it rough and simple—to nourish everyone and not just a few. Offering a barley bread, Dante sheds his own ostentation and takes no shame in consuming the bread of the masses if it means he can feed them too.

Anthropologists and historians have repeatedly demonstrated that taxonomies are never neutral, but rather serve to establish and naturalize hierarchic structures.[54] Mutton and partridge, or wheat bread and whole grain bread, are figures in a classification that records and reinforces a system of community organization. As figures, these foods can absorb more nuanced

49   de Lubac, *Medieval Exegesis,* vol. 2, p. 59.
50   Aquinas, *Summa,* 3a, q.74, a.3, ad3.
51   Henisch, *Fast and Feast,* p. 157.
52   Le Goff, *La civilisation de l'occident médiéval,* p. 290.
53   Dameron, "Feeding the Medieval Italian City-State," p. 1004.
54   See the classic study by Mary Douglas, "Deciphering a Meal," pp. 61–81, and Bruce Lincoln, *Discourse and the Construction of Society,* pp. 131–141.

or different meanings, responding to changes in social composition or a desire to effect change. Moreover, they are not only reflections of, but also reiterations of—even, at times, determinations of—the values of the author and his community, able to act as a shorthand that can express a breadth and profundity of meaning. Once decoded in the context of their historical moment, mutton, partridge, and bread might permit a better understanding of a poem and the poet's finesse; more critically, they point to a code that Dante himself is inscribing, one that he already began to give shape to in the first verses he composed, and that he used to create a language that spoke clearly and simultaneously on literal and metaphoric planes.

Teodolinda Barolini has suggested that the *tenzone* is a locus of significance for Dante's poetics, in that it "helps us construe the passage from the narrow, circumscribed world of the *Vita nuova* to the philosophically inclusive and socially differentiated universe of the *Commedia*."[55] The *Comedy* presents Dante's fully imagined hierarchy of this world and the next, but the inhabitants of each space are illustrative rather than essential. The *tenzone* begins this work: while the existence of a hierarchy, or the severity with which it is implemented, might not change, the representative artifacts can. In the *Convivio*, Dante positions himself as the one responsible for providing food and protecting those who are unable to feed themselves. Unlike the foolish King Roberto in Sercambi's tale, Dante sees the significance and not just the sign—neither rich clothes nor rich foods can manufacture virtue. Perhaps those who are sloppy eat like animals, even accepting the rough grain of a bread made with animal fodder, because they've been left with no choice but to root around under the table for crumbs. Real gluttony is the behavior of those at the high table, eating delicately and wasting food, letting it drop around them. Noble men always eat noble fare, but nobility is defined in the eyes of the beholder as Dante himself insists, and historical men are as fleeting and ephemeral as their meals.

In the fourth book of the *Convivio*, just before abandoning the philosophical treatise to take a journey toward a more complete knowledge in a new format, Dante lists the virtues laid out by Aristotle and the vices they act upon, noting that temperance, second on his list, "è regola e freno de la nostra gulositade e de la nostra soperchievole astinenza ne le cose che conservano la nostra vita" (this acts as a guide and a rein for our gluttony and our excessive abstinence with respect to things that preserve our life) (*Conv.* 4.17.4). As the thing that preserves life, upon which all other functions depend, food is the most intimate friend and, as must follow,

55   Barolini, "From Editorial History to Hermeneutic Failure," p. 5.

the most dangerous enemy. What one eats is important because it defines one's identity and one's role with respect to others; it becomes a part of the self and the means by which the self is articulated and perceived. By taking up food and the human relationship with eating, Dante expresses his values and his preoccupations through each edible item and each practice, sometimes using his platform to modify or push back against expectations. Yet in doing so he is also establishing a model for how food can create a literary language and a literary community—how on the page it can be used to communicate and to form the bonds that tie us together just as it does in life.

Works Cited

Albala, Ken. *Eating Right in the Renaissance.* Berkeley: University of California Press, 2002.

Alfie, Fabian. *Dante's* Tenzone *with Forese Donati: The Reprehension of Vice.* Toronto: University of Toronto Press, 2011.

Alighieri, Dante. *The Banquet.* Translated by Christopher Ryan. Saratoga, CA: Amma Libri, 1989.

Aquinas, Thomas. *Summa Theologica.* 3 vols. Translated by the Fathers of the English Dominican Province. New York: Benziger Brothers, 1948.

Ascoli, Albert. "Ponete mente almeno come io son bella: Prose and Poetry, 'pane' and 'vivanda,' Goodness and Beauty, in *Convivio* 1." In *Dante's* Convivio: *or How to Restart a Career in Exile*, edited by Franziska Meier, 115–143. Bern: Lang, 2018.

Baldelli, Ignazio. "Castrone." In *Enciclopedia Dantesca*, edited by Umberto Bosco. Rome: Istituto della Enciclopedia italiana, 1970–1975.

Barolini, Teodolinda. *Dante and the Origins of Italian Literary Culture.* Fordham: Fordham University Press, 2006.

Barolini, Teodolinda. "From Editorial History to Hermeneutic Failure." In *Dante's Lyric Poetry: Poems of Youth and of the Vita Nuova*, edited by Teodolinda Barolini and translated by Richard Lansing, 3–28. Toronto: University of Toronto Press, 2014.

Bianchi, Luca. "*Noli comedere panem philosophorum inutiliter*: Dante Alighieri and John of Jandun on Philosophical 'Bread.'" *Tijdschrift voor Filosofie* 75 (2013): 335–355.

Boggioni, Valter and Giovanni Casalengo. *Dizionario storico del lessico erotico italiano: Metafore, eufemismi, oscenità, doppi sensi, parole dotte, parole basse in otto secoli di letteratura italiana.* Milan: Longanesi, 1996.

Capatti, Alberto and Massimo Montanari. *La cucina italiana: Storia di una cultura.* Rome: Laterza, 1999.

Cherubini, Giovanni. *Agricoltura e società nel medioevo*. Florence: Sansoni, 1977.

Cherubini, Giovanni. "The Peasant and Agriculture." In *Medieval Callings*, edited by Jacques Le Goff, 112–136. Chicago: University of Chicago Press, 1990.

Camporesi, Piero. *The Magic Harvest: Food, Folklore and Society*. New York: Polity, 1998.

Douglas, Mary. "Deciphering a Meal." *Daedalus* 101, no. 1 (Winter 1972): 61–81.

Dameron, George. "Feeding the Medieval Italian City-State: Grain, War, and Political Legitimacy in Tuscany, c. 1150–c. 1350." *Speculum* 92, no. 4 (October 2017): 976–1019.

Flandrin, Jean-Louis and Massimo Montanari, eds. *Storia dell'alimentazione*. Rome: Laterza, 1997.

Foster, Kenelm and Patrick Boyde, eds. and trans. *Dante's Lyric Poetry*, 2 vols. Oxford: Clarendon Press, 1967.

Frosini, Giovanna. *Il cibo e i signori: La mensa dei priori di Firenze nel quinto decennio del sec. XIV*. Florence: Accademia della Crusca, 1993.

Giagnacovo, Maria. "Due 'alimentazioni' del basso Medioevo: la tavola dei mercanti e la tavola dei ceti subalterni." *Alimentazione e nutrizione secc. XIII-XVIII*, edited by Silvia Cavaciocchi, 821–830. Florence: Le Monnier, 1997.

Giagnacovo, Maria. *Mercanti a tavola: prezzi e consumi alimentari dell'azienda Datini di Pisa*. Florence: Opus, 2002.

Gilson, Etienne. *Dante et la philosophie*. Paris: Vrin, 1972.

Gilson, Simon. "The Anatomy and Physiology of the Human Body in the *Commedia*." In *Dante and the Human Body: Eight Essays*, edited by John C. Barnes and Jennifer Petrie, 11–44. Dublin: Four Courts Press, 2007.

Goody, Jack. *Cooking, Cuisine and Class: A Study in Comparative Sociology*. Cambridge: Cambridge University Press, 1982.

Grieco, Allen J. "Alimentazione e classi sociali nel tardo Medioevo e nel Rinascimento in Italia." In *Storia dell'alimentazione,* edited by Jean-Louis Flandrin and Massimo Montanari, 371–380. Rome: Laterza, 1996.

Grieco, Allen J. "Menu, Banchetti e Tavole Imbandite in Toscana." In *Et coquatur ponendo: cultura della cucina e della tavola in Europa tra medioevo e eta moderna,* eds. Orazio Bagnasco, et. al., 373–379. Prato: Istituto internazionale di storia economica 'Francesco Datini,' 1996.

Grieco, Allen J. "From Roosters to Cocks: Italian Renaissance Fowl and Sexuality." In *Erotic Cultures of Renaissance Italy*, edited by Sara F. Matthews-Grieco, 110–122. Surrey: Ashgate, 2010.

Henderson, John. *Piety and Charity in Late Medieval Florence*. Chicago: University of Chicago Press, 1994.

Henisch, Bridget. *Fast and Feast: Food in Medieval Society*. University Park: The Pennsylvania State University, 1976.

Ito, Marie D'Aguanno. "Orsanmichele – The Florentine Grain Market: Trade and Worship in the Later Middle Ages," Ph.D. diss, The Catholic University of America, January 2014.

La Roncière, Charles M. de. *Florence: centre economique regional au XIVe siecele: le marche des denrees de premiere necessite a Florence et dans sa campagne et les conditions de la vie des salaries, 1320–1380*. 3 vols. Aix-en-Provence: S.O.D.E.B., 1976.

La Roncière, Charles M. de. *Prix et salaires à Florence au XIVe siècle (1280–1380)*. Rome: École Française de Rome, 1982.

Le Goff, Jacques. *La civilisation de l'occident médiéval*. Paris: Arthaud, 1964.

Le Goff, Jacques, ed. *Dizionario dell'occidente medievale*. 2 vols. Turin: Einaudi, 2011.

Lincoln, Bruce. *Discourse and the Construction of Society: Comparative Studies of Myth, Ritual, and Classification*. Oxford: Oxford University Press, 2014.

Lubac, Henri de. *Medieval Exegesis: The Four Senses of Scripture*. 3 vols. Translated by E.M. Macierowski. Grand Rapids, MI: Eerdsman Publishing, 2000.

Malgarini, Patrizia Bertini. "Il linguaggio medico e anatomico nelle opere di Dante." *Studi Danteschi* 61 (1989): 1–108.

Martellotti, Anna. *I ricettari di Federico II. Dal* Meridionale *al* Liber de coquina. Florence: Olschki, 2005.

Montanari, Massimo. *Campagne medievali: Struttura produttive, rapporti di lavoro, sistemi alimentari*. Turin: Einaudi, 1984.

Montanari, Massimo. "Strutture di produzione e sistemi alimentari nell'alto Medioevo." In *Storia dell'alimentazione,* edited by Jean-Louis Flandrin and Massimo Montanari, 217-225. Rome: Laterza, 1997.

Najemy, John. *A History of Florence, 1200–1575*. Oxford: Blackwell, 2008.

Noakes, Susan. "Virility, Nobility, and Banking: The Crossing of Discourses in the *Tenzone* with Forese." In *Dante for the New Millennium*, edited by Teodolinda Barolini and H. Wayne Storey, 241–258. New York: Fordham University Press, 2003.

Olson, Kristina. "Shoes, Gowns and Turncoats: Reconsidering Cacciaguida's History of Florentine Fashion and Politics." *Dante Studies* 134 (2016): 26–47.

Origo Iris. *The Merchant of Prato: Francesco di Marco Datini, 1335-1410*. Jaffrey, NH: Nonpareil, 1986. First published 1917.

Pinto, Giuliano. *Il libro del biadaiolo. Carestie e Annona a Firenze dalla metà del '200 al 1318*. Florence: Olschki, 1978.

Pinto, Giuliano. *Toscano medievale: paesaggi e realtà sociali*. Florence: Le Lettere, 1993.

Scully, Terence. *The Art of Cookery in the Middle Ages*. Woodbridge, UK: Boydell, 1995.

Sercambi, Giovanni. *Il novelliere.* Edited by Luciano Rossi. Rome: Salerno Editrice, 1974.

Toussaint-Samat, Maguelonne. *A History of Food.* Translated by Anthea Bell. London: Wiley, 2009.

Tucci, Hannelore Zug. "La caccia, da bene comune a privilegio." In *Storia d'Italia: Annali,* vol. 6, edited by Ruggiero Romano and Ugo Tucci, 397–445. Turin: Einaudi, 1983.

William of Conches. *Glossae super Boethium.* Turnhout: Brepols, 2010.

3. Infernal Gluttony

Abstract

This chapter begins the exploration of gluttony in the *Comedy* with a focus on the first canticle, *Inferno*. The barren wasteland to which the unrepentant are condemned is, like the individual *contrapassi* (just punishments) to which they are subjected, a perfect infernal imitation of the diseased community they created with their actions on earth. In Hell, Dante's gluttons demonstrate how the relationship with food can either aid or undermine the recreation of the city of God in the city of man. Engaging directly with the debate over the essential nature of humanity and the threshold between body and soul, Dante portrays the infernal glutton with the eroded identity and loss of reason that are the inevitable results of indiscriminate consumption, results that prompt an indigestion that will poison not just this generation but also the next.

Keywords: cannibalism, communion, essence, progeny, reason, will

The *Convivio* is a failed experiment in at least one respect: the poet's abandonment of its composition cannot but lend credence to the suggestion that it was incapable of acting as a grain store for the new community Dante had envisioned. This rustic bread of mixed grains exposes a great deal about the server and the served, however, and it remains an important point of reference even as the philosopher becomes the poet of the *Comedy*. Regaining his footing after the unfinished *Convivio*, the pilgrim begins the journey toward the head of a new table, passing first through a landscape of lack that represents the realization of the unprovisioned city. The barren wasteland to which the unrepentant are condemned is, like the individual *contrapassi* to which they are subjected, a perfect infernal imitation of the diseased community they created with their actions on earth. As the poem begins to weave political philosophy with spiritual understanding, Dante's gluttons will demonstrate how consumption practices structure individual and group identities alike, and either aid or undermine the recreation of the city of God in the city of man.

Callegari, D., *Dante's Gluttons: Food and Society from the* Convivio *to the* Comedy.
Taylor & Francis Group, 2022
DOI 10.5117/9789463720427_CH03

The souls Dante encounters in *Inferno* 6 are the first group the poet explicitly defines as gluttons, yet the message to be distilled from his exchange with them is far from transparent, and the context in which their exchange takes place only provokes further questions. The representative soul condemned for this sin is the still-elusive Ciacco, whom scholars have never successfully aligned with a historical person despite the emphasis in his lines on identity, and who suffers a perplexing contrapasso. Departing from the framework of the *Convivio*, however, in which Dante sets out how self-care and self-knowledge are both established and maintained through diet, and where Dante confirms the relationship between leading and provisioning a community, the thread that ties together eating practice, personhood, and politics becomes almost immediately clear. As the pilgrim's journey through *Inferno* progresses, the parallels between the individual body and the body politic only grow stronger, until he reaches the lowest circles—what Robert Durling has usefully designated the "belly of Hell"—the place where body and soul, politics and faith, and individual and community all perfectly converge.[1]

The figure of Count Ugolino—whom Dante encounters chewing on his nemesis in *Inferno* 32—has in fact been recognized as a gluttonous nexus, an intersection of all hunger-related terms in the *Comedy*.[2] After betraying his city of Pisa, Ugolino was double-crossed by his soon-to-be infernal companion, then jailed and left to starve to death with his family. Biting his hands as his children cried out for bread with their last breaths, the count infamously traded gnawing on his own skin for the flesh of his dead progeny. In Ugolino's wake come Fra' Alberigo, who murdered his dining companions, in *Inferno* 33, and the three-mouthed Lucifer, who eternally masticates the bodies of the great traitors of Church and State in *Inferno* 34. The Eucharistic parody generated by the insatiable consumption of other humans in the final cantos of *Inferno* is clearly recognizable, but this spiritual metaphor is underpinned by the real threat of starvation under a gluttonous leader, as Ciacco pronounces long before the pilgrim broaches the last circle. Equally troubling is the possibility that we are all truly what we eat—that is to say, diet can and must affect the essence of our humanity. Against the specter of the cannibal that inhabits the infertile plains of Hell, Dante proposes that a community thrives when those with abundance perform their duty of feeding those who lack. This model is not casual or metaphoric, but rather a direct result of his

---

1   Durling, "Deceit and Digestion in the Belly of Hell," pp. 61–93.
2   As Barolini points out, "All the threads of the semantic field of hunger converge in [Ugolino's] episode," in "'Only Historicize'," p. 48. See also Purdy Moudarres, "Bodily Starvation and the Ravaging of the Will," pp. 205–228.

knowledge and experience as a member of a community and as an exile forced out of one, all within a historical moment when developing effective food policy was tantamount to the act of governing and theophilosophical debates focused intensely on the boundaries between body and soul.

Ciacco marks the "official" introduction to infernal gluttony, explaining how the city of Florence will buckle under its useless, gluttonous leaders; this thread leads next to Ugolino and Fra' Alberigo, who together act as stepping stones to the poet's concluding image of the gaping, forever-unsatisfied mouths of Lucifer, a counter-image of the social harmony effected through feeding at the bottom of *Inferno*. The unchecked appetites here demonstrate the multifold and profound consequences of gluttonous behavior on the health of the human body and the human city, but they also begin the work of extending those outcomes to the physiological model used for the production of new bodies—the paradigm of reproduction that Dante delineates for humans and their creative impulses, whether flesh or art—and the fully realized anatomy that maps onto his literary production. Like a human belly, the belly of Hell is the first organ in a reproductive process that results in new bodies and new spirits. Engaging directly with the debate over the essential nature of humanity and the threshold between body and mind/soul, Dante portrays the infernal glutton with the eroded identity of the individual who consumes indiscriminately and becomes something less than human. Then, in an analogy rooted in dietary science, Dante shows his reader how the act of overstuffing the stomach jeopardizes the body's natural functions and its ability to procreate, creating an indigestion that will poison not just this generation but also the next.

Who Weeps for the Gluttons?

As the menacing presence of the insatiable *lupa* announces in *Inferno* 1, even before the three-throated Cerberus blocks the pilgrim's passage in *Inferno* 6, gluttony is a driving force in the first canticle. Yet the gluttons themselves are best remembered for just how unmemorable they are, and the perfunctory 115 lines the poet dedicates to them (the fewest in the canticle alongside *Inferno* 11) after the devastatingly pathetic ending of canto 5 does little to encourage readers to give the sin examined in *Inferno* 6 much attention.[3] Of the many acts that are punished in Hell, overeating seems too banal, too

3   Purdy Moudarres observes this is in fact a tactic rather than a misfire: "The ease with which the gluttons slip from our memory is not accidental." "Devouring Selves," p. 3.

quotidian and familiar to impress or provoke fear, particularly from a modern perspective. The threat of gluttony feels petty in the grand scheme: given how common such behavior is, what real harm can it do? As Lino Pertile asked in his examination of Ciacco and Dante's teacher Brunetto Latini: "If you are a Catholic, when was the last time you confessed to having added double cream to your spaghetti sauce, and drunk more Cabernet than you needed to quench your thirst? Gluttony is no longer felt to be a sin, let alone a mortal one. We may still shed a tear for Dante's Lustful, but who weeps for the Gluttons?"[4]

If the infernal order in which gluttony must be punished is perhaps met with a feeling of indifference by readers today, one person who very much does still weep for the gluttons is the pilgrim. After Dante and his guide wander under "la piova / etterna, maladetta, fredda e greve" (eternal, cursed, cold, and heavy rain; *Inf.* 6.7–8), listening to the howling of the punished souls, Virgil's mud-slinging silences the thundering of three-headed Cerberus who guards the entrance to the circle, setting the stage for the conversation between the pilgrim and Ciacco, the only figure with whom Dante speaks directly:

> Ed elli a me: "La tua città, ch'è piena
>   d'invidia sì che già trabocca il sacco,
>   seco mi tenne in la vita serena.
> Voi cittadini mi chiamaste Ciacco:
>   per la dannosa colpa de la gola,
>   come tu vedi, a la pioggia mi fiacco.
> E io anima trista non son sola,
>   ché tutte queste a simil pena stanno
>   per simil colpa." E più non fé parola.
> Io li rispuosi: "Ciacco, il tuo affanno
>   mi pesa sì, ch'a lagrimar mi 'nvita"
>   *Inf.* 6.49–59

(And he to me: "Your city, which is so full of envy that the sack already overflows, kept me with her during my sunny life. You citizens called me Ciacco; because of the damnable sin of the gullet, as you see, I am broken by the rain. And I, wretched soul, am not alone, for all these endure similar punishment for similar guilt." And he spoke no further word. I replied, "Ciacco, your trouble weighs on me so that it calls me to weep.")

4   Pertile, "Ciacco, Brunetto and the Voice of God," p. 158.

Scholars have mostly disregarded Dante's tears in favor of contending with the obscurity of the lines that follow, struggling in particular to understand who "Ciacco" is meant to be. Because this name might equally be a nickname, a given name, or an insulting moniker, the primary exponent of the circle of gluttony has proved challenging to pin down. The poet's very act of naming him should ostensibly confirm that his identity is important while reminding the reader of the importance of identity more broadly—of the crucial question, that is, of what makes us who we are. It is a question that the pilgrim must constantly confront in his journey through the afterlife as a simultaneously embodied and ensouled person surrounded by aerial bodies. The expectation that substance, in multiple senses, will be found among the gluttons is instead met with the radically insubstantial Ciacco. His contrapasso has likewise puzzled readers: the driving rain seems inadequate to the tortures of Hell, even if it is brutal and causes the earth to stink ("pute la terra che questo riceve," *Inf.* 6.12), and is strangely nonspecific given the exquisite perfection of Dante's other punishments. Even as critics have proposed useful glosses for the punishment of the gluttons, the conclusions have not entirely managed to capture what makes the canto relevant, if only because upon closer scrutiny, *Inferno* 6 prompts many unexpected questions, none of which are intelligibly related to one another.

The strangeness of the gluttons' contrapasso notwithstanding, the very presence of a contrapasso provides a point of departure: the filthy rain that falls down upon the gluttons must somehow be equally perfect in its inversion and perversion of the way in which these individuals treated the body and soul that God granted them. Pertile has suggested that we might look first to the body and its interaction with food, noting that according to Ambrose (who quotes from Jeremiah 25:27: "Drink, be drunken, and vomit, and fall to never rise again"), the impact of gluttony on the individual body is indigestion and expulsion of the excess, giving the first glimmer of a larger process that Dante would have had present as he fashioned this punishment.[5] Taking a similar tack, Simone Marchesi has argued that the apparent slipperiness of the name "Ciacco" is likely due to the fact that it is meant to function on multiple levels, legible as a real name or nickname that also does the work of connecting him and the other gluttons with hogs (for which *ciacco* was a slang term in the contemporary Florentine dialect), following a tradition of equating Epicureans, or those who saw food as an end rather than a means, with hogs. His punishment could then be explained

---

5   Pertile, "Ciacco, Brunetto and the Voice of God," pp. 166–168. Pertile sees gluttony as a "symptom," while I would point to it as the cause.

through the same tradition, as Isidore of Seville and Augustine both held that the Epicureans rolled around in carnal filth—essentially, vomit, as Ambrose had understood Jeremiah 25 to indicate.[6]

The curiosity, in any case, is that the punishment is not just a precipitation of dirty water, but more precisely a "foul" mixture of the souls *and* the rain. As Christiana Purdy Moudarres has observed, the presence of moisture in the body, and especially too much moisture, was for Dante's contemporaries quickly recognizable as the result of overeating, given their familiarity with Avicenna's theory of digestion.[7] Following a Galenic model, Avicenna held that food went through a four-part digestion, being "concocted" into "chyle" and then "blood" (neither substance being synonymous with modern usage) which was distributed through the veins to other parts of the body before passing through yet another digestion to render the "blood" more solid and "perfect" for each organ's specific nutritional needs. All nutriment was in this sense moisture first and foremost, as food became a nutrimental liquid that traveled the body to arrive at and nourish its component parts, and all people contained the moisture that was used to render their bodies in the first place—what Avicenna referred to as "radical moisture." Being "watery" was thus a sign of a body out of equilibrium as a result of the introduction of too much external nutrient. Indeed, this was the first explanation early commentators provided for the contrapasso of the gluttons; as Pietro Alighieri wrote, "in hoc mundo, vivendo in vitio gule, marcescunt in aquositade" (in this world, living in the vice of gluttony, they languish in wateriness).[8] The shades thrashing about, mixing with the excess water that rains down upon them in *Inferno* 6, are enacting the process by which the body attempts to incorporate excess food, fails, and creates a cold, watery imbalance in the system.

An overload of nutriment disturbed the body's ability to nourish itself properly, but it was yet more dangerous because it led to a series of other imbalances, one of the prime reasons that gluttony was considered the "gateway sin." More pointedly, the very basis for considering it a sin was the fact that overeating diverted or stunted the digestive process, leading to the vomiting Ambrose imagined, in contrast to healthy digestion which

---

6   Marchesi, "'Epicuri de grege porcus': Ciacco Epicurus and Isidore of Seville," pp. 117–131.

7   Purdy Moudarres, "Devouring Selves," p. 5; she is citing *Petri Allegherii super Dantis...* on *Inf.* 6.7–15. Her essay provides a comprehensive introduction to the landscape and the relevant bibliography.

8   As discussed in Chapter 1, this was most likely filtered to Dante through Albertus Magnus; see Nardi, *Studi di filosofia medievale*, pp. 49–51. This subject will be taken up at length again in the next chapter.

would instead have as its end the production of human life, as Statius will demonstrate in *Purgatorio* 25. The connection to *Purgatorio* is in no way casual or indirect here, and it is the crucial piece that must be added to the reading of Ciacco and the infernal gluttons. Though *Inferno* 6 is rarely considered as philosophically or theologically provocative as *Purgatorio* 25—in fact it has only infrequently even been brought into discussion with the later canto—it is here that Dante begins to trace the outline of his position in the charged debate over the interaction of food with body and then the essence of human identity, in the form of radical moisture, and then perhaps, still more vexingly, soul itself. And if the connection between gluttony and the seed of human nature is perhaps less immediately obvious to the modern reader, Dante was nonetheless careful to insert a signpost to ensure it couldn't be missed. At the end of *Inferno* 6, as Ciacco falls back into the filthy mud, Virgil turns to the pilgrim and observes without prompting:

E 'l duca disse a me: "Più non si desta
    di qua dal suon de l'angelica tromba,
    quando verrà la nimica podesta:
ciascun rivederà la trista tomba,
    ripiglierà sua carne e sua figura,
    udirà quel ch'in etterno rimbomba."
                     Inf. 6.94–99

(And my leader said to me: "Never again will he arise this side of the angelic trumpet, when he will see the enemy governor: each will see again his sad tomb, will take again his flesh and his shape, will hear what resounds eternally.")

Dante should foresee how the reuniting of every soul with its body that will occur at the end of time will guarantee the exquisite perfection of both the contentment of beatification and the pain of condemnation, as Virgil reminds him: "Ritorna a tua scïenza, / che vuol, quanto la cosa è più perfetta, / più senta il bene, e così la doglienza" ('Return to your philosophy, which teaches that the more perfect a thing is, the more it feels what is good, and the same for pain,'" *Inf.* 6.107–108). God created humans with unmarked bodies and unblemished souls; the divine perfection of beatification and damnation alike is contingent, the ancient poet stresses, on the unification of the soul with the reconstituted body at the end of time. While it is not made fully explicit, the need to introduce this question in the canto of the gluttons is not hard to extrapolate, as eating practices could clearly be shown to have some effect on the body—and quite possibly on the soul.

Early Scholastic theologians frequently discussed this hypothetically permeable boundary between material food and spiritual essence. The movement from external to internal was considered the most elementary of human acts as well as the most inscrutable; indeed, the very idea of digestion suggested something supernatural, or possibly unnatural, in its ability to make matter change, to unite disparate bodies, or even to inspire creation. In the Scholastic debates of the late twelfth century, Caroline Walker Bynum has emphasized that "organic processes, especially those, such as eating, in which one substance disappeared into another, were both mysterious and threatening."[9] Though the change and growth that occurred following consumption was evidently connected to the assimilation of food, the possibility of a digestion that interacted directly with the flesh remained problematic for theologians, who were at that time highly preoccupied with the pure, unadulterated resurrection of the body. How would this process affect the moment when body and soul were resurrected together? As Peter of Poitiers famously pointed out to those who would have it that food became a part of man:

> But it may be objected that by eating the flesh of pork it becomes part of the human flesh, and all human flesh will be resurrected. Therefore also the flesh of pigs will rise in the resurrection, though in human and not porcine form [...] But the Truth resolves this objection, as it says in the Evangelist, Do you not understand that whatsoever enters into the mouth goes into the belly and is cast out into the privy?[10]

Others attempted to draw a line rather arbitrarily with regard to the digestion process. In order to refute the possibility that cannibalism, for example, would affect the reconstitution of the flesh, some exegetes argued that because human flesh was consumed unnaturally, it was never truly assimilated. This proposition had already led Augustine to write:

> Now surely no one will maintain, with truth or reason, that the whole of a body so digested passes through the intestinal tract without any

---

9   Bynum, *The Resurrection of the Body in Western Christianity*, p. 136.
10   "Sed objicitur: Porcina caro comedendo transit in carnem hominis et tota caro hominis resurget. Ergo et caro porcina, non porcina, sed humana... Sed hanc objectionem solvit Veritas, dicendo in Evangelio, quia omne quod in os intrat foras vadit et in secessum emittitur (Matth. XV)," *Sententiae* 5.18.1264D–1265A.

change or conversion into the flesh of the consumer? That the consumer was once emaciated and is no longer will be sufficient to indicate that physical deficiencies are supplied by such nutriment.[11]

The potential corruption of the flesh was itself troublesome, but the next layer was where the debate became truly determinative. If food mixed with and became part of the body, there was then at least a possibility that it reached the spiritual essence, the kind of "medieval DNA," as Purdy Moudarres has described it, that defined an individual. In that case, diet would ultimately exercise influence over the core of one's identity. The watery excess nutriment that floated around the body would not then simply be a threat to the body—disturbing digestion and leading to a series of physical ailments and stunted productivity—but could indeed cause a literal dilution of the self. Dante's description of the gluttons as wallowing in a mixture of water and the deteriorated matter of their bodies would seem to fit neatly into this debate. This is further confirmed, Purdy Moudarres notes, by the fact that Dante's representative glutton Ciacco remains unidentifiable—having allowed his diet to dilute his very essence.[12]

As the conversation between Ciacco and the pilgrim progresses, one thing that becomes clear is that in the canto of the gluttons, gluttony will be little discussed. Instead, the conversation between Dante and Ciacco revolves around politics, specifically those of the city of Florence. Whoever Ciacco may be, he is certainly someone with an intimate relationship to Dante's native city, and he wastes no time in asserting that Florence will suffer at the hands of the unjust men who lead it:

E quelli a me: "Dopo lunga tencione
    verranno al sangue, e la parte selvaggia
    caccerà l'altra con molta offensione.
Poi appresso convien che questa caggia
    infra tre soli, e che l'altra sormonti
    con la forza di tal che testé piaggia.
Alte terrà lungo tempo le fronti,
    tenendo l'altra sotto gravi pesi,
    come che di ciò pianga o che n'aonti.

---

11 "Num quisquam veridica ratione contendet totum digestum fuisse per imos meatus, nihil inde in eius carnem mutatum atque conversum, cum ipsa macies, quae fuit et non est, satis indicet quae illis escis detrimenta suppleta sint," *De civitate Dei* 22.20.18.
12 Purdy Moudarres, "Devouring Selves in the Circle of Gluttony," p. 18.

Giusti son due, e non vi sono intesi;
   superbia, invidia e avarizia sono
   le tre faville c'hanno i cuori accesi."
                    Inf. 6.64–75

(And he to me: "After much quarreling they will come to blood; the party
from the woods will drive out the other with much harm. Then later
this party must fall within three suns and the other rise, with the power
of one who now hugs the shore. Long will they hold high their brows,
keeping others down under heavy weights, no matter how they weep or
are shamed. Two are just, and no one heeds them; pride, envy, and greed
are the three sparks that have set hearts ablaze.")

Pertile has articulated the questions that most frequently leap to mind after
absorbing these lines: "What is the connection, if any, between gluttony and
Florentine political rivalry? [...] What authority has [Ciacco] got to speak
about politics?"[13] As a Florentine, Ciacco may have a right to speak about his
city's grave political turmoil, but as a glutton what gives him the privilege
to prophesy the city's fall? More importantly still, how do the eating habits
of an individual connect to the stability of the surrounding community? If
Ciacco and his companions in the circle of gluttons are guilty of eating "too
soon, too expensively, too much, too eagerly, or too daintily" (as Aquinas
would have it), the means by which they doomed themselves are clear; the
means by which they are attached to the city they now deem beyond saving
are much harder to discern.[14]

   The relationship between this sin and political disaster is one that can be
drawn from the work Dante has already begun, establishing how indulgence
in food is bound up with duty and responsibility to the community. Ciacco
performs the next step for the poet, laying a foundation within the *Comedy*
that can support the construction of a more sophisticated network of
gluttony's roots and fruits. In his entry on gluttony in the *Enciclopedia
dantesca*, André Pézard notes that Ciacco's introductory lines affirm that
his discourse will address how gluttony affects the health of the city and the
health of the body: the "sunny life" ("la vita serena," *Inf.* 6.51) Ciacco recalls in
Florence actually refers to a specific historical moment, the period between
1266 and 1283 when Florence was at peace, sometimes also referred to with

---

13   Pertile, "Ciacco, Brunetto and the Voice of God," p. 164. As Pertile notes, these questions
have been posed in several commentaries and critical contributions.
14   Aquinas, *Summa* 2a 2ae q.148 a.4 ad.1.

the medieval commonplace of the "popolo grasso." As Pézard acknowledges, "il popolo grasso s'ingrassa a spese del popolo magro" (the fat always fatten themselves at the expense of the thin), and Ciacco and his companions' unapologetic self-gratification came at a cost that affected the whole and not just the individuals at fault.[15] Invoking Saint Ambrose, Pertile has emphasized that "gluttony is not a private vice, but a public evil," one that, like the rain that assails the gluttons in *Inferno* 6, saturates everyone, even as it is practiced by only a few.[16] As Robert Dombroski notes, the constant rain that constitutes the gluttons' contrapasso might be interpreted as a kind of anti-manna, the opposite of the heavenly food God provided to the Jews in Exodus 16:4: "Then the Lord said to Moses, 'I will rain down bread from heaven for you. The people are to go out each day and gather enough for that day. In this way I will test them and see whether they will follow my instructions.'"[17] Pertile expands on this reading by placing the passage from Exodus alongside the book of Numbers, again with the help of Ambrose. In the version of the story that continues in Numbers 11:4, the Israelites disdain the manna, lamenting that they had meat and a variety of other foods while still in Egypt and asking: "Who shall give us flesh to eat?". In response, God sends them "flesh" in the form of quails, promising that they will have so much they will vomit it from their nostrils.[18] Enraged by their unchecked appetites and desire for more delicate foods, the Lord then smites the Israelites with a plague. Only two elders remain back in the camp, and they prophesy with the help of the spirit of the Lord while the Israelites are left to bury those "who had yielded to craving," giving the place the name *Kibroth Hattaavah* (graves of craving).[19] Ambrose distills the story into a simple cause and effect relationship: "But when they began to desire flesh and were turned by their desires to Egypt, out of so many thousands of men not more than two deserved to enter the land of promise."[20]

Like Forese or the unspecified indiscriminate consumers in Dante's *Convivio*, the Israelites' unchecked appetites distract them from God and from their greater purpose, which is to arrive at the Promised Land and establish their city. Their gluttony has led them to believe they would prefer enslavement to freedom, to remain subject to another's rule rather

15 Pézard, "Ciacco," in *Enciclopedia dantesca*, 1:984.
16 Pertile, "Ciacco, Brunetto and the Voice of God," p. 168.
17 Dombroski, "The Grain of Hell," p. 105; Exod. 16.4.
18 Num. 11:18–20.
19 Num. 11.33–34.
20 Ambrose, *De Helia* 18.68.

than to govern themselves. Ciacco, who may remain unidentifiable in many ways but is firmly Florentine, and his compatriots have in their gluttony done the same. Their appetites led them to take more than their fair share at the expense of others, to grow fat while others grew thin, and moreover to lose sight of the privilege of having a city of their own. When Ciacco informs the pilgrim that just as in the Old Testament account so too in Florence only two just men are left ("Giusti son due," *Inf.* 6.73), it would seem that the gluttonous citizens have already provoked the wrath of God, and the deterioration of their city, now fallen from His grace, has begun.[21]

The means by which gluttony weaves together all of these threads—community, governance, identity, and (re)productivity—will not be entirely visible until the end of the canticle, largely because digestion (and the physical reactions that overeating prompts) plays a key role in developing the poem's structure and argument as a whole. In his anatomical account of *Inferno*, Robert Durling advances this template as a way of reading the canticle, designating the bottom of Hell as its "belly" and demonstrating how Dante used the process of eating as an essential framework for both *Inferno* and his broader conception of poetry at once. Master Adam and his dropsy-distended stomach in *Inferno* 30 show how "the state of his body mirrors the state of his soul, the technology of his crime, and the effects of his crime on society," while digestion begins the work of procreation in Statius's discussion of embryology to come.[22] In ways equally ironic and coincidental, Ciacco has been left out of these larger discussions, isolated in *Inferno* 6 and eliminated from the community of canti just as a glutton must be excised from any community. The gastric/gastronomic through line must necessarily be anchored in the circle of gluttons, however, and Ciacco quite literally embodies the message Dante intends to deliver through his language of food: hunger and justice are bound together, and by hungering for more than what is just, both the individual body and the collective body suffer. With the first gluttons the poet describes in his major work, Dante confirms that the ability to recognize an appropriate diet—and to hold the appetite with neither too firm nor too slack a rein—will be the essence of both his poetry and his politics.

---

21   Dombroski, "The Grain of Hell," pp. 103–108.
22   In this important essay, Durling insists that exploring food imagery in the *Comedy* can almost certainly lead us closer to "some of the fundamental issues of [Dante's] poetics." See Durling, "Deceit and Digestion in the Belly of Hell," p. 72.

Gluttons for Flesh

Count Ugolino could not represent a better contrast to Ciacco, at least in the critical tradition. Where Ciacco announces crucial prophetic information for both the pilgrim and the reader but has received limited consideration, Ugolino presents an appendix, if a lengthy one, to an already well-known story but has been the subject of obsessive, persistent attention. This attention has been somewhat blinkered, however, as readings of the count's tragic tale have not often considered him as a piece of the larger whole, despite the fact that his magnetism is born from his ability to capture the poem's greater themes. Understanding Ugolino as the next glutton in a chain of many—from Forese Donati to those disdainful of mixed-grain bread in the *Convivio* to Ciacco—who finally give way to the relentless consumption of Hell's last inhabitants builds a rich interpretative foundation that functions both materially and spiritually, and like the relationship with food on which it is based, to readers past and present.

Ciacco's eroded human identity and his foretelling of the fall of Florence to its gluttonous inhabitants, with its recollection of the biblical moment in which the Israelites demanded flesh, sets the stage for the explicit statements of the last cantos of *Inferno*. If the bottom of Hell portrays the cold reality of the city of man stripped of its humanity, it is only appropriate that its most famous figure would be the most feared product of a culture of starvation. The point farthest from God is represented as a place where there is no common table and nothing to eat but each other. In Dante's vision, Ugolino thus appears consuming human flesh as the climax of the human descent into the inhuman in *Inferno* 33, his grotesque gluttony positioning him deep in the intestinal tract of the "belly" of Hell, where the fraudulent "sins of the gut" are punished.[23] When the pilgrim comes upon Ugolino, the count is in that very moment engaged in eating, and his meal is the flesh of another man. Forever tied to his archenemy by his teeth, Ugolino gnaws on Archbishop Ruggieri, enacting his place in Dante's system of gluttony:

e come 'l pan per fame si manduca
 così 'l sovran li denti a l'altro pose
 là 've 'l cervel s'aggiungne con la nuca
non altrimenti Tidëo si rose
 le tempie a Menalippo per disdegno,

---

23 Durling explains the connection between fraud and sins of the "gut" in "Deceit and Digestion," p. 61.

che quei faceva il teschio e l'altre cose.
Inf. 32.127

(And as bread is eaten by the starving, so the one above put his teeth to
the other, there where the brain joins the nape: not otherwise did Tydeus
gnaw Menalippus' temples in his rage, than this one did the skull and
the other things.)

Having been double-crossed by Ruggieri in the midst of his treasonous plot
to win complete control over Pisa, the count was imprisoned with his family
by his enemies, and ultimately left to starve. Pushed to recount his last days
on earth, the count remembers vividly a dream he had while locked in the
"tower of hunger." Ugolino's dream foretells the conditions of his death and
his contrapasso at once:

Questi pareva a me maestro e donno,
   cacciando il lupo e' lupicini al monte
   per che i Pisan veder Lucca non ponno.
Con cagne magre, studïose e conte
   Gualandi con Sismondi e con Lanfranchi
   s'avea messi dinanzi da la fronte.
In picciol corso mi parieno stanchi
   lo padre e' figli, e con l'agute scane
   mi parea lor veder fender li fianchi.
Inf. 33.28–36

(This man appeared to me as master and lord, hunting the wolf and
his little cubs on the mountain for which the Pisans cannot see Lucca.
With lean, eager, alert bitches, he had put Gualandi with Sismondi and
Lanfranchi before his face. In brief course the father and his sons seemed
to tire, and I seemed to see the sharp fangs tearing their flanks.)

His dream of flesh torn from the innocent to feed a ravenous beast will soon
come true, but not before he is given a crucial last chance to recognize the
value of food. The next thing Ugolino remembers is his children wailing
for bread, "pianger senti' fra 'l sonno i miei figliuoli, / ch'eran con meco, e
dimandar del pane" (I heard my sons, who were with me, crying in their
sleep and asking for bread; *Inf.* 33-39), their empty bellies a consummate
reminder of the selfishness that precipitated their unnecessary deaths.
When they then offer up their own bodies to him in an act of self-sacrifice

that puts Ugolino's empty gestures in stark relief, the count is incapable of understanding that sustenance given is more valuable than sustenance stolen:

> ambo le man per lo dolor mi morsi;
>   ed ei, pensando ch'io 'l fessi per voglia
>   di manicar, di sùbito levorsi
> e disser: "Padre, assai ci fia men doglia
>   se tu mangi di noi: tu ne vestisti
>   queste misere carni, e tu le spoglia."
>   *Inf.* 33.58–63

(Both my hands I bit for rage; and they, thinking that I must be doing it out of a desire to eat, suddenly stood up and said: "Father, it will be much less pain for us if you eat of us: you clothed us with this wretched flesh, so do you divest us of it.")

Too blind to perceive this opportunity to partake in the communion that binds the father of the whole world with his many children, or even to accept his immediate role as provider in his own children's lives, Ugolino not only took the bread out of his children's mouths with his political treachery but literally used them as his own meal:

> ond'io mi diedi,
> già cieco, a brancolar, sovra ciascuno,
>   e due dì li chiamai, poi che fur morti.
>   Poscia, più che 'l dolor, poté 'l digiuno.
>   *Inf.* 33.72–75

(and I, already blind, took to groping over each of them, and for two days I called them, after they were dead. Then fasting had more power than grief.)

The question of whether the poet truly intended this last, ambiguous line as a euphemism for cannibalism has long troubled Dante scholars.[24] The count

24 See Singleton's reading: "Some commentators have held the curious view that by this last line of Ugolino's narrative Dante meant to imply that the count, in the extremity of starvation, did actually attempt to prolong his life by feeding upon the bodies of his sons, as they had begged him to do while they were yet alive (vv. 61–63)—that 'hunger' prevailed over grief in that sense. But such a view of the meaning here is hardly worth a serious rebuttal." *The Divine Comedy:* 1, *Inferno*, p. 617. On the disagreement over the meaning of Ugolino's phrase, "poi più che 'l dolor

does not say explicitly what his last act was, and the poet chooses language that permits both readings, letting the absence of words become more telling than their presence. Yet the argument over whether Dante intended Ugolino to be read as a cannibal obscures a more compelling question: why did Dante allow for the possibility of this reading in the first place? That is, whatever truly happened in the tower before his death on earth, Ugolino is unequivocally engaged in cannibalism when the pilgrim stumbles across him, so the question is not so much whether Ugolino is a "real" cannibal, but rather, why should a sinner located at this level of Hell be portrayed as a cannibal? A wider historical and geographic lens can be helpful here, as scholarship on the accusations of cannibalism advanced arbitrarily at indigenous Americans by European imperialists is a useful reminder that the cannibal has often been a stand-in for threatening otherness.[25] As William Chester Jordan has proposed in his expansive study of the effect of famine in the late Middle Ages, reports of cannibals might be better accounted for by the often murky causes of disappearance and death during times of famine and the general confusion of such historical moments. The importance of news of cannibalism lies in the use of the cannibal as an indicator of social deterioration.[26] Taking a similarly comprehensive view, John Henderson has emphasized that while the term "famine" is used often and indiscriminately to describe conditions during food shortages in pre- and early modern Europe, true famine was characterized by two main features: "a substantial increase in mortality and a breakdown in the social and political order."[27] The appearance of the cannibal, both historically and as a literary trope, is a marker of this breakdown. The cannibal is at once a justified fear of a potentially real person and a projected personification of an earthly existence, a representative of an alternate universe that can and has descended upon the city of man.

The uncanny similarity between a human and a human-eater, and the shrinking grey area between the two, became significantly more ominous in moments of extreme deprivation. Contemplating the frightening yet

poté il digiuno," see the summary of the two traditional positions in Herzman, "Cannibalism and Communion in *Inferno* XXXIII," pp. 53–78, and the conclusions drawn by Yowell, "Ugolino della Gherardesca," p. 841.

25   See the comprehensive study by Barker, Hulme, and Iversen, eds., *Cannibalism and the Colonial World*, and especially Hulme's introduction, "The Cannibal Scene," pp. 1–38.

26   Jordan, *The Great Famine*, pp. 148–150.

27   Henderson, *Piety and Charity in Late Medieval Florence*, pp. 273–278. Henderson also points out that grain dearth is itself sometimes misinterpreted as "famine." Dameron similarly notes the problematic inconsistency with which the term is used in chronicles and in the historiography, in "Feeding the Medieval Italian City-State," pp. 987–988. Both Dameron and Henderson rely on the comprehensive overview provided by Ó Gráda in *Famine: A Short History*.

attractive familiarity of the figure of the cannibal through the present, Kristen Guest notes that "ultimately it is the shared humanness of cannibals and their victims that draws our attention to the problems raised by the notion of absolute difference."[28] That is, while the cannibal is often invoked in an effort to anchor a transcendent theophagy in contrast to the Other's savage and unpredictable anthropophagy, the efficaciousness of the figure is dependent upon our recognition of the similarity it bears to ourselves. In the medieval universe of hunger, Ugolino's crime is unspeakable, but it is not *unimaginable*—hence the reader's ability to fill in the rest of his story where he leaves off. As Borges famously put it, uncertainty is part of the design.[29] Whether or not a cannibal has existed is much less important than the certainty inherent in a population that their community is always on the brink of breeding one.

This process is more easily visible when one sets cannibalism alongside its nearby and natural opposite, communion. The presence of and participation in the Eucharist marks the successful Christian community, well-fed on the bread of Christ, joining together without fear around a food that only becomes more abundant as it is consumed. John Freccero has established the foundational nature of this opposition in the *Comedy*, and has shown moreover that as a poetic device, the count's flesh-eating sets up a contrast between the sacrificial Eucharist that forges bonds and the lifeless meat that erodes them.[30] Ugolino chooses to eat the dead flesh of his children when compelled by his bestial physical hunger rather than their living flesh when it was offered to him, a gesture of sacrifice that would extend an unqualified love between them. His painfully literal understanding of the act of eating—a self-involved and self-serving action—drives him inevitably to occupy the greatest distance from the community of the beatified.

As with Ciacco, part of Ugolino's humanity is missing as a result of his inability to control his appetite for food: he has forfeited a piece of what makes him a complete human in exchange for a piece of flesh. Also like Ciacco, Ugolino points forward to the pilgrim's encounter with Statius, in this case not only in the themes his episode evokes but more directly in the citation of the *Thebaid* Dante weaves into the initial sighting of the Count and the Archbishop, alerting the reader to the thread tying together all the figures of indiscriminate dietary practices with the later explanation of body and soul creation. Where Ciacco introduces the link between the individual

---

28   Guest, *Eating Their Words*, p. 3.
29   Borges, *Selected Non-Fictions*, p. 278.
30   Freccero, *The Poetics of Conversion*, pp. 152–166.

body and the community, showing how food can dilute the essence of what makes one human and becoming at once unidentifiable and incapable of citizenship as a result, Ugolino reveals the glutton's loss of will and intellect, the very elements that connect each human with the divine, and illustrates the physiological way in which the glutton is less than human.

Returning to the description of Ugolino's unequivocal man-eating in the circle of treachery, it is important to remember that the count specifically targets Archbishop Ruggieri's "nuca"—the beginning of the spinal cord—because it was understood to be the source of the marrow that controlled the body's activity through the influence of the sensitive soul as well as the point where the spinal cord and the brain connected. The *nuca* represented a threshold, one of the spaces where body and soul interacted, and where the former possibly had an impact on the latter given its proximity to the brain, the seat of the rational soul. It was Bruno Nardi who once again drew attention to Dante's reliance on the Arabic physicians here, in this case not only Avicenna but also Haly Abbas and Rhazes, in exploring the *nuca* and its uncomfortable implications.[31] As Purdy Moudarres has pointed out more recently, the term in fact appeared in even earlier Latin sources familiar to Dante, and had prompted a series of challenging questions.[32] If the rational soul, which controlled will and intellect (the part of humans that defined them as superior to and more divine than animals) shared a boundary with the sensitive soul (the part of humans that was shared with other sentient creatures), then it was possible that the appetites of the sensitive soul affected the rational soul, and thus the intellect and the will. More simply put, though there remained some doubt and the debate raged on during Dante's lifetime, the *nuca* suggested that the body could have some power over the mind. In that case, as with digestion, what was absorbed into the body would have an effect not only on an individual's physical essence but also on one's mental and spiritual essences.

As with digestion again, the questions that arose were myriad and received all manner of response. If it was impossible to avoid noticing the body grow and change because of food, which required theophilosophers to grapple with the place food had in the perfect resurrection of the body and the creation of the soul, so too the desire for food felt by the sensitive soul and the satisfaction (or lack thereof) of that desire had to be confronted in considering the rational soul—and thus the intellect and the will. The radical Aristotelian principle of a shared rational soul allowed for the possibility of a clear distinction from the

31   Nardi, *Nel mondo di Dante*, pp. 249–257.
32   Purdy Moudarres, "Bodily Starvation," p. 207.

sensitive soul of any given individual, with no interaction; but that proposition was equally troubling, as it eliminated the clear chain of development of the soul from inception. Yet if the rational soul absorbed the other souls into itself, as Aquinas would have it (hewing more closely to the Aristotelian original), then the sensitive soul must have some connection to the rational soul.[33] None of the answers were reassuring, but Dante's description of Ugolino gnawing at this anatomically highly specific point does the same thing as the suggestion, however unprovable, of cannibalism: it affirms for the reader that Dante is aware of and concerned about this grey area. To anyone who believed there was a chance that the sensitive soul wielded influence over the rational soul, the imbalance in Ugolino's body introduced by his forced starvation would at least provide the conditions for a physical deterioration that would in turn jeopardize the mind and the spirit.[34] What is more important than determining if the poet stood on one side or the other of this debate is acknowledging that Dante saw this as a possibility, and concluding, as Purdy Moudarres does, that he demands "a sharpening of our sensitivity to the power the body wields over the mind, and thus, to the iniquity of its mistreatment."[35]

Ugolino's mistreatment of his own body, and then his children's bodies, will by extension cost the body politic; as Freccero has stressed, Ugolino's story is more than a tragedy of an individual man's inability to see the divine in the human, but rather a "paradigm of political understanding."[36] Gluttony is always politicized, as Dante firmly establishes in *Inferno* 6, and contemporary descriptions of Ugolino's conduct as a public official confirm that his unfettered appetite was reflected in the decisions he made for his community. Reasserting the need to read Ugolino's last words as an indication of his descent into anthropophagy, William Cook and Ronald Herzman have highlighted a quote from the Pseudo-Brunetto Latini chronicle (c. 1300) which demonstrates how notorious the count was as a local leader, but not before retelling the tale of his horrible death:

> At that time Count Ugolino, being lord of Pisa, because of the bad treatment he was in the habit of showing them, the people rose up in anger,

---

33 Aquinas, *Summa* 1a q. 84 art. 7–8.
34 Purdy Moudarres explains the very specific ways in which Ugolino's symptoms, especially but not exclusively the blindness that descends upon him just prior to death, track with a Galenic understanding of the process by which a body denied adequate nourishment eventually produces too much black bile, which in turn clouds the area of the brain that can think or reason, causing the person to behave irrationally or bestially, in "Bodily Starvation," pp. 221–224.
35 Purdy Moudarres, "Bodily Starvation," p. 209.
36 Freccero, "Bestial Sign and Bread of Angels," pp. 152–153.

coming with force and great uproar to the Archbishop Ruggiero Ubaldini, crying out: "May he die! May he die!" He was taken and put in prison with two of his sons and two grandchildren, and they were made to die of hunger in prison [...] Then Guido, Count of Montefeltro, commanded that Count Ugolino and his two children and two grandchildren not be given any more to eat, and so all five died of wretched hunger. That is Count Ugolino and Uguccione, Brigata, Anselmuccio and Guelfo, and it was found that the one had eaten the flesh of the other, and finally the last rites were denied to them and one morning all five were dragged dead from prison. This Count Ugolino was a man of such cruelty that he made the people of Pisa die of hunger while at the same time having a great abundance of grain, such that it cost seven pounds to buy a *staio* of grain in Pisa; then finally he himself died of hunger with all his family. In this year in Florence the loggia of Orsanmichele was constructed with ten pillars, all of stone.[37]

The fluidity with which the Pseudo-Latini account moves—from the circumstances of Ugolino's death to a description of his neglect of Pisa's food economy and his personal hoarding, then to the construction of a grain store in Florence in the same year—perfectly illustrates the relationship between the glutton and the failed city of Pisa, contrasted with the foresighted and successful Florence. Hoarding for himself, the count not only committed

37 "In questo tempo il conte Ugolino esendo singnore di Pisa per la mala singnoria chelli usava a furore di popolo colla forza dello arcivescovo di Ubaldini con grande romore gridando: Muoia! muoia! fu preso e messo in prigione con II tra i' filli et II nepoti fecero di fame morire in prigione [...] Allora tantosto Guido conte di Montefeltro comandò ke mai al conte Ugolino e a suoi figli & 2 nepoti fosse dato mangiare, e così morirono dinopia fame tutti i cinque. Ciò fue il conte Ugolino e Ugoccione, Brigata, Aselmuccio e Guelfo, e qui si trovò kelluno mangiò de le carne all'altro, e finalmente fu loro dinegato [...] il loro peccato et tutti i V un uno mattino fuoro tratti morti di prigione. Questo conte Ugolino fue homo di così fatta maniera chelli facea morire il popolo di Pisa di fame ed al suo tempo avendo grande abondanza di formento fu sì crudelmente che VII lib. facea conperare lo staio del grano in Pisa, poi finalmente per fame morio con tutta sua famiglia. In questo anno in firenze si fece la loggia d'orto San Michele ornatamente in X pilastri tutta di pietra." The original text is found in the Biblioteca Nazionale Magl. II.IV.323, fol. 10v, but several scholars have cited part or all of this passage in relation to other critical concerns, including Herlihy, *Pisa in the Early Renaissance*, p. 109, and Holloway, *Twice-Told Tales*, p. 153. Early twentieth-century Dante scholars, offended by the idea of cannibalism in the poem, argued over its validity as proof that Ugolino had eaten his children; see D'Ovidio, *Nuovi studii danteschi: Ugolino, Pier della Vigna, i Simoniaci*, pp. 63–116. More recently, Cook and Herzman have inserted the passage into their wider argument for receiving Ugolino as a cannibal, a component of the deterioration of the city of man seen in the last cantos of *Inferno*, in "Inferno XXXIII: The Past and Present in Dante's Imagery of Betrayal," p. 378.

an act of inhuman neglect of his brethren, he inadvertently undermined his own claim to authority. His people depended upon him and found him unwilling to provide, leaving them like the hungry who flocked to Dante's table in the *Convivio* desperate for bread. The apparent non sequitur in the final line of the passage, where Pseudo-Brunetto underlines the fact that Florence built its now-famous grain store, Orsanmichele, in this year, is instead an important recognition of a related decision in policy-making—in this case, a successful one. The chronicler perhaps takes pride, or heed, in noting that while Ugolino starved Pisa, the leaders of Florence took action to protect their citizens from hunger.

Ugolino thus acts out the dangers of an indiscriminate diet on two planes, demonstrating the effects on himself and on his city. As an individual he was responsible for nourishing his body in order to maintain its health and protect the sanctity of his soul; his political appointment required that he provide for his people to ensure the health and growth of that larger body politic. The count's gruesome gluttony in Hell is not only an ironic twist on his rejection of communion with Christ, but also a reminder of the agreement he broke with his people in choosing to let them starve while indulging in political factionalism. When he should have fed others, Ugolino ate for himself; later, when his children offered to feed him, Ugolino refused to engage in the exchange. Even more telling is how the loss of humanity that transpires during his earthly imprisonment is visited first upon his children in the tower, consumed before they ever have a chance to participate in the community, and then upon his betrayer in Hell, who loses not just reason but also voice and presence, allowing the reader to trace the far-reaching and devastating consequences of a diet gone wrong.

Bring the Fruit!

The tendency to isolate Ugolino as a self-contained epic is no doubt one of the reasons this reading has rarely been extended to the rest of the canto, much less the rest of the poem. However, the count, the most notorious of all the souls found at the bottom of Hell for his pathetic tale and his anthropophagic tendencies, is in reality at the heart of a sequence of crucial dramas around the table that concludes *Inferno*, leading up to the eerily silent meal of Lucifer.[38] In fact, Ugolino's infernal home of Antenora gives

---

38   See Durling's powerful reading of Master Adam's distended belly in "Deceit and Digestion," p. 62.

way to a section specifically defined as the final resting place for those who betrayed their dining companions, and the only speaking inhabitant in this subsection of the ninth circle, Fra' Alberigo, discloses that this kind of betrayal is a sin for which no forgiveness exists. Still, despite his shocking contrapasso and his suggestive positioning between the cannibalistic count and the insatiable Satan, Fra' Alberigo remains an oft-ignored link in the chain of tragic anti-banquets.[39]

If it is perhaps not surprising that Ugolino's parting allusion to cannibalism leads both pilgrim and reader to believe the count is the finale of *Inferno* 33, it is also true that the meeting with Fra' Alberigo, the jovial friar of Faenza, does little to draw attention to itself. Like the encounter with Ciacco in *Inferno* 6, it is neither traumatic nor especially memorable, and easily overshadowed by the count's revelation of a hunger more powerful than grief that comes immediately before it. Nonetheless, as Alfred Triolo has taken pains to emphasize, "the Fra' Alberigo episode is, in its somewhat muted way, quite as explosive as its predecessor," and while he is not accused of cannibalism, Alberigo also exchanges feeding for faithlessness, creating a telling complement to the preceding episode and adding a crucial layer to the theme of gluttony that builds throughout *Inferno*.[40] Condemned to the level just before the amorphous colossus of Lucifer, Alberigo is both the last soul to exchange words with Dante in Hell and the only speaking representative of Ptolomea, where he resides with the other traitors to dinner guests. Denied even the relief of weeping in the frozen prison of the penultimate region, Alberigo attempts to broker a deal, which the pilgrim repays with the ambiguous "cortesia" of refusing to remove the icy mask of tears from his face. Anticipating a moment's liberation from his suffering, the friar guarantees the pilgrim whatever information he might desire, freely giving up his name and the details of his fate:

> I' son frate Alberigo;
> i' son quel da le frutta del mal orto,

---

39 In addition to Triolo's dedicated article, "Inferno 33: Fra Alberigo in Context," studies that have given fuller attention to Alberigo include the discussion of his place in the canto by Herzman, "Cannibalism and Communion in *Inferno* 33," pp. 53–78; a brief but valuable summary of his singularity by Gilson in "Medieval Magical Lore and Dante's *Commedia*," pp. 45–48; Chiodo's consideration of Alberigo and the significance of fruit and plant life in his anecdote, in "Tutti i frutti," pp. 97–110; and the *lectura dantis* focused on Alberigo and his silent companion Branca Doria by Fiorilla, "Frate Alberigo e Branca Doria fra tradizioni antiche e riscritture moderne," pp. 155–177.

40 Triolo, "Inferno 33: Fra Alberigo in Context," p. 39.

che qui riprendo dattero per figo.

Inf. 33.118–120

I am Brother Alberigo, I am he of the fruits of the evil orchard, and I receive a date for every fig.

A member of the generally intemperate "frati gaudenti" (jovial friars), Alberigo dei Manfredi was a Guelph lord of Faenza whose power was contested by his cousin Manfredo. Following Giovanni Villani's account in the *Nuova cronica*, it seems that during an argument between the two men Manfredo's young son Alberghetto struck Alberigo in a fit of rage. Pretending to forgive the youth's insolence, Alberigo invited him and his father to a banquet in May of 1285, where at his call for dessert, "Vengan le frutta!" (Bring the fruit!) his assassins emerged and slayed the two hapless guests.[41] Further chronicles confirm the other guests present were also ruthlessly slaughtered, with the exception of a young boy, who was spared only to be sent back to the city to tell the tale, should anyone think to question Alberigo's power again.[42] It is for this "bad fruit," as he discloses, that the friar is condemned to Ptolomea, where the severity of his punishment exceeds his crime to the degree that a date is sweeter than a fig.

Much like the narrative of Ugolino, Alberigo's story was too notorious to be news to his contemporary the pilgrim, even if it is less familiar to the modern reader of Dante. However, it nonetheless arouses interest in the pilgrim, who is surprised to find someone he thought was still alive among the shades. The prompt allows the friar to explain further:

"Cotal vantaggio ha questa Ptolomea,
    che spesse volte l'anima ci cade
    innanzi ch'Atropòs mossa le dea.
E perché tu più volontier mi rade
    le 'nvetrïate lagrime dal volto,
    sappie che, tosto che l'anima trade
come fec'ïo, il corpo suo l'è tolto
    da un demonio, che poscia il governa
    mentre che 'l tempo suo tutto sia vòlto;
ella ruina in sì fatta cisterna."

Inf. 33.124–133

---

41 Villani, *Nuova cronica*, vol. 3, p. 27.
42 See the brief summary by Zama, *I Manfredi, signori di Faenza*, pp. 60–61.

(Ptolomea has this advantage, that often the soul falls here before Atropos has sent it off. And that you may more willingly shave the glass tears from my eyes, know that, as soon as the soul betrays as I did, its body is taken over by a demon, who then governs it until his time has all revolved; the soul falls down to this cistern.)

Like Ptolemy, son of Abubus, who murdered Simon of Macabee and his sons at the banquet to which he had invited them, the souls that fall to Ptolomea are guilty of having treacherously killed their guests at dinner.[43] But while all residents of the ninth circle are traitors of the most delicate trust, it is apparently only those who betray their dining companions who are denied any chance of repentance, falling instantly to Hell and leaving a demonically possessed body in their wake. Apart from its lack of a firm scriptural foundation, this twist creates a surprising discontinuity with Dante's own well-documented emphasis on the power of penance, best characterized by the last act of contrition of Buonconte da Montefeltro, whose soul is found in *Purgatorio* 5, saved by "una lacrimetta" (a little teardrop; *Purg.* 5.107). Ptolomea is a glaring contradiction to this rule and the prevailing doctrine of the time, a section defined by a sin so grave that the sinner is deprived of any opportunity for atonement and any chance to appeal to God's otherwise-infinite mercy.

Though neither demonic possession nor re-animated corpses were understood as *a priori* absurd or unlikely in the late Middle Ages, a demon taking control of a human body after the soul has already been banished to Hell is a unique and likely unorthodox concept. Relying on the classic study by Arturo Graf, Simon Gilson has suggested that this manipulation of accepted contemporary demonologies "seems to be unprecedented, certainly in medieval scholastic writings and [...] in more popularizing genres too."[44] The subtle differences that divide the sinners in the ninth circle render the punishment still more striking. Though there are several episodes in which the pilgrim displays an irrational sympathy for the condemned souls, he takes solace in his belief that Divine Justice has been done. Even Ugolino,

---

43 Some commentators have suggested the section was named instead for Ptolemy XII who murdered Pompey when he arrived in Egypt expecting hospitality, but consensus holds that Dante relied primarily on the Biblical Ptolomy, who invited guests to a banquet and subsequently killed them. For more on the subject see the entry "Ptolomea," in Bosco, ed., *Enciclopedia Dantesca*, pp. 617–618.

44 Gilson, "Medieval Magical Lore and Dante's *Commedia*," p. 47. See also the same sentiment expressed by Triolo, who turns to the still-earlier work by Filomusi-Guelfi to conclude that there is no direct source for the idea, in "Inferno 33: Fra Alberigo in Context," pp. 63–70.

who is often perceived as a victim, is ultimately recognized as a perpetrator; though the thought of his bitter end causes him immense grief, he never expresses regret for his crime in Hell, nor did he request forgiveness in life. The souls in Ptolomea are given no opportunity to repent for so similar a crime. Instead, their lives are cut from them instantly, as Alberigo makes clear when he identifies Branca D'Oria, whose soul fell to join the friar even before his intended victim was dead:

> "Nel fosso sù," diss'el, "de' Malebranche,
>   là dove bolle la tenace pece,
>   non era ancor giunto Michel Zanche
> che questi lasciò il diavolo in sua vece
>   nel corpo suo e un suo prossimano
>   che 'l tradimento insieme con lui fece."
>   *Inf.* 33.142–147

("Up in the ditch," he said, "of the Evil Claws, there where the sticky pitch is boiling, Michel Zanche had not yet arrived, when this one left a devil in his stead, in his body and that of a relative of his who committed the betrayal along with him.")

The complication presented by such a declaration is twofold. Not only is it unclear why Dante would have felt compelled to oppose generally accepted dogma in his development of this punishment, but his reason for choosing to single out this specific group as its recipient is also mysterious.[45] In fact, the introduction of Ptolomea's "vantaggio" seems to announce in itself the poet's intention to create a foil between Ugolino, who suffers an all too appropriate punishment, and Alberigo, who instead receives much more than he could have ever bargained for.

In commenting on this section, most early readers of Dante proposed that the banquet in question is not an earthly event but rather the "mensa dell'amore," as in *Paradiso* 24 when Beatrice invites the beatified elect to the "gran cena del benedetto Agnello" (*Par.* 24.1–9). Thus the sin committed is against both literal "commensali" as well as the brothers and sisters at the

---

45 Pietrobono articulated the question succinctly nearly a hundred years ago: "Perché qual differenza porremo tra i traditori della Caina e quelli della Ptolomea, se gli uni tradirono i congiunti e gli altri i commensali? I congiunti sono essi pure e in primo grado nostri commensali; e il tradirli sarebbe certo colpa assai più grave del tradimento dei semplici commensali, se dovessimo stare al senso letterale della parola e non intendere con essa qualcosa di più sacro della stessa famiglia." In Pietrobono, *Dal centro al cerchio*, p. 59.

table to which God has invited all men.[46] The only major Biblical example of a demon possessing a body at the moment of sin is the case of Judas at the Last Supper, as recorded in passages from Luke and John (John 13:21-30; Luke 22:3-6); there, Satan entered the body of Judas upon his decision to betray Christ, after he received the Eucharist falsely, which makes the association with the earthly version of the "mensa dell'amore" more evident. The impression is strengthened when considering that the friar appears immediately following Ugolino's allusion to cannibalism, and just preceding Lucifer's infernal inversion of communion in *Inferno* 34. There is, however, a fundamental difference: neither Alberigo nor Branca Doria, nor the Ptolemy from whom the section gets its name, can be properly represented as Judas figures, as they were not guests who betrayed their hosts but rather hosts who betrayed their guests. The Ptolomeans did not rebuke hospitality; they extended it treacherously. The friar himself underlines this when he ironically remarks that in Hell he is given a "dattero" in exchange for the "figo" he offered his guests.

Other scholarly considerations of the exceptional punishment reserved for traitors of dining companions have proposed that the violation of this intrinsic trust was in itself enough to define the Ptolomeans as substantially worse than other traitors. These readings underline that the guest-host relationship constituted a sacred bond in ancient cultures, one enhanced by a special trust within the context of a meal.[47] This may have been an accurate description of the Roman *convivium*, which Cicero portrayed in his *Familiares* as "tum maxime simul vivitur" (9.24, the time we most truly coexist together). Though the ideal was perhaps seldom a reality, the convivium was at least intended to mirror the Republic, giving everyone equal place and equal access to food.[48] Yet the application of this ancient vision of a group meal, where the table acted as the primary setting for cementing friendships and encouraging equality, neglects both the contemporary reality and the

---

46 Herzman elaborates this idea considerably when he arrives at his discussion of Alberigo in "Cannibalism and Communion in *Inferno* 33," pp. 69–78.

47 "The guest-host relationship constitutes a deep and sacred value in ancient cultures [...] enhanced by a special trust within the context of a meal or banquet." Triolo, "Ptolomea," in *The Dante Encyclopedia*, p. 722. See also the *lectura dantis* of Di Pietro, who concludes: "To commit acts of treachery under the guise of hospitality is so evil in such a cultural context that we can understand why Dante would not even feel a modicum of compassion for those souls who must remain frozen in this godless lake for all eternity." Di Pietro, "Lectura Dantis: Inferno 33," pp. 73–84.

48 In her book on the Roman table in literature, Emily Gowers emphasizes: "Where the principle of an equal elite was essential for political coherence, the domineering host (or *rex*) became a sinister reminder of monarchy." Gowers, *The Loaded Table*, pp. 25–26.

context of Alberigo's meal as presented by the poet. Dante's *Convivio* is a translation of the ancient concept of *convivium* into a contemporary context, and the meal he describes in his philosophical treatise acknowledges the distinctions in class and power among those seated at the table. So too the table at which Fra' Alberigo hosted his guests is not imagined to be an organic union of likeminded men, where one man counted another as his equal, but the offer of food from his table nonetheless harbors significance in light of this accepted asymmetrical relationship.

In the tightly bound food-power relationship of thirteenth-century Italy, the table constantly reenacted the dynamic of dependency between provisioner and provisioned. Dante's *Convivio* recreates this tension for his reader: his philosophical treatise based on a shared meal attempts to bring the access and balance of the Roman convivium to a late medieval context that recognized a very different political reality.[49] The ability to provide sustenance was the ultimate demonstration of legitimate power, and the table, where one hosted a meal, was the place where that power was exhibited and confirmed. A host established stability and extended security to his guests; if he lavished them with generous feasts of the most exotic ingredients, it was not to thank them for their camaraderie, but so that they should see his power manifested in the abundance he provided. As a significant reinforcement to this political-gastronomic hierarchy, the structure of the dining room and the seating at table changed dramatically in this period, in response to this interpretation of duty-bound nourishment. Whereas Romans had typically reclined on three large couches arranged in a horseshoe (*triclinium*), with the guest of honor seated to the extreme left, over time the Carolingian tradition of the lord or king seated upright in the center of a central table, often elevated above the others on a dais, became the standard.[50] The resulting image is clear: at table, the dominant position was reserved for the leader of the community, the one who provisioned and thus protected his citizens, and in doing so affirmed his right to occupy that seat.

Though the threat of being deprived remained potent, these clearly defined roles at the table did not necessarily engender discontent or fear;

---

49 Considering the changing meaning of the feast on the continent from antiquity to the present, Strong defines the late Middle Ages as the moment when the table was used almost exclusively for the symbolic reiteration of power: "Through the eleventh century and into the twelfth, the feast became a quintessential part of the fabric of feudalism, a massive periodic culinary event celebrating the relationship between a lord and his vassals, and the power this relationship engendered." Strong, *Feast: A History of Grand Eating*, p. 66.

50 Strong, *Feast*, p. 28.

while Dante's *Convivio* is not a Roman republican ideal, it is a place where true nourishment and conviviality are meant to be found. The gesture of feeding, to give food instead of keeping it for oneself, afforded the opportunity to model good leadership by being a reliable provider and inclined toward charity; it could just as easily run parallel to the image of the "mensa dell'amore" as contrary to it. The table did undoubtedly recall the final promise Christ made to his disciples, "Ye may eat and drink at my table in my kingdom" (Luke 22:30), but the host at the table was aligned not with the disciples, Judas or otherwise, but with Christ. The meal on earth was in anticipation of the heavenly banquet, where everyone would indulge together in the bread of life made available by the ultimate provider, God. Hosting was a means for reinforcing and reenacting the divine feast to bind and grow the community. In hoarding food, a leader both missed the chance to extend the most essential Christian gesture of sodality and tarnished the reflection of the city of God meant to be seen in the city of man.

The superhuman image associated with the dominant position at the table and in turn with the head of a community was thus very much in keeping with the established responsibilities of that role. If Ugolino's contemporary in the Pseudo-Latini chronicle observed the inhumanity of the count's practice of grain hoarding, his judgment of Alberigo would have no doubt been much harsher. A good prince fed his people, and a bad prince let them starve, so it could only be a demonic prince who fed fatal blows in place of food. If the head of the community must take his seat at the dining table and enforce cohesion by providing the meal, the progression from a sinful leader to an unforgivable one becomes clear. Ciacco announces the fate of the community led by gluttons; Ugolino, who gorged on his children's flesh and let his people starve when he should have been their source of abundance, is condemned to eternal suffering; Alberigo, who presented himself as a legitimate and benevolent provider but acted with malicious intentions, is rightly replaced with a demon, because he poisoned the food at the table which he had been granted the chance to head. The total loss of self that befalls the Ptolomeans is the logical conclusion of the process by which individual identity is diluted through uncontrolled eating. Both nutritional values and agreed upon social and economic values make the "date" that Alberigo must digest in place of the "fig" of his crime richer than his complexion can bear.

Ciacco has been seen as so generic as to be essentially unidentifiable, and the contrapasso to which he and his companions are subjected registers as little more than an unfortunate weather pattern. But envisioning *Inferno*

6 as the introduction to a much larger conversation about gluttony and its effects not just on the individual but on the community at large clarifies the conclusions of the last canticle and their purpose. Indeed, the planting of "bad seeds" that bear ill fruit is frequently employed in the first canticle. In *Inferno* 28, for example, Mosca de' Lamberti, mentioned by Ciacco in *Inferno* 6 among the Florentine ancestors whom Dante believes to have been good men but who in fact inhabit lower circles of Hell, is charged with planting the "mal seme per la gente Tosca" (the seed of evil for the Tuscans; *Inf* 28.107), setting off the Guelf-Ghibelline factionalism that would plague Florence for decades. Similarly, when the pilgrim encounters the members of the excessive, wasteful group of wealthy young Sienese nobles known as the *brigata spendereccia* in *Inferno* 29, he is reminded that their gluttonous attachment to cloves was especially dangerous because the practice would "take root" and grow in the community: "ne l'orto dove tal seme s'appicca" (in the garden where that seed takes root [i.e. their city of Siena]; *Inf.* 29.129).

As the pilgrim progresses to the last circle, the prophecy first pronounced by Ciacco becomes more chillingly real. Scholars have in fact noted that there is broader prophetic gravity that also characterizes *Inferno* 33 and 34, through both classical and biblical allusions. Ronald Herzman has suggested that the cannibalism to which Ugolino is reduced by his enemy harkens to the similar fate of the doomed city of Jerusalem described in Jeremiah 19:8-9, in an intertext closely related to the gloss for Ciacco's punishment found in Jeremiah 25:27:

> I will devastate this city and make it an object of horror and scorn; all who pass by will be appalled and will scoff because of all its wounds. I will make them eat the flesh of their sons and daughters, and they will eat one another's flesh because their enemies will press the siege so hard against them to destroy them.[51]

Through his actions Ugolino has rendered Pisa the Jerusalem of the Jeremiad, a "novella Tebe" (new Thebes; *Inf.* 33.89). In response to his betrayal of the commune, he is locked away in a structure meant to

---

51   "Et ponam civitatem hanc in stuporem, et in sibilum; omnis qui praeterierit per eam obstupescet, et sibilabit super universa plaga eius. Et cibabo eos carnibus filiorum suorum et carnibus filiarum suarum; et unusquisque carnem amici sui comedet in obsidione, et in angustia in qua concludent eos inimici eorum, et qui quaerunt animas eorum." Herzman, "Cannibalism and Communion in *Inferno* XXXIII," pp. 35–36.

protect his community for the future, which he then renders the site of the consumption of its progeny.[52] The new Thebes that he reigns over will be the cause of its own destruction, consuming indiscriminately until it ultimately chews through its only means for survival. Drawn together, the gluttonous figures the pilgrim meets on his journey through Hell perform the legacy of the glutton: the insatiable eater who preys on the weak not only fails to satisfy himself, but furthermore incurs a debt with the next generation.

Dante's progressing antitype, moving from Ugolino to Alberigo and eventually concluding with the eternally masticating Satan, is a perfect contrast with the successful head of the community, who is powerful through providing and enforcing cohesion through communion in food. Gluttony, which results in impotence or violence in the role of provisioner, pushes past the individual, and even the present generation. It creates an anti-community, an alternate genealogy of the city in which men become man-eaters and children become the next meal instead of the future. As Dante's first glutton Forese Donati will tell the pilgrim when they meet again on the terrace of gluttony in *Purgatorio*, echoing the prophecy of Ciacco among the gluttons of *Inferno*, if the people in Florence knew what destiny awaited them, their mouths would already hang open—not to seek manna, but to wail: "già per urlare avrian le bocche aperte" (they would already have opened their mouths to howl; *Purg.* 23.108).[53]

Works Cited

Alighieri, Dante. *The Divine Comedy of Dante Alighieri.* Edited and translated by Robert M. Durling, with introduction and notes by Ronald L. Martinez and Robert M. Durling. 3 vols. New York: Oxford University Press, 1996.

Alighieri, Dante. *The Divine Comedy: 1. Inferno.* Translated, and with a commentary, by Charles S. Singleton. Princeton: Princeton University Press, 1970.

Ambrose. *De Helia et ieiunio.* Turnhout: Brepols, 2010.

52   On the extensive imagery drawn from Seneca and the broader Tantalean themes in Ugolino's narrative, see Villa, "Rileggere gli archetipi," pp. 122–129, and "Unicuique suum: Observations on Dante as a Reader of Classical Authors," pp. 150–151. Villa points out that among the classical themes Dante exploits in Ugolino's narrative, there is the expression of a special "ira" for communities that cannot manage to live according to justice but instead use their communal structures to carry out terrible misdeeds.

53   The correspondence between *Inferno* 23 and *Purgatorio* 23 and the connection to the Fall of Jerusalem is carefully elaborated in Martinez, "Dante's Jeremiads," pp. 304–307.

Aquinas, Thomas. *Summa Theologiae*. Translated by Fathers of the English Domenican Province. 3 vols. New York: Benziger, 1948.

Augustine. *The City of God Against the Pagans*. 7 vols. Translated by George E.
McCracken, et. al. Cambridge, Mass.: Harvard University Press, 1957–1972.

Barker, Francis, Peter Hulme, and Margaret Iversen, eds. *Cannibalism and the
Colonial World*. Cambridge: Cambridge University Press, 1998.

Bynum, Caroline Walker. *The Resurrection of the Body in Western Christianity,
200-1336*. New York: Columbia University Press, 1995.

Bosco, Umberto, ed. *Enciclopedia Dantesca*. 6 vols. Rome: Istituto della Enciclopedia
italiana, 1970-75.

Barolini, Teodolina. "'Only Historicize': History, Material Culture and the Future
of Dante Studies." *Dante Studies* 127 (2009): 37–54.

Borges Jorge Luis. *Selected Non-Fictions*. Edited by Eliot Weinberger. New York:
Viking, 1999.

Chiodo, Carol. "Tutti i frutti: The Fruits of Treachery and the Roots of the Soul in
Inferno 33." In *Table Talk: Perspectives on Food in Medieval Italian Literature*,
edited by Christiana Purdy Moudarres, 97-110. Cambridge: Cambridge Scholars
Press, 2010.

Cook, William R. and Ronald B. Herzman. "Inferno XXXIII: The Past and Present
in Dante's Imagery of Betrayal." *Italica* 56, No. 4 (Winter 1979): 377–383.

Dameron, George. "Feeding the Medieval Italian City-State: Grain, War, and Political
Legitimacy in Tuscany, c. 1150–c. 1350." *Speculum* 92, no. 4 (October 2017): 976–1019.

Di Pietro, Robert J. "Lectura Dantis: Inferno 33." *Lectura Dantis: A Forum for Dante
Research and Interpretation* 1, no. 1 (1987): 73-84.

Dombroski, Robert. "The Grain of Hell: A Note on Retribution in *Inferno* 6." *Dante
Studies* 88 (1970): 103–108.

D'Ovidio, Francesco. *Nuovi studii danteschi: Ugolino, Pier della Vigna, i Simoniaci*.
Milan: Hoepli, 1907.

Durling, Robert. "Deceit and Digestion in the Belly of Hell." In *Allegory and
Representation: Selected Papers from the English Institute*, edited by Stephen
Greenblatt, 61–93. Baltimore: Johns Hopkins University Press, 1981.

Fiorilla, Maurizio. "Frate Alberigo e Branca Doria fra tradizioni antiche e riscritture
moderne." In *Lectura Dantis Interamnensis*, edited by Giancarlo Rati, 155-177.
Rome: Bulzoni, 2010.

Freccero, John. *The Poetics of Conversion*. Edited and with an introduction by Rachel
Jacoff. Cambridge: Harvard University Press, 1986.

Gilson, Simon A. "Medieval Magical Lore and Dante's *Commedia*: Divination and
Demonic Agency." *Dante Studies* 119 (2001): 27-66.

Gowers, Emily. *The Loaded Table: Representations of Food in Roman Literature*.
Oxford: Oxford University Press, 1997.

Guest, Kristen, ed. *Eating Their Words: Cannibalism and the Boundaries of Cultural Identity*. Albany: State University of New York Press, 2001.

Henderson John. *Piety and Charity in Late Medieval Florence*. Oxford: Clarendon Press, 1997.

Herlihy, David. *Pisa in the Early Renaissance: A Study in Urban Growth*. New Haven: Yale University Press, 1958.

Herzman, Ronald. "Cannibalism and Communion in *Inferno* XXXIII." *Dante Studies* 98 (1980): 53-78.

Holloway, Julia Bolton. *Twice-Told Tales: Brunetto Latini and Dante Alighieri*. New York: Peter Lang, 1993.

Jordan, William Chester. *The Great Famine: Northern Europe in the Early Fourteenth Century*. Princeton: Princeton University Press, 1996.

Marchesi, Simone. "'Epicuri de grege porcus': Ciacco Epicurus and Isidore of Seville." *Dante Studies* 117 (1999): 117–131.

Martinez, Ronald L. "Dante's Jeremiads: The Fall of Jerusalem and the Burden of the Pharisees, the Capetians, and Florence." In *Dante for the New Millennium*, edited by Teodolinda Barolini and Wayne H. Storey, 301–319. New York: Fordham University Press, 2003.

Nardi, Bruno. *Studi di filosofia medievale*. Rome: Edizioni di Storia e Letteratura, 1960.

Nardi, Bruno. *Nel mondo di Dante*. Rome: Edizioni di Storia e Letteratura, 1944.

Ó Gráda, Cormac. *Famine: A Short History*. Princeton: Princeton University Press, 2009.

Pertile, Lino. "Ciacco, Brunetto and the Voice of God." In *Legato con Amore in un Volume: Essays in Honor of John A. Scott,* edited by John J. Kinder and Diana Glenn, 157-174. Florence: Leo S. Olschki, 2013.

Peter of Poitiers. *Sententiae Petri Pictaviensis*. Edited by Marthe Dulong and Philip S. Moore. Notre Dame: University of Notre Dame Press, 1943–50.

Pietrobono, Luigi. *Dal centro al cerchio: la struttura morale della Commedia*. Turin: Società editrice internazionale, 1956.

Purdy Moudarres, Christiana. "Bodily Starvation and the Ravaging of the Will: A Reading of Inferno 32-33." *Viator* 47, no. 1 (2016): 205-228.

Purdy Moudarres, Christiana. "Devouring Selves in the Circle of Gluttony: A Gloss on the Contrapasso of *Inferno* 6." In *Table Talk: Perspectives on Food in Medieval Italian Literature*. Edited by Christiana Purdy Moudarres, 3-18. Newcastle upon Tyne: Cambridge Scholars Publishing, 2010.

Strong, Roy. *Feast: A History of Grand Eating*. London: Jonathan Cape, 2002.

Triolo, Alfred. "Inferno 33: Fra Alberigo in Context." *L'Alighieri* 11 (1970): 39-70.

Villa, Claudia. "Rileggere gli archetipi: la dismisura di Ugolino." In *Leggere Dante*, edited by Lucia Battaglia Ricci, 113-129. Ravenna: Longo, 2003.

Villa, Claudia. "'Unicuique suum': Observations on Dante as a Reader of Classical Authors." In *Italy and the Classical Tradition: Language, Thought, and Poetry, 1300-1600*. Edited by Carlo Caruso and Andrew Laird. London: Bloomsbury, 2013.

Villani, Giovanni. *Nuova cronica*. Edited by Giuseppe Porta. 3 vols. Parma: Fondazione Pietro Bembo, 2007.

Yowell, Donna. "Ugolino della Gherardesca." In *The Dante Encyclopedia,* edited by Richard Lansing, 1586-1591. New York: Routledge, 2010.

Zama, Piero. *I Manfredi, signori di Faenza*. Faenza: Fratelli Lega, 1954.

4. Purgatorial Gluttony

Abstract

After *Inferno* demonstrates how the unrepentant gluttons dilute their essence, descending into a bestial consumption that leads them to eat the flesh of their own loins, in *Purgatorio* Dante models how gluttony can be corrected and channeled into productivity. Coding the poetry of his former cohort as the consequence of overeating, Dante contrasts their now-obsolete poetic production with his own successful composition in the *dolce stil novo*. Turning once more to the question of procreation, but in the form of bodies and souls, Dante emphatically confirms the connection between consuming and creating, and insists that anyone who knows how to eat can contribute to the formation of a lasting human community, be it through poetry, politics, or procreation.

Keywords: embryology, poetics, politics, procreation, productivity

The affinity between Ciacco's pronouncement in *Inferno* 6 and Forese Donati's lines in *Purgatorio* 23 is not only generated by the repeated prophecy of Florence's demise. Just as the ostensible disconnect between Ciacco's sin and his speech organized a demonstration of the correlation between gluttony, identity, and civic duty, so too the peculiar selection of a place dedicated to punishing gluttons for a conversation about body and soul will reveal itself to articulate gluttony's crucial role in human reproduction and salvation. As Dante will learn when he nears the top of the purgatorial mountain, body and soul are first joined when God infuses a soul into the embryo—formed from male and female contributions that are themselves the result of the digestion of food. This explanation is delivered in a memorable and much-discussed monologue by the Roman poet Statius, who responds to the pilgrim's query about the shades' bodies made thin by a lack of food, despite no longer requiring earthly sustenance: "Como si può far magro / là dove uopo di nodrir non tocca?" (How can thinness occur where there is no need for nourishment?; *Purg.* 25.20–21). At this prompting, Statius

Callegari, D., *Dante's Gluttons: Food and Society from the* Convivio *to the* Comedy.
Taylor & Francis Group, 2022
DOI 10.5117/9789463720427_CH04

reveals a comprehensive embryology that demonstrates how the process of eating leads first to the production of human bodies, then to the infusion of human souls, then to the death of the body, the projection of souls into shades, and finally, to the reunification of body and soul at the end of time. Scholars have further noted that the vast and complex path from life to afterlife that Dante lays out in the voice of Statius does double duty for the poet, describing not one but two acts of creation: human and poetic.

Where in the first canticle the connection between Ciacco's political speech and gluttony is not immediately clear and requires significant unpacking to interpret, in the second canticle the relationship between gluttony and producing poetry is made explicit, and to be sure it has been noted on many occasions. Robert Durling and many others have shown that the potential pitfalls of the indiscriminate ingestion of humans are addressed repeatedly in Dante's work, and while they come through most powerfully in the "belly" of Hell, they also form a line stretching from Dante's earliest experiments in lyric to his eventual encounter with the poets on the purgatorial mountain—a line that can be traced quite literally, as gluttony is an accusation Dante makes against Forese Donati in the *tenzone* and once more against his poetic peers in the figure of Donati in the *Comedy*. The link between food consumption and the creation of souls has garnered even more critical attention, not least because Statius's embryology treads difficult theological territory, possibly derived from heterodox sources, and places no clear boundary between the human physiological processes and the divine intervention that leads to a complete body and soul. That the purging of gluttony must be the backdrop against which embryology and ensoulment are explained becomes clear when placed in context with the steps Dante has taken so far to establish the role that food has in defining the relationship between body and soul, between individual and community. In *Purgatorio* this will be elaborated, by adding the conclusion to the process of consuming, nourishing, and growing: creativity.

The long path to understanding the process from consumption to creation, whether of humans or art, is mapped across an equally long portion of the poem. Statius won't furnish the pilgrim with the complete embryology that also explains the generation of shade bodies and human bodies until *Purgatorio* 25. But even if readers limit their gaze to the second canticle, it is necessary to reach back several cantos in order to appreciate the implications of Dante's fully realized network of physical and spiritual development. After *Inferno* reveals the fate of gluttons who either overeat and regurgitate, or who go on consuming until they eat the flesh of their own loins (condemning both themselves and their progeny), *Purgatorio* now models how gluttony can be corrected. Coding the poetry of his former cohort as the consequence of overeating, Dante contrasts their now-obsolete poetic production with his own successful composition, a product of a judicious appetite. Turning once more to the question of production, but in the form of bodies and souls, Dante emphatically confirms the connection between consuming and creating, and insists that anyone who knows how to eat can contribute to the formation of a lasting human community, be it through poetry, politics, or procreation.

Mother's Milk

The relationship between gluttony and productivity that is alluded to in *Inferno* and firmly established in *Purgatorio* is not Dante's invention. As noted in Chapter 1, the human proclivity to overeat and its inevitable consequence of stunting the longevity of the species has long been associated with a parallel stunting of creative capability, famously outlined by Plato in the *Timaeus*.[1] As the dysfunctional intestines of the Malebolge—which Durling calls the "most gigantic case of constipation on record"—demonstrate dramatically, it is a human impulse to devour insatiably until pain or even death occurs, and Dante played frequently with the parallel between material food consumption and metaphoric consumption.[2] Dante's purgatorial gluttons have thus been interpreted in light of a deeply rooted tradition, making their appearance on the terrace of gluttony part of a much larger conversation about consumption, digestion, and reproduction. The poets who came before Dante were, like all humans, prone to overeating, and through their gluttony they were rendered, as Plato would have it, "unphilosophical and unmusical." The lengthy monologue Statius delivers in *Purgatorio* 25, which presents an inversion of this process such that digestion leads instead to human birth, can in turn be seen as a reflection and a corrective at once. As Statius discusses the growth of the fetus through to birth, he reveals the natural process by which Dante has "given birth" to his verses.[3] A temperate diet will lead to healthy digestion and successful parturition: using sexual reproduction as a veiled description of the poetic gesture, Statius confirms that just as babies are born, so too

---

1   Plato, *Timaeus 73a*. See also the first chapter of this book.
2   Durling, "Deceit and Digestion," p. 65.
3   The moment in the poem is summarized by Freccero as "the *askesis* that will bring the body of the text closer to the spirit which informs it." *The Poetics of Conversion*, p. 205.

Dante's method of composition gives new life. To be sure, the Roman poet who will soon replace Virgil as the pilgrim's guide gives much more than a metaphoric parallel to Dante's poetic production. Beginning in *Purgatorio* 21 and running through the end of the canticle, Statius will articulate the way that gluttony and its opposite, a controlled appetite, dictate the very terms of human existence.

Before lecturing on human and literary reproduction, it is the same Statius who more subtly discusses the first step in the digestive process: consumption, whether it leads to death or life. The allusion to the meeting with Christ on the road to Emmaus in his initial appearance signals that Statius's role as a guide is bipartite. Before he reveals the complex, organic process by which new men and new words are made, he first models proper engagement with a primary text, demonstrating how to use words like food to inspire generation:

> Ed ecco, sì come ne scrive Luca
> > che Cristo apparve a' due ch'erano in via,
> > già surto fuor de la sepulcral buca,
> ci apparve un'ombra, e dietro a noi venìa,
> > dal piè guardando la turba che giace;
> > né ci addemmo di lei, sì parlò pria,
> dicendo: "O frati miei, Dio vi dea pace."
> > > > > *Purg.* 21.7–13

(And behold, just as Luke writes for us that Christ appeared to the two who were on the way, when he was just risen from the hollow tomb, a shade appeared to us, coming behind us, and we were avoiding the crowd lying at our feet, unaware of the shade until it spoke, saying, "O my brothers, God give you peace.")

Like the disciples, the pilgrim and Virgil do not recognize Statius at first, but in their exchange, Statius divulges not only his identity but also his gratitude to Virgil:

> Tu prima m'invïasti
> > verso Parnaso a ber ne le sue grotte,
> > e prima appresso Dio m'alluminasti.
> Facesti come quei che va di notte,
> > che porta il lume dietro e sé non giova,
> > ma dopo sé fa le persone dotte,

quando dicesti: 'Secol si rinova;
 torna giustizia e primo tempo umano,
 e progenïe scende da ciel nova.'
Per te poeta fui, per te cristiano.
Purg. 22.64–73

(You first sent me to Parnassus to drink from its springs, and you first lit the way for me toward God. You did as one who walks at night, who carries the light behind him and does not help himself, but instructs the persons coming after, when you said: 'The age begins anew; justice returns and the first human time, and a new offspring comes down from Heaven.' Through you I became a poet, through you a Christian.)

By reading correctly, as Statius explains with a parallel to consumption, the text was able to act as the foundation for later (re)generation, in the form of new poetry. All creation requires a prior digestion, and Statius affirms that the *Aeneid* was to him both "mamma" (mother) and "nutrice" (wet-nurse), a text by which he was gestated and then given the nourishment he used to produce his own poetry (*Purg.* 21.97–98). Furthermore, as Christ teaches his disciples how to see his flesh behind the words in the Old Testament, so Statius recounts how he was made not just a new poet but a new man, reborn in Christ through consuming and digesting Virgil's line: "Quid non mortalia pectora cogis, / auri sacra fames!" (To what end do you not drive the hearts of men / o cursed hunger for gold!; *Aen.* 3.57). Recalling the verse that laments Polymestor's decision to kill his friend's son in order to take his gold, Statius is set right by interpreting it not as a censure of men's desire for wealth but of intemperance in appetite:

E se non fosse ch'io drizzai mia cura,
 quand'io intesi là dove tu chiame,
 crucciato quasi a l'umana natura:
'Per che non reggi tu, o sacra fame
 de l'oro, l'appetito de' mortali?'
 voltando scniteri le giostre grame.
Purg. 22.37–42

(And had it not been that I straightened out my desires, when I understood the place where you cry out, almost angry at human nature: 'Why do you, O holy hunger for gold, not govern the appetite of mortals?' I would be turning about, feeling the grim jousts.)

Reinterpreting the same Latin word with another valence incidentally revealed by the Italian translation he chooses, Statius sees the "sacra" as sacred—"holy" or "just" in the modern sense—rather than "accursed" or "detestable," as Virgil had first intended it. This spectacularly suggestive misprision serves to mark Statius as the anti-glutton in both its content and its design: reading about a dangerous kind of hunger, Statius understands how to curb his appetite and consume in a way that allows him to grow and become not just a great poet, but also a Christian. In striking the Aristotelian mean, Statius vaults the ultimate obstacle, the one that Cassian described as the "first struggle." He has found the way to consume consciously, to foster a just hunger that is procreative, in contrast with the cursed hunger that led first Polymestor, and then Ciacco and those who follow after him in Hell, to consume indiscriminately and leave behind a sterile wasteland.

A Knot in the Stomach

Following not one but two ancient poets now, the pilgrim proceeds to the terrace of gluttony where he encounters still more poets, specifically his early companions in composition. Those who once dedicated themselves to amorous verses in the first Tuscan school now find themselves in Purgatory purging not their lust, but their desire for food. Commentators have often glossed the unusual combination of love poets and gluttons through the figure of Forese, noting that he was an infamous overeater, though this is a reputation for Forese built by Dante himself in their *tenzone* of some years earlier.[4] An overriding focus on poetics has led scholars to remove food entirely from the equation here, assuming only a metaphoric interpretation of gluttony and a superficial relationship between speech and eating, which both involve the mouth. While metaphor is clearly at play, this leap ignores the bookends that Statius presents for the episode, as he shows how he was "nursed" in canto 21 and then reveals how digestion forms human bodies in canto 25. Eating and the bodily functions that succeed it, as understood by medieval dietary science, in fact form the essential framework for this crucial, controversial, and revelatory section of the poem.

---

4   Singleton cites Dante's accusation of Forese in his *tenzone* as proof of his gluttony and reinforces that with commentary from the Anonimo Fiorentino and Benvenuto da Imola, who also use Dante as their source for information on Forese's gluttony. In Singleton, *The Divine Comedy: 2, Purgatorio*, pp. 548–549.

As the pilgrim walks behind Virgil and Statius, listening to the conversation that instructs him in "poetar" (writing poetry; *Purg.* 22.131), their entry onto the terrace of gluttony is marked by a sudden encounter with a fruit tree that seems to cry out, "Di questo cibo avrete caro" (You shall not eat this food; *Purg.* 22.140) and then, "Più pensava Maria onde / fosser le nozze orrevoli e intere / ch'a la sua bocca, ch'or per voi risponde" (Mary thought more about how the wedding could be made honorable and complete than about her mouth, which now answers for you; *Purg.* 142-144). Invoking the wedding at Cana, and Mary's request that her son intervene to spare the newly married couple the embarrassment of running out of wine, the disembodied voice begins the work of building a series of counterexamples to the gluttons that have been witnessed so far. A judicious appetite for the drink that seals a bond tying together new kin, legitimizing a new generation in the eyes of the community, will now contrast the unfettered appetites that chewed through those ties and consumed the next generation. Morever, through the brief reference to Cana, Dante acknowledges that the use of the mouth is twofold, to consume and to communicate, preparing his reader for the next crucial leap connecting gluttony to parturition and poetics.

As Virgil urges the pilgrim forward beyond the tree, they hear first the quiet song of the penitent, asking God to open their mouths once again, but this time to produce and give back rather than consume:

> Ed ecco piangere e cantar s'udìe
>   "Labïa mëa, Domine," per odo
>   tal che diletto e doglia parturìe.
> "O dolce padre, che è quel ch'i' odo?"
>   comincia' io; ed elli: "Ombre che vanno
>   forse di lor dover solvendo il nodo."
>   *Purg.* 23.10–15

(And behold, we heard weeping and singing of "Labïa mëa, Domine," in a manner that gave birth to both delight and woe. "Oh sweet father, what is that I hear?" I began; and he: "Shades who perhaps go untying the knot of their debt.")

The knot here has been variously identified as the knot in the tongue of a person unable to speak or the knot of the falcon's leash that holds it back from soaring as it should. Fabian Alfie has identified a yet more direct line to the *tenzone* with Forese Donati, pointing to Dante's insistence that Forese would be trussed in a knot of subjugation if he continued his gluttonous behavior (as noted in Chapter 2).[5] If nothing else, the connection to the *tenzone* with Forese, and the very first accusation of gluttony in Dante's lyric can hardly be casual here, since not only does the knot appear, but Forese himself will shortly become the pilgrim's primary interlocutor throughout the terrace of gluttony. First, though, Dante continues to set the stage with further references to the gluttonous contexts that have appeared up to this point:

> Ne li occhi era ciascuna oscura e cava,
>   palida ne la faccia e tanto scema
>   che da l'ossa la pelle s'informava:
> Non credo che così a bucca strema
>   Eristtone fosse fatto secco
>   per digiunar, quando più n'ebbe tema.
> Io dicea fra me stesso pensando: "Ecco
>   la gente che perdé Ierusalemme,
>   quando Maria nel figlio diè di becco."
>   *Purg.* 23.22–30

(Each was dark and hollow about the eyes, with faces pallid and so wasted that the skin took its shape from the bones: I do not think that Erysichthon was so dried up into his outer rind by fasting, when it made him most afraid. I was saying in my thoughts: "Behold the people who lost Jerusalem, when Mary put her beak into her son.")

In a feat of poetic prowess that recalls the density and potency of his words in the *tenzone,* Dante succeeds in using a single name to draw together every element of destruction that occurs as a result of gluttony that has been identified within the poem. Erysichthon was punished by the nymph he had killed when chopping down Demeter's grove, who then called upon Limos to enter the king's stomach and curse him with eternal insatiability. After selling everything he owned in exchange for food, including his own daughter, Erysichthon eventually ate himself alive entirely. Dante's mythological intertext retraces the gluttonous path through *Inferno,* moving from the desire to deny others the possibility of sharing in the harvest to

---

5   Alfie, *Dante's* Tenzone *with Forese Donati,* pp. 85–86. For the knot as a metaphor for being "tongue-tied" and a dedicated study to the knot of language, see Gorni, *Il nodo della lingua e il verbo d'amore;* for the extended falconry metaphor, see Pertile, "Il nodo di Bonagiunta, le penne di Dante e il Dolce Stil Novo," pp. 44–75.

the insatiability that ends with the sacrifice of one's own children, to the drying and overheating of the body provoked by starvation contrasted with the watery dampness that comes of overeating, to the cannibalistic act that erases individual identity and severs the bond with a community. The return to the jeremiad that connects all the disordered eating and dire political prophesies of the first canticle immediately conjures the wider landscape of unchecked consumption, in which the the telos of gluttony is borne out with the appearance of the cannibal and the ultimate fall of the city. It is against this now-thoroughly established motif that the pilgrim finally engages with one of the shades, none other than his very first glutton, Forese Donati:

> Già era in ammirar che sì li affama,
>> per la cagione ancor non manifesta
>> di lor magrezza e di lor trista squama,
> ed ecco del profondo de la testa
>> volse a me li occhi un'ombra e guardò fiso;
>> poi gridò forte: "Qual grazia m'è questa!"
> Mai non l'avrei riconosciuto al viso,
>> ma ne la voce sua mi fu palese
>> ciò che l'aspetto in sé avea conquiso.
> Questa favilla tutta mi raccese
>> mia conoscenza a la cangiata labbia
>> e ravvisai la faccia di Forese.
>> > > *Purg.* 23.37–48

(Already I was wondering what makes them hunger so, for the cause of their leanness and sad scurf was not yet manifest, and behold, one shade from the depths of his head turned his eyes toward me and stared fixedly; then he cried loudly: "What grace this is for me!" Never would I have recognized him by his face, but in his voice was evident to me what his appearance had ravaged in itself. This spark rekindled all my recognition for his changed features, and I made out the face of Forese.)

As discussed in Chapter 2, Dante considers Forese a glutton in their youthful poetic exchange inasmuch as he eats foods reserved for those engaged in the service of his community, and in so doing takes away from the common good instead of contributing to it. On the terrace of gluttony in *Purgatorio*, Forese returns to help Dante comment once again on consumption and community construction, this time specifically with regard to literary community. While naming those around him, their faces too emaciated to be identifiable, Forese points out infamous indulgers whose presence might be expected, but also other love poets who, like himself, are similarly purged by starvation: "Qui non si vieta / di nominar ciascun, da ch'è sì munta / nostra sembianza via per la dieta" (Here it is not forbidden to name each one, since our appearance has been so milked dry by fasting; *Purg.* 24.16–19). Forese thus announces the perfect purgatorial inversion of this defining feature of the infernal gluttons, whose core identities have been diluted and who remain nameless, along with the names of several of Dante's primary contemporary interlocutors. Among them is Bonagiunta da Lucca, who, along with the other poets of the Tuscan school, including two Forese mentions explicitly, Guittone d'Arezzo and Giacomo da Lentini, insisted love poetry was no place for science or learning.

Science and learning, however, were precisely where the link between love poetry, or lust, and gluttony was to be found, as the relationship between lustful activities and gluttony was first and foremost a bodily one. As explored in Chapter 1, gluttony was understood to provoke lust not simply because the "gateway" sin of gluttony opened the door to all manner of immoral behavior, but rather because it was explicitly based on an understanding of medical science and a physiological operation that could be tracked through the body. By the later Middle Ages, this idea had been widely diffused, primarily through the Arabic commentator Avicenna's careful tracing of Aristotelian digestion from food to sperm and in his more general appropriations of Galen's dietary codes, which linked overeating with lustful behavior. Excessive eating produced excessive reproductive material through the process of digestion, by which food became blood and then either male or female semen. Theologians were quick to remind overeaters that diet was as crucial to spiritual health as it was to physical health. Indeed, Aquinas arrived at his memorable definition of lust as "the daughter of gluttony" because in the attempt to satisfy an appetite for food, one could incidentally provoke an appetite for sex through an analogous (if immoral) perversion of the process by which children were conceived.[6]

If Forese, Bonagiunta, and the other poets produced lustful poetry with no desire for self-betterment or learning, they must have been gluttons, as the unchanneled sexual passions they wrote about were naturally the product of too much food. The buildup of excess sexual material is inevitably expressed in a carnal gesture, the lustful poetry of their youth. It is not surprising, then, that Dante employs parallel language to explain the misstep to Bonagiunta.

6   Aquinas, *De Malo* q. 14 art. 4 ad. 3. See also Chapter 1 of this book.

When asked to illustrate plainly how the *dolce stil novo* came to life, Dante uses a metaphor that mirrors the consumption-to-composition process, which results not in the useless yearnings of Bonagiunta and his school of poetry but instead in the new verses of Dante's sweet style that inspires others to action. Akin to the last step in the digestion of food, the pilgrim explains that the natural seed of inspiration born from Love is planted within him and causes him to generate verse: "I' mi son un che, quando / Amor mi spira, noto, e a quel modo / ch'e' ditta dentro vo significando" (I in myself am one who, when Love breathes within me, takes note, and to that measure which he dictates within, I go signifying; *Purg.* 24.52–54). Upon receiving these words, Bonagiunta responds excitedly:

"O Frate, issa vegg'io," diss'elli, "il nodo
    che 'l Notaro e Guittone e me ritenne
    di qua dal dolce stil novo ch'i'odo!
Io veggio ben come le vostre penne
    di retro al dittator sen vanno strette,
    che de le nostre certo non avvenne;
e qual più a gradire oltre si mette,
    non vede più da l'uno a l'altro stilo";
    e, quasi contentato, si tacette.
Purg. 24.55–63

("O my brother, now I see," said he, "the knot that held the Notary and Guittone and me back on this side of the sweet new style I hear. I see well how your pens follow close behind him who dictates, which with ours certainly did not happen; and whoever most sets himself to looking further will not see any other difference between the one style and the other." And, as if satisfied, he fell silent.)

Studying this passage, Teodolinda Barolini has pointed out that the crucial moment of change for Bonagiunta—the loosening of his "knot"—occurs when the example of Dante's poem "Donne ch'avete" leads Bonagiunta to understand his error. As Barolini clarifies, the gluttons in *Purgatorio* are rehabilitated by the poetic artifact that marks Dante's own conversion from self-indulgence to disinterested attention:

The gluttons of canto 23 have turned their mouths from the basest of concerns—"eating," or unrelieved self-involvement—to praising God, in the same way that the discovery of the *stil novo* turns the Italian lyric from the conventional poetics of the "I" to the deflection of the "I" in the poetry of praise. Thus, the gluttons chanting their Psalm are described as souls who are loosening the knot of their obligation, "forse di lor dover solvendo il nodo" (23.15), in a paraphrasing that anticipates the loosening of Bonagiunta's "knot" (his uncertainty regarding the reasons for his poetic failure) by the pilgrim. The artifact that symbolizes the conversion that the gluttons have only now achieved—away from the self toward a disinterested focusing on the Other—is "Donne ch'avete," which attains its prominence within the *Comedy* precisely because it marks the moment in which Dante first opens his mouth in a song of praise.[7]

The love poets in Purgatory are men who consumed indiscriminately, needlessly taking in sustenance without the hope or intention to produce material that might be useful to others. They produced futile and hollow verses by concentrating their attention on their own hunger for things beyond their needs, and, like the gluttons of *Inferno* or the ill-disposed of *Convivio*, gave nothing back to the community.[8] Between this self-indulgence and productivity there must be a loosening of the knot; the obstacle to free movement must be removed. On the stylistic level, this would be a *denouement* in the full sense, a climactic moment in which Bonagiunta feels the untying of the compositional complications that prevented him from achieving the *dolce stil novo*. Yet the presence of the shade bodies, which allow the souls the sensation that is fundamental to the purgatorial experience, calls attention to the acutely physical element that remains. Alison Cornish has emphasized that it is the poem's ultimate composition of "both flesh *and* spirit" that creates the foundation for the sort of textual descendants Dante desires.[9] Like the knot Dante had used to mock Forese in their infamous *tenzone*, those who gave themselves over to excess would find themselves bound up, and stopped up, by their indiscriminate ingestion: "Ben ti faranno il nodo Salamone / Bicci novello, e' petti de le starne" (Partridge breasts, young Bicci, will truss you in Solomon's knot all right; *Rime* 73.1–2). The knot in his bowels has now loosened, allowing the balanced body to digest healthily and leave Bonagiunta "satisfied."

Bonagiunta's ultimate satiation comes as a result of Dante's just hunger and conscious consumption: waiting for inspiration to fill him, he is

7   Barolini, *Dante's Poets,* p. 52.
8   For a discussion of the "contingenze," as Dante describes them, that distract men from directing desire towards things that move them closer to divine understanding and grace, see Treherne, "Liturgical Personhood," pp. 139–142.
9   Cornish, *Vernacular Translation in Dante's Italy,* p. 156.

prompted to compose for others that they too might get their fill. In the same way that the governing body distributes food to maintain and reinforce the city, so too Dante's poetic leadership turns from the autonomous act of feeding and growing the self to feeding and growing a literary community. The question is one of contributive potential, be it to the civic, earthly society to which all humans belong, or in the case of the purgatorial souls the pilgrim speaks with here, to the society of the "sweet new style." That the path he takes them on leads toward a familiar, healthy appetite and not a transcendent, food-less existence is reiterated in the last lines of *Purgatorio* 24:

> E sentì dir: "Beati cui alluma
> 　　tanto di grazia, che l'amor del gusto
> 　　nel petto lor troppo disir non fuma,
> esurïendo sempre quanto è giusto!"
> 　　　　　　　　　　　*Purg.* 24.151–154

(And I heard: "Blessed are those whom so much grace illuminates that love of the palate does not smoke with too much desire in their breasts, hungering always for what is just.")

The final verse can be read flexibly, either as "those who exhibit just hunger," never indulging beyond necessity, or "those who hunger for what is just," channeling their appetite toward the common good. Taking the words that inspired Statius, Dante now "overhears" the poets on the terrace of gluttony learning precisely how to correct the missteps he identified in his first exchange with Forese and applying the model he constructed in his *Convivio*, always relying on real food to anchor metaphoric understanding. Both their material food and their intellectual stimulation must be appropriate to this purpose: the gluttons of Purgatory learn first how to control their appetites, and then how to use that judicious hunger to energize themselves and serve the community at large.

A Poetics of Parturition

What doubts might remain about Dante's insistence on the physical digestion of food as the framework for these grander schemes of life and learning are quickly dispersed when in *Purgatorio* 25, the same Statius explains how digestion creates humans and explicitly connects the practice of eating to making bodies and infusing souls. Tellingly, the monologue is prompted by the pilgrim's question about food—"Como si può far magro / là dove uopo di nodrir non tocca?" (How can [the shades] become thin, where need of nourishment does not touch them?; *Purg.* 25.20–21)—and Statius opens with words that presume a biological (not theological) understanding of digestion on the part of the reader:

> Sangue perfetto, che poi non si beve
>   da l'assetate vene, e si rimane
>   quasi alimento che di mensa leve,
> prende nel core a tutte membra umane
>   virtute informativa, come quello
>   ch'a farsi quelle per le vene vane.
> Ancora digesto, scende ov'è più bello
>   tacer che dire; e quindi poscia geme
>   sovr'altrui sangue in natural vasello
>   *Purg.* 25.37–45

(Perfected blood, never drunk by the thirsty veins, but left, like food one carries back from the table, takes on within the heart the power to shape all human members, as does that which goes out through the veins to become members. Digested further, it descends to the place of which it is better to be silent than to speak, and then from there it flows onto another's blood in a natural vessel.)

This description relies once again on Avicenna's commentary on Aristotle's *De generatione animalium.*[10] According to Avicenna's Galenic model, the penultimate step in the multi-part digestion of food into "blood" rendered it "perfect" for the specific nutritional needs of the body's various parts. This model provides the foundation for what Statius goes on to explain directly, that a part of the perfect blood continues through a last digestion where it is transformed into semen. This is why Avicenna had defined the male donation to the embryo (what Dante calls the "virtù informativa") as "superfluitas digestionis quartae residuans," the surplus of the remainder of the fourth digestion; Albertus Magnus had called it, quite literally, the "superfluitas ultimi cibi," what remains of the final food, or "superfluitas

---

10   Nardi, *Studi di filosofia medievale,* pp. 49–51. Boyde, among others, further traced this influence in his study of the generation of man in the *Comedy* in *Dante Philomythes and Philosopher,* pp. 271–273.

quartae digestionis," what remains of the fourth digestion.[11] After reaching the predisposed container in the female, Statius reveals, the male seminal fluid instigates a process that both generates a vegetative soul and sets it in motion toward the formation of a new body:

> comincia ad operare
>> coagolando prima, e poi avviva
>> ciò che per sua matera fé constare.
> Anima fatta la virtute attiva
>> qual d'una pianta, in tanto differente,
>> che questa è in via e quella è già a riva,
> tanto ovra poi, che già si move e sente,
>> come fungo marino; e indi imprende
>> ad organar le posse ond'è semente.
>
> *Purg.* 25.49–57

(and, once arrived, it begins to operate by coagulating first, and then it quickens what it has made firm to be its matter. This active power, having become a soul like that of a plant, but different in so far as it is still under way, while the other is already in port, next works until it moves and has feeling like a sea sponge, and then it undertakes to shape organs for the faculties of which it is the seed.)

Commentators and scholars have at various points been scandalized by the apparently unorthodox elements contained within Statius's discourse, particularly the incorporation of Avicenna's stress on continuity from the generation of the embryo's flesh to its soul; this is especially apparent in the final step of the process, when the vegetative and sensitive souls are taken up by the intellectual soul: "ciò che trova attivo quivi, tira / in sua sustanzia, e fassi un'alma sola / che vive e sente e sé in sé rigira" ([it] absorbs that which is active there into its own substance, and makes one single soul which lives and feels and circles on itself; *Purg.* 25.73–75). This explanation was problematic because it presumed the vegetative and sensitive souls evolved into the rational soul while remaining present themselves in potency.[12] More

---

11   Albertus Magnus, Canon III, fen 19, tr.1, c.3; *De animalibus* 3.2.8; *De nutrimento* 2.2.

12   Gragnolati helpfully condenses the pluralist position: "Those who asserted plurality of forms stressed the empirical sense of change as a continuous process in which something evolves on the basis of the concept of act and potency. When the vegetative soul of an embryo is in an active state, the sensitive is in a state of potency, and when the sensitive is active, the rational

to the point, this model maintained a constant bond between body and soul, with no clean break between the physiological processes that produced the embryo from digested food and the divine intervention that introduced the intellect and the will. As with the question of identity, Aquinas suggested a more clearly punctuated explanation which, despite not resolving the controversy, was eventually accepted as doctrine: "when a more perfect form supervenes, the previous form is corrupted; however, it does so in such a way that the supervening form contains whatever the first one does and something in addition."[13] The question nonetheless continued to provoke debate and discomfort, as no solution proved equally able to recognize the obvious truths that Augustine had acknowledged while also eliminating the troubling suggestion that everyday eating habits could somehow direct the most wondrous aspect of human life—its creation.[14]

Where in *Inferno* there might remain some doubt about Dante's interpretation of the boundary between body and soul—and thus what substances might or might not be incorporated into the core of an individual, affecting their identity or ability to reason—*Purgatorio* no longer leaves room for hesitation. The critical obsession with orthodoxy in this section of the poem has distracted readers from the fact that Dante's unapologetic presentation of a straight line from food to body to soul weaves the embryological discourse into a grander, more profound and elaborate philosophy. Precisely like the poetry creation Dante models in this section of *Purgatorio*, soul creation is posited as a natural process that begins with convivial consumption (the gesture of nourishment that is the ultimate means of bonding within a human community), continues with digestion, and is occasioned by the joining of digested materials through intercourse. Just as Dante had shown in the *Convivio* that he would feed everyone hearty barley bread even if it wasn't the marker of "nobility," so that they might thrive and enable their

---

is in potency." Gragnolati, "From Plurality to (Near) Unicity of Forms: Embryology in *Purgatorio* 25," p. 197.

13   "Quando perfectior forma advenit, fit corruptio prioris ita tamen quod sequens forma habet quidquid habebat prima, et adhuc amplius." *Summa* 1a, q.118, a.2, ad2.

14   On the many, varied arguments advanced on the topic, see Bynum, *The Resurrection of the Body in Western Christianity*, pp. 117–155, and Reynolds, *Food and the Body,* pp. 50–66. More recently, Purdy Moudarres has considered these discussions with regard to radical moisture for a very useful reading of the *contrapasso* of the gluttons, in "Devouring Selves in the Circle of Gluttony." Bynum sums up the argument and subsequent mixed feelings regarding the resolution: "Although discussion stayed in the narrow confines of the university and theologians indeed remained uncomfortable with some of its ramifications, unicity of form and formal identity became fairly widespread assumptions by 1330." *The Resurrection of the Body in Western Christianity*, p. 277.

intellect to grow, and in *Inferno* had relived the pain of a city oppressed by gluttons who consumed until they lost their humanity and had nothing left to eat but their own flesh and blood, now, in *Purgatorio,* he shows how a nourishing process will give life to a healthy community of citizens and poets.

While Statius's embryology may be the most transparent and significant commentary on procreation, images and descriptions of births appear in all three canticles. As Giuseppe Mazzotta has established, births and origins are essential to the framework of the *Comedy*, precisely because they point to a future: Ciacco, in the circle of gluttony in *Inferno*, is among the first to call Dante's attention to the "making" and "unmaking of humans": "Tu fosti, prima che io disfatto, fatto" (You were made before I was unmade; *Inf.* 6.42 [translation mine]).[15] Heather Webb has further noted that the last cantos of *Inferno*, especially the lines introducing that most gruesome of gluttons, Ugolino, rely heavily on an inverted language of reproduction, contrasting the fecundity of Mary's womb with the barrenness of Hell.[16] While recounting his tragedy to the pilgrim, Ugolino first describes his heart proclaiming the pain of his fate, "ciò che 'l mio cor s'annunziava" (what my heart was announcing to me; *Inf.* 33.41). His words recall the most important conception of life in Christian history, the Annunciation—with an impregnation akin to the one Dante describes in *Purgatorio* 24—and yet they convert the dialogue of life that marks the Annunciation moment into a self-contained death sentence. Where the word of the Lord, as announced by the angel Gabriel, fills the Virgin with life, the announcement delivered to Ugolino foretells his death and the deaths of his children. His self-reflexive actions have not only alienated him from a living community but have left him sterile and bereft of his progeny, incapable of participating in the reproduction that continues the cycle of life in this world or the next. Later in the same canto, Alberigo feels "'l duol che 'l cor m'impregna" (the pain that impregnates my heart; *Inf.* 33.113 [translation mine]), and describes the action that makes his sin more grievous; the sterility of Ugolino thus gives way to the fertility of Alberigo. The count cannot extend his spiritual blindness and devastation, but Alberigo plants the poison seed in his successors, passing on a legacy of depravity to the next generation.

The reproductive descriptions in *Inferno* have a very direct correspond-ence with the birth that results from a balanced diet (which permits a healthy, undisturbed digestion process, as Statius lays out in *Purgatorio* 25). The canto that opposes the explanation of poetic inspiration and creation is,

---

15   Mazzotta, "Dante's Poetics of Births and Foundations," p. 129.
16   Webb, "Dante's Stone Cold Rhymes," p. 164.

not coincidentally, home to the inversion of this birth. *Inferno* 24 illustrates the frightening possibility of those who consume indiscriminately, and the bestial birth they inspire, in the *contrapasso* of the thieves:

> Né O sì tosto mai né I si scrisse,
> > com'el s'accese e arse, e cener tutto
> > convenne che cascando divenisse;
> e poi che fu a terra sì distrutto,
> > la polver si raccolse per sé stessa
> > e 'n quel medesmo ritornò di butto.
> Così per li gran savi si confessa
> > che la fenice more e poi rinasce,
> > quando al cinquecentesimo anno appressa;
> erba né biado in sua vita non pasce,
> > ma sol d'incenso lagrime e d'amomo,
> > e nardo e mirra son l'ultime fasce.
> > > *Inf.* 24.100–111

(Neither *O* nor *I* has ever been written so fast as he caught fire and burned and was all consumed, falling, to ashes; and when he was on the ground, destroyed the dust gathered together by itself and instantly became the same one again. Thus the great sages profess that the Phoenix dies and is reborn, when it approaches its five hundredth year; in its life it eats neither grass nor grain but only tears of incense and of balsam, and nard and myrrh are its winding sheet.)

In his analysis of several important illuminations in late medieval manuscripts of the *Comedy*, R. Allen Shoaf has tied this first infernal "birth scene," which imagines the thieves reborn from an insubstantial consumption, to the one that will appear in the corresponding canto of *Purgatorio*. In reviewing the words exchanged between Dante and Bonagiunta, Shoaf considers this crucial moment in *Purgatorio* 24 a foundation for what he calls the "poetics of parturition," drawn from the birth narrative that can be seen to run through the poem and that is highlighted by its later illuminations.[17] The thieves in *Inferno* 24 are transformed in a "hellish parody of 'birth'" for having stolen and tried to keep for themselves what was not theirs, while in *Purgatorio* 24 the pilgrim describes how he is impregnated by the material he has consumed, giving life to his new poetry, revealing the expected conversion

---

17   Shoaf, "Delivering Dante: Representations of Reproduction in the *Commedia*," p. S85.

of the perversion. Neither starving nor gorging, the poets of the new style will be the forefathers of a growing community. Modeling the method for the gluttonous poets, Dante instructs his reader in how to consume, digest, and give birth, using a knowledge of the body and its interaction with food to approach the ineffability of the soul.

Food to Humans, Grapes to Wine

Dante's use of the scientific understanding of the means by which the consumption and digestion of food creates humans, and his parallel explanation of how poetry is born the same way, is also a reminder of his persistent effort to make the inaccessible accessible through the familiarity and universality of food. Indeed, anticipating the pilgrim's confusion over the digestive-reproductive processes, Statius pauses to provide Dante with what he imagines will be an obvious comparison. The development of an embryo into an ensouled fetus is hard to grasp, Statius acknowledges, but the pilgrim need only liken it to the transformation of grapes into wine:

> E perché meno ammiri la parola,
> > guarda il calor del sol che si fa vino,
> > giunto a l'omor che de la vite cola.
> > > *Purg.* 25.76–78

(And that you may wonder less at my words, look how the heat of the sun becomes wine, joined with the liquid that flows from the grape.)

Though Statius poses this comparison as if it will clarify everything that has come before in short order—which is to say, the process by which human reproductive matter becomes a fetus with a divine soul—few commentators have accepted it as a "less perplexing" alternative to the decidedly complex physical and metaphysical descriptions contained in the canto, proposing instead many possible interpretations. The enological analogy can most succinctly be seen as a parallel between the powers of God and the sun: the former acts on the embryo just as the latter acts on the fruit of the vine. Many readers have suggested that it points still further, to the fact that the change God performs on the embryo is like the one his Son enacts on the water at the marriage feast at Cana described in the Gospel of John. Modern commentators have even occasionally imagined this to mean that medieval people simply thought wine production was itself miraculous and inexplicable; Singleton, for example, glossed verse 78 by stating simply: "the process of fermentation was not understood at this time."[18]

The irony of these readings is that they complicate rather than clarify Statius's simple analogy. While the phenomenon of fermentation might have aroused wonder then as now, by invoking wine-making, Dante takes advantage of a recognizable touchstone for his contemporaries. Like digestion, the making of wine was both quotidian and connected to the mystical; like food, it allows Dante (through the voice of Statius) to broach the mysteries of the soul while reiterating the persistent importance of the body and its fleshliness, tracing the contours of the bonds of human community while anticipating the seamless unity promised in the city of God. Indeed, there are many nods to wine culture in these cantos before the analogy Statius presents to Dante in *Purgatorio* 25. In *Purgatorio* 24, as Forese Donati helps the pilgrim to identify the souls rendered unrecognizable by emaciation in the afterlife, he points to one among them who does penance for having enjoyed wine too much:

> e quella faccia
> di là da lui più che l'altre trapunta
>   ebbe la Santa Chiesa in le sue braccia:
> dal Torso fu, e purga per digiuno
> l'anguille di Bolsena e la vernaccia.
> *Purg.* 24.21–24

(The one beyond him, even more emaciated than the rest, had clasped the Holy Church; he was from Tours; his fast purges Bolsena's eels, Vernaccia's wine.)

The face more emaciated than all others is Martin IV, the Frenchman raised to the papacy by Charles of Anjou against the will of several cardinals and so disliked by Rome that he was forced to take his crown at Orvieto. There were many reasons Martin was perhaps a less than exemplary pope, but like Forese, he does not seem to have had a reputation as a glutton outside of Dante's accusation. Early commentators of the *Comedy* provided some embellishment; Jacopo della Lana supplies the most colorful of these in a gloss cited frequently by later commentators, asserting that the pope didn't drink his Vernaccia, but insisted on boiling the eels alive in it. Moreover, he did this in his private rooms, so as to be able to enjoy them fresh and undisturbed: "facea torre l'anguille del lago da Bolsena, e quelle facea annegare e morire

---

18   Singleton, *The Divine Comedy: 2, Purgatorio* 25.78.

nel vino della vernaccia, poi fatte arrosto le mangiava; ed era tanto sollicito a quel boccone che continua ne volea, e faceale curare e annegare nella sua camera" (he had the eels brought in from the lake of Bolsena, and he had them drowned and killed in the wine from the Vernaccia grape, and having been roasted thus he ate them; and he was so desirous of that mouthful that he wanted to continue with more, and he had them taken and drowned in his chambers).[19] The context here points the reader back toward the social hierarchy of food and the actions of an individual unconcerned with the role they are meant to play in the larger community—once again, just like Forese. And as with Forese's partridge and mutton, Martin IV's eels and wine have specific values that Dante and his readers would have been aware of. In the case of the eels, they are well-represented in the *Liber de coquina*, appearing in at least three recipes, one of which is directly followed by a recipe for "brodio martino," apparently named for the very same pope. Eels that were part of a collection of recipes associated with a powerful court and high culture act as a sign of unseemly indulgence for a man who would do better to devote his energy to his civic and spiritual duties. The following terzina provides further corroboration, when Ubaldino de la Pila (de'Ubaldini) appears next to Martin IV. Unlike Martin and the many others accused by Dante of giving in to gluttonous proclivities, Ubaldino was known as a great lover of food and appreciator of food culture—so much so that it seems he commissioned a Tuscanized copy of the *Liber de coquina*, known as the *Libro de la cocina*, providing an even more direct link.[20]

Martin IV's Vernaccia builds on this symbolic density, becoming an even more charged figure here. Massimo Montanari points out that wine was particularly evocative when it came to the gastro-social hierarchy: "Wine in the medieval imagination thus constitutes a decisive reference point with regard to identity. Its prestige gave it a paradigmatic value, according to which *other* realities are defined in opposite terms, which is to say negative. This is, above all, relevant to geography and territory."[21] Montanari observes that

---

19   "Comedia di Dante degli Allaghieri col Commento di Jacopo della Lana bolognese," last accessed July 7, 2021, Dartmouth Dante Project.

20   Many critics have made this connection, though Martellotti is not convinced that the original author of the *Liber de coquina* sourced the recipe from Martin IV (which is to say, his head of household or cook): it is probably better to state that the dish appeared in multiple vernacular versions of the most popular culinary text and that the name-dish association was a commonplace that Dante could rely on, rather than having any profound historical rooting. The "frittelle ubaldine" that appear instead in the Tuscan redaction of the *Liber de coquina* do seem to be strong evidence that the copy was commissioned by Ubaldino degli Ubaldine, as discussed in Chapter 1.

21   Montanari, *Medieval Tastes,* p. 138.

many miracles related to the appearance of wine when none could be had, as reported in High and late medieval hagiographies and in the Gospels, emphasize not only that wine was found or delivered by divine source, but also that the wine was of fine quality. Wine was preferred because it was nutritious, medicinal, and sacred, but most of all, because it communicated identity—an attachment to a space, and to a value within the organization of that space. In his *Cronica* (c. 1282), Salimbene de Adam reports on the excitement born around the production of Vernaccia, confirming that at the time Dante was writing it had become much coveted.[22] By the time Sante Lancerio, bottigliere to Pope Paul III, wrote his now famous letter to Cardinal Guido Ascanio Sforza, listing and rating all the wines in the pope's vast cellar, he underlined that Vernaccia was "una perfetta bevanda da Signori" (a perfect drink for Lords).[23]

Pope Martin IV's tastes thus betray him, not as a drunk, but as ostentatious and incompetent, lacking in self-awareness and placing personal pleasure above duty. Indulging in wine was one thing, but drinking Vernaccia broadcast a host of other implications: a desire to be perceived as cultured, imprudence with Church funds, and disregard for the humility appropriate to the clergy. Repeating Della Lana's comment on these lines, the commentator Francesco da Buti adds with further wonder: "vernaccia è vino che nasce ne la riviera di Genova, millior vino che si trovi, e forsi che anco ne bea volontieri" (Vernaccia is a wine born in the Genoan riviera, the best wine that exists, and one that might be drunk voluntarily).[24] If Martin IV wasn't drinking the Vernaccia but rather using it for cooking, all the worse that Christ's vicar on earth would waste excellent wine on a pot of eels, when there were many who had no wine at all. In this case, Dante's poem does not just reinscribe the current economic and perceived social value of this wine, but adds a moral and aesthetic judgment: good wine should be appreciated by those who recognize and deserve it.

Statius's grapes-to-wine analogy is on a continuum, then, carefully threading together references to food, wine, digestion, and growth, but also making the leap to connect the human community to the heavenly one. If we return to Statius's evocation of the wedding feast at Cana and Christ's miracle of turning water into wine, it is worth noting that the first allusion to this Biblical episode actually comes much earlier, in *Purgatorio* 13, on the

---

22 Hanska, "'Volebam tamen ut nomen michi esset Dyonisius': Fra Salimbene, Wine and Well-Being," pp. 138–141.

23 Lancerio, *I vini d'Italia giudicati da papa Paolo III Farnese e dal suo bottigliere Sante Lancerio*, p. 58.

24 "Commento di Francesco da Buti sopra La Divina Commedia di Dante Allighieri," last accessed July 7, 2021, Dartmouth Dante Project.

terrace of envy, where disembodied voices cry out around the repentant souls "vinum non habent" (they do not have wine; John 2:3). As reported in the Gospel of John, these are the words Mary spoke to her son in concern at the wedding feast upon realizing that the wine had run out. In response, Jesus performs what will be recorded as the first of seven miracles that mark him as the divine son of God: he turns water into wine. In the context of Dante's poem, on the terrace of envy, the miracle is recalled not to guarantee Christ's divinity, but as a model for giving something of value without envy or ulterior motive. Dante employs the intertext of the miracle at Cana as a lesson about defining the self and giving of the self through wine. The Virgin Mary feels pain knowing that the young couple will be disgraced and that their marriage, a ceremony that establishes their place in their community, will be undermined by the lack of the drink that distinguishes celebration from normalcy. When Christ performs the miracle, he both reinforces the importance of the bond of marriage and reinscribes the social, now sacred significance of the wine itself. It is, furthermore, a social faux pas through which the miracle is revealed. Upon tasting the water become wine, the wine steward comments that the bridegroom has departed from custom and served the best wine last rather than first: "and the master of the banquet tasted the water that had been turned into wine. He did not realize where it had come from, though the servants who had drawn the water knew. Then he called the bridegroom aside and said, 'Everyone brings out the choice wine first and then the cheaper wine after the guests have had too much to drink; but you have saved the best till now'" (John 2:9–10).

In the lines following his original analogy, Statius articulates this connection between the flesh and the spirit for the pilgrim one final time:

> Quando Làchesis non ha più del lino,
> solvesi da la carne, e in virtute
> ne porta seco e l'umano e 'l divino:
> l'altre potenze tutte quante mute;
> memoria, intelligenza e volontade
> in atto molto più che prima agute.
> *Purg.* 25.79–84

(When Lachesis has no more thread, the soul is released from the flesh, and it carries off in its powers both the human and the divine: the other powers, all of them, are mute; memory, understanding, and will are much sharper in action than before.)

In the moment of the severing of flesh and spirit, Statius states once again that even when the soul leaves the body in death, it maintains something human within—the food that nourished the flesh and gave rise to the spirit. The ability to contain the human and the divine together is the very definition of human existence, and the tension between these potentialities is maintained as each remains in virtue, alternately exercising their power in this world and then the next. Beginning with the gluttonous poets of Purgatory and concluding with Statius's grapes to wine analogy, the power of food and hunger is what carries human life from this world into the next, allowing Dante's verses to remain accessible even as they inch toward the indescribable.

The arrival in *Purgatorio* is expected to coincide with a fundamental change in perspective, a shift from concern for earthly matters and earthly sustenance to a post-corporeal existence where "l'uopo di nodrir non tocca" (*Purg.* 25.21), particularly as the pilgrim arrives in the upper terraces described in the final cantos of the canticle, nearly ready for his passage into heaven. Yet Dante's own words, which appear to confirm that expectation, in fact reveal themselves to be a provocation. It is not the answer to the question of the role of nourishment to which the poet wishes to draw our attention, but the question itself. The pilgrim has predicated his query on a flawed pretense: need of nourishment *does* touch the souls in Purgatory, as it touches all of our souls. The implication that food drives procreation and ensoulment is not a worry for Dante, but a necessity. For Dante, the permeable boundary, and the closeness to food, was the fundamental point of departure. The far-reaching effects of dietary choices, however heretical they may have appeared to medieval theologians—or however frivolous they may seem to the modern reader—are precisely what the poet wished to assert and are the foundation on which he builds a poetics of generation and a philosophy of corporeal citizenship.[25]

Despite the trappings of poetry and the distance of time, the first component of what Dante presents in the embryology of Statius remains as true now as it did when he was writing, and no doctrinal or metaphoric

---

25 Corporeality has frequently been the subject of feminist scholarship which notes the preoccupation with the female relationship to the body, and the suggestion that women have long been perceived as "more biological" or more weighed down and distracted by their attachment to nature, thus making them less rational (for example, see Grosz, *Volatile Bodies*), an idea that has also been applied to colonial subjecthood. Dante's confirmation of the continued importance of the body even in the afterlife, and his unwavering faith in the need for human civic participation, has been explored at length by many scholars; see Gragnolati, *Experiencing the Afterlife: Soul and Body in Dante and Medieval Culture,* and Shapiro, *Dante and the Knot of Body and Soul.*

acrobatics can change the fact that—at least when it comes to our flesh and blood—we are what we eat. Asserting the more ambiguous second part of the process, and validating the extension of this truth to contain the soul as a product of digestion, Dante reins in the abstract, ethereal soul, and anchors it to the seemingly ignoble moment of food entering the body. In doing so, he reasserts the presence of human will and responsibility in the process. A. N. Williams has suggested that their performance of volition is exactly why "the souls in the middle canticle could be seen as the most fully human of any in the poem," and *Purgatorio* is first and foremost a journey to the restoration of the will.[26] It cannot surprise us that Dante answers the question of how body and soul work together with a firm declaration that the hunger that defines the physical human condition is the driving force behind the creation, or the destruction, of human community.

Works Cited

Albertus Magnus. *Opera omnia*. Edited by Auguste Borgnet. 9 vols. Paris: Ludovicum Vives, 1890.

Alfie, Fabian. *Dante's* Tenzone *with Forese Donati: The Reprehension of Vice*. Toronto: University of Toronto Press, 2011.

Aquinas, Thomas. *On Evil*. Edited and with an introduction by Brian Davies. Translated by Richard Regan. Oxford: Oxford University Press, 2003.

Barolini, Teodolinda. *Dante's Poets: Textuality and Truth in the Divine Comedy*. Princeton: Princeton University Press, 1984.

Boyde, Patrick. *Dante Philomythes and Philosopher: Man in the Cosmos*. Cambridge: Cambridge University Press, 1981.

Bynum, Caroline Walker. *The Resurrection of the Body in Western Christianity: 200-1336*. New York: Columbia University Press, 1995.

Carruthers, Mary. *The Book of Memory: A Study of Memory in Medieval Culture*. Cambridge: Cambridge University Press, 1990.

Cornish, Alison. *Vernacular Translation in Dante's Italy: Illiterature Literature*. Cambridge: Cambridge University Press, 2011.

Dartmouth Dante Project. "Comedia di Dante degli Allaghieri col Commento di Jacopo della Lana bolognese." Accessed July 7, 2021. https://dante.dartmouth.edu.

Dartmouth Dante Project. Commento di Francesco da Buti sopra La Divina Commedia di Dante Allighieri." Accessed July 7, 2021. https://dante.dartmouth.edu.

26   Williams, "The Theology of the *Comedy*," p. 211.

Durling, Robert. "Deceit and Digestion in the Belly of Hell." In *Allegory and Representation: Selected Papers from the English Institute*, edited by Stephen Greenblatt, 61–93. Baltimore: Johns Hopkins University Press, 1981.

Freccero, John. *The Poetics of Conversion*. Edited by Rachel Jacoff. Cambridge, Mass.: Harvard University Press, 1986.

Gorni, Guglielmo. *Il nodo della lingua e il verbo d'amore: Studi su Dante e altri duecentisti*. Florence: Olschki, 1981.

Gragnolati, Manuele. "From Plurality to (Near) Unicity of Forms: Embryology in *Purgatorio* 25." In *Dante for the New Millenium*. Edited by Wayne Storey and Teodolinda Barolini, 192-210. New York: Fordham University Press, 2003.

Gragnolati, Manuele. *Experiencing the Afterlife: Soul and Body in Dante and Medieval Culture*. South Bend: University of Notre Dame Press, 2005.

Grosz, Elizabeth. *Volatile Bodies: Towards a Corporeal Feminism* London: Routledge, 1994.

Hanska, Jussi. "'Volebam tamen ut nomen michi esset Dyonisius': Fra Salimbene, Wine and Well-Being." In *Mental (Dis)Order in Later Medieval Europe*. Edited by Sari Katajala-Peltomaa and Susanna Niiranen, 128-150. Leiden: Brill, 2014.

Lancerio, Sante. *I vini d'Italia giudicati da papa Paolo III Farnese e dal suo bottigliere Sante Lancerio*. Livorno: Bastogi, 1890. Reprinted with an introduction by Arturo Celentano. Capri (Naples): La Conchiglia, 2004. Page references are to the 2004 edition.

Mazzotta, Giuseppe. "Dante's Poetics of Births and Foundations." *Dante Studies* 127 (2009): 129–146.

Montanari, Massimo. *Medieval Tastes: Food, Cooking, and the Table*. Translated by Beth Archer Brombert. New York: Columbia University Press, 2015.

Pertile, Lino. "Il nodo di Bonagiunta, le penne di Dante e il Dolce Stil Novo." *Lettere italiane* 46 (1994): 44–75.

Plato, *Timaeus, Critias, Cleitophon, Menexenus, Epistles*. Edited and translated by R. G. Bury. Cambridge, Mass.: Loeb Classical Library, 1960.

Purdy Moudarres, Christiana. "Devouring Selves in the Circle of Gluttony: A Gloss on the Contrapasso of *Inferno* 6." In *Table Talk: Perspectives on Food in Medieval Italian Literature*. Edited by Christiana Purdy Moudarres, 3-18. Newcastle upon Tyne: Cambridge Scholars Publishing, 2010.

Reynolds, Philip Lyndon. *Food and the Body: Some Peculiar Questions in High Medieval Theology*. Leiden: Brill, 1999.

Shapiro, Marianne. *Dante and the Knot of Body and Soul*. New York: St. Martin's Press, 1998.

Shoaf, R. Allen. "Delivering Dante: Representations of Reproduction in the *Commedia*." *MLN* 127, no. S1 (January 2012): S81-90.

Treherne, Matthew. "Liturgical Personhood: Creation, Penitence, and Praise in the *Commedia*." In *Dante's* Commedia: *Theology as Poetry*, edited by Vittorio Montemaggi and Matthew Treherne, 131-160. South Bend: University of Notre Dame Press, 2010.

Webb, Heather. "Dante's Stone Cold Rhymes." *Dante Studies* 121 (2003): 149–168.

Williams, A. N. "The Theology of the *Comedy*." In *The Cambridge Companion to Dante*, 2nd ed., edited by Rachel Jacoff, 201-217. Cambridge: Cambridge University Press, 2007.

5. Heavenly Gluttony

Abstract

Paradiso necessarily turns away from the appetites for food that have appeared so far in the poem, yet it is also where Dante confirms definitively how good provisioning and convivial consumption strengthen the bonds of community. This occurs most crucially in the prophecy of his exile through a food-based metaphor, but also in the presentation of the poet's body as it shrinks in the face of a lean diet. Pouring himself into his work, the last self-portrait Dante paints in the *Comedy* is of a man who finds himself finally beyond the reach of gluttony: through his poem, he has found the means for a fruitful fast, a method of channeling his appetite into work that produces for the community.

Keywords: authority, civitas, contemplation, conversion, exile, prophecy

In making a purely divine repast its goal, *Paradiso* takes a firm turn away from the appetites for food that have been seen so far in the poem. When, in *Paradiso* 2, Dante addresses those who "drizzaste il collo" (stretched out your necks) toward the "pan de li angeli" (bread of the angels), he warns that they are "non sen vien satollo" (never sated by it; *Par.* 2.10–12): a rejection, it may seem, of both the tangible human food through which he has commented on creativity and community and the metaphoric nourishment he has woven into his poetics. At the same time, the pilgrim undergoes a process of self-reflection in heaven that leads him to comment more than ever before on his expectations in this life, and his exposure to the perfection of the city of God enables him to imagine what the human city on earth might become. As he progresses into the inexpressible abstraction of *Paradiso*, the poet attempts to say what has never been said before, but his human language nevertheless engages the human concerns of appetite, provisioning, and nourishment while speaking through food and eating practices.

Callegari, D., *Dante's Gluttons: Food and Society from the* Convivio *to the* Comedy.
Taylor & Francis Group, 2022
DOI 10.5117/9789463720427_CH05

Before his arrival in heaven, the pilgrim must pass through the Earthly Paradise—perhaps the most evocative space for gluttony within the poem. The Garden of Eden is the only place humankind has ever experienced the contentment of a perfectly satisfied appetite, the only place body and soul enjoyed the quietude permitted by an utter lack of desire. In the prelapsarian state, the first man existed momentarily before and outside of the "first struggle" of gluttony, while everyone who has followed him has been defined by the yearning to return to that state. The pilgrim, having successfully navigated the seven terraces of the purgatorial mountain and reached its peak, is thus presumably perfect upon entering the garden at the top, unspoiled in the way that God had intended. As Jeffrey Schnapp describes in his overview of *Purgatorio*, "When he reaches his destination, Dante has been remade. He is a new man, a perfect double of Adam before the Fall."[1] Yet there is a conspicuous difference between Adam and Dante: unlike his Edenic forerunner, the pilgrim is tired. He has not been placed in the garden by the grace of God, but rather he has arrived the way Adam's postlapsarian counterpart must, after a difficult physical journey, weighed down by the body and its needs. As Dante laments in *Purgatorio* 27, the effort of the climb forces him to rest even when his desire drives him forward, as "la natura del monte ci affranse / la possa del salir più e 'l diletto" (the nature of the mountain had broken our power to climb further and our delight in it; *Purg.* 27.74-75). When Virgil tells the pilgrim that "libero, dritto e sano è tuo arbitrio" (free, upright, and whole is your will; *Purg.* 27.140), he confirms that Dante's soul has been cleansed of any weakness and restored to full strength, allowing him to pass through the cleansing fires into the Earthly Paradise in *Purgatorio* 28, but physical strength—the human "virtù" that complements the divine "virtù," as Statius repeatedly explained in his embryology—is depleted.

The baptismal scene that follows further highlights the double nature of the pilgrim's existence, body and soul, and the simultaneous presence of each. Lifted by the beautiful Matelda into the cleansing waters of the river, Dante is bathed in them, but he also slakes his thirst, swallowing the water as he swims in it:

La bella donna ne le braccia aprissi;
    abbracciommi la testa e mi sommerse
    ove convenne ch'io l'acqua inghiottissi.
Indi mi tolse, e bagnato m'offerse

---

1   Schnapp, "Introduction to *Purgatorio*," p. 93.

dentro a la danza de le quattro belle,
e ciascuna del braccio mi coperse.
                    Purg. 31.100–105

(The beautiful lady opened her arms, embraced my head, and submerged
me, so that I had to swallow some of the water. Then she took me and,
drenched as I was, inserted me into the dance of the four beauties, and
each of them covered me with her arm.)

Emerging from Eünoe, the poet tells us he was "rifatto sì come piante novella,
rinovellate di novella fronda" (remade, as new trees are renewed when
they bring forth new boughs; *Purg.* 33.143–144). After stepping out of the
revitalizing waters of the Earthly Paradise, the pilgrim prompts us to think
not just of his fresh spirit but also of his newly strong body, pushing forth
new growth like a young tree.

This acknowledgment of the need to consume and refresh bodily weakness intimates that a focus on food and physicality will remain with Dante,
even as he embarks upon his flight through the heavens. Recalling his final
rite of passage in the Earthly Paradise, he conveys his feelings through the
same sensations of bodily hunger and thirst that he has relied on up to
this point:

S'io avessi, lettor, più lungo spazio
    da scrivere, i' pur cantere' in parte
    lo dolce ber che mai non m'avria sazio
                    Purg. 33.136–138

(If, reader, I had more space to write, I would continue to sing in part the
sweet drink that could never satiate me.)

The reference here to insatiability would seem to contrast with what has
been said and what is to come; Eden is a place where the unchecked desire
for food has never existed, and the abundance of the garden and its promise
of immaculate satiation will shortly give way to the canticle where consumption and nourishment become increasingly less tangible. Yet *Paradiso* will
not only continue the discourse on gluttony, but amplify it, delivering the
final word on Dante's complete vision of consumption and community.

The first canto of *Paradiso* immediately begins to play with the tension
between heavenly expectations and earthly needs that will characterize this
space. While there is no place for human food in heaven, the relationship

with food remains crucial to the human ability to understand it. Indeed, the paradigmatic analogy that Dante furnishes so that his readers might understand the poetry of Paradise is based on eating:

> Nel suo aspetto tal dentro mi fei,
>   qual si fé Glauco nel gustar de l'erba
>   che 'l fé consorto in mar de li altri dèi.
> Trasumanar significar per verba
>   non si poria; però l'essemplo basti
>   a cui esperïenza grazia serba.
>   *Par.* 1.67–72

(Gazing at her I became within what Glaucus became tasting the herb that made him a consort of the other gods in the sea. To signify transhuman-izing *per verba* is impossible; therefore let the comparison suffice for those to whom grace reserves the experience.)

To broach the divine, Dante must change himself in a manner that cannot be put into words—his most famous neologism, "transumanar," is born here—but he can best help his readers imagine the process by reminding them of the ways in which eating provokes growth and change, whether naturally (like a tree absorbing water) or supernaturally (like Glaucus and his herbs).

Having set these as its opening terms, the last canticle will proceed to see Dante undoing the myths that surround moon spots (*lunar maria*) with a parallel to the human body as it fluctuates between lean and fat in *Paradiso* 2. It will witness Dante's ancestor foretelling the poet's exile through the contrast between the bread of strangers and the bread of home and how the palate might become accustomed to an unfamiliar taste in *Paradiso* 17. It will allow Dante to thoroughly confirm how good provisioning and convivial consumption first create and then strengthen the bonds of community. Most tellingly, it will finally give space for Dante to once again condemn those who grow fat on the food they immorally co-opt for themselves, and defend the power structures they (at times consciously, at times inadvertently) undermine. Yet here, those bodies will be set against the image of the poet's own body as it shrinks in the face of a lean diet in *Paradiso* 25. Pouring himself into his work, the last self-portrait Dante paints in the *Comedy* is of a man who finds himself finally beyond the reach of gluttony. Through his poem, he has found the means to triumph over the first struggle, channeling his appetite into work that feeds the community, and digesting what he needs in order to produce for others.

Citizenship and Gluttony

Dante's misgivings about the potential for civic participation in the city of man are made exquisitely clear throughout the poem, and indeed, it is gluttony that frequently enables him to voice his bitter disappointment in what prospects there are for anyone who wishes to imitate the great shared feast that will be enjoyed in the city of God. The uncanny similarity between a contemporary terrestrial urban landscape and what the pilgrim sees in Hell, where souls are so deteriorated from their excessive, violent consumption that their demonically possessed bodies are all that's left to govern, bodes poorly for the future, to say the least. Nonetheless, the optimism of the philosopher of the *Convivio* with his promise to provide bread for the many, not just the few, is still present in the poet of the *Comedy*, especially in *Paradiso*. As Peter Hawkins has underlined, Dante remains deeply convinced that "whatever the actualities of civic life on earth, no matter how unrealized their potential or perverted their expression, it is still better to be a citizen, a member of a community, than not."[2] By the time he reaches the last canticle, Dante has established that reliable provisioning underpins any community, and that a glutton in its midst will threaten its survival. It thus follows that even in this rarefied space, questions of food consumption and distribution will remain a primary preoccupation.

Hawkins's observation comes directly from the poet himself, in fact, in an exceptionally intimate moment in *Paradiso* 8. In the heaven of Venus, the pilgrim must respond to the interrogations of Charles Martel, the son of Charles II of Anjou, a figure who represented the hope for a just and stable imperial rule in Dante's lifetime but whose premature death quickly dashed those hopes. Martel recognizes Dante's love for him as the pilgrim turns his gaze toward the spirit encased in rays, and he confirms that had he lived, the world might have been a better place: "e se più fosse stato, / molto sarà di mal, che non sarebbe" (had it been longer much evil to come would not exist; *Par.* 8.50–51). Knowing that the existence to which Dante will return is colored by the cruel politics that will lead to his exile, Martel asks the pilgrim, "Or dì: sarebbe peggio / per l'omo in terra, se non fosse cive?" (Now tell me: would it be worse for man on earth, if he were not a citizen?). The response comes unexpectedly from the writing Dante—not the pilgrim—who rebuts with his most vulnerable and honest intervention: "sì [...] e qui ragion non cheggio" (Yes [...] and here I ask for no proof;

---

2   Hawkins, "Nightmare and Dream," p. 72. It is also Hawkins who uses the term "word city," coined by Pike in *The Image of the City in Modern Literature*, in relation to the *Comedy*.

Par. 8.115–17). This, as Hawkins reiterates, can be seen as proof of Dante's conviction that *civitas* and *humanitas* are one, an idea that reveals the influence of one of Dante's teachers, Remigio de' Girolami, who had stressed the city as more perfect than the individual.[3] In the *Tractatus de bono communi*, Girolami had affirmed: "qui erat civis Florentinus per destructionem Florentiae iam non sit Florentinus dicendus [...] Et si non est civis, non est homo, quia homo est naturaliter animal civile" (He who was a Florentine citizen could no longer be called a Florentine if Florence were destroyed [...] And if he is not a citizen, he is not a man, because man is naturally a civic animal; 9.80–81). To live together—*convivere*—Dante knows that we must sometimes suffer violence at our banquets and demons in our midst, but it is the act of sharing space, of conviviality, that gives us our identities and shapes our very existence.

It is just after this revelatory moment in *Paradiso* 8 that Dante explicitly sets a table for the first time since the *Convivio*. In *Paradiso* 10, Dante explains that while he provides the nourishment, he leaves the eating up to the readers themselves:

> Or ti riman, lettor, sovra 'l tuo banco,
>   dietro pensando a ciò che si preliba,
>   s'esser vuoi lieto assai prima che stanco.
> Messo t'ho innanzi: omai per te ti ciba.
>   *Par.* 10.22–25

(Now remain, reader, upon your bench, reflecting on this of which you have a foretaste, if you would be glad far sooner than weary. I have set before you; now feed yourself.)

Returning to the post he occupied in his philosophical banquet, and acknowledging again the tired postlapsarian body, Dante begins to draw together the nutritional threads that have run through his work from the very beginning, tying up the dangers of injudicious consumption with the means to create and construct community. The table, the crucial site where Dante first aligned his intention of distributing knowledge to a wide new audience with the civic duty of food distribution, is where he will now leave his readers to sit and feed themselves. As the poet unfolds the final cantos of his major work, his reader may reflect on the struggle to restrain

---

3   Hawkins, "Nightmare and Dream," p. 80. Kantorowicz calls Girolami "proto-Hegelian" for his conviction that the community is the final goal in *The King's Two Bodies*, p. 479.

the appetite in the places where gluttony lurks. With the table freshly set, and the profound importance of citizenship in the city of man confirmed, Dante once again uses bread to define the boundaries and the bonds of his community—but in *Paradiso,* the stakes have been raised. No longer just an experiment in learning and self-discovery, the bread Dante invokes in heaven points to earthly consumption, this time as a real expression of the fate Dante will face as one expelled from his city and forced to beg for his meals.

As Robert Durling affirmed, it is not simply the figure of bread but indeed the relationship with food more generally that achieves its greatest prominence in Dante's work in the climactic conversation between the pilgrim and Cacciaguida in the central cantos of *Paradiso.*[4] The revelatory and awe-inspiring meeting with Dante's great-great-grandfather is characterized by straightforward and simple language that returns to the gesture of bread distribution. In the heaven of Mars, Cacciaguida will treat the pilgrim to a sprawling history of his family and native city, followed by a vast, often-brutal vision of the future, including his own destiny to never return home. While reflecting on their home, Dante's crusader ancestor recalls a moment of happiness and sobriety in Florence, before unfettered consumption began to deteriorate the foundations of that peaceful existence:

Fiorenza dentro da la cerchia antica,
   ond' ella toglie ancora e terza e nona,
   si stava in pace, sobria e pudica.
Non avea catenella, non corona,
   non gonne contigiate, non cintura
   che fosse a veder più che la persona.
Non faceva, nascendo, ancor paura
   la figlia al padre, che 'l tempo e la dote
   non fuggien quinci e quindi la misura.
                      Par. 15.97–105

(Florence, within her ancient ring of walls—that ring from which she still draws tierce and nones—sober and chaste, lived in tranquillity. No necklace and no coronal were there, and no embroidered gowns; there was no girdle that caught the eye more than the one who wore it. No daughter's birth brought fear unto her father, for age and dowry then did not imbalance—to this side and to that—the proper measure.)

4   Durling, "Deceit and Digestion," pp. 63–65.

The Florence that existed for Cacciaguida is, however, much changed, as Dante already knows. Their city has become worldly, obsessed with material gain, and a few families have become fat on the backs of the many.[5] Factionalism has led to instability, violence, and even bloodshed, and Dante himself will soon be victimized by the now faithless, fierce city, as Cacciaguida reveals:

> Tu lascerai ogne cosa diletta
>   più caramente; e questo è quello strale
>   che l'arco de lo essilio pria saetta.
> Tu proverai sì come sa di sale
>   lo pane altrui, e come è duro calle
>   lo scendere e 'l salir per l'altrui scale.
>   *Par.* 17.55–60

(You will leave behind everything beloved most dearly, and this is the arrow that the bow of exile first lets fly. You will experience how salty tastes the bread of another, and what a hard path it is to descend and mount by another's stairs.)

Though the pilgrim has received many hints along the way, this is the first time the truth of his exile is laid bare for him; the poet, in contrast, is well aware of what the future holds, as he writes these lines from the very state of exile that Cacciaguida here predicts. Like the response to Charles Martel in *Paradiso* 8, these lines span the distance between naïve pilgrim and knowing poet, and food is the means by which this distance is traveled. When, in the voice of the ancient Florentine, Dante divulges with unsparing honesty the pain of his current state to his past self, he does so with an image of an unfamiliar type of bread: "lo pane altrui." As the poet declares, the prophecy is meant to be quite transparent; Dante will know exile in the future by the foreign taste that greets him in the bread he receives. But if the prophecy is clear, the reader must return to Dante's other meditations on food and security to appreciate the full significance of the bread. The poet's vulnerability in his lived exile is writ large as he underscores the ties of community created through food, which generate closeness where geographical proximity can no longer be had (or perhaps never existed).

---

5   These verses also confirm in short order the crucial role of the material studies lens, as witnessed by Olson's close reading of the changes in fashion referenced here, in Olson, "Shoes, Gowns and Turncoats."

The full extent of Cacciaguida's prophecy is more easily understood when one connects it to the motif of exile that recurs throughout the *Comedy*, a motif articulated through bread more than once. Seeking to dissect another prophecy of exile that occurs earlier in the poem, William A. Stephany has called attention to the fact that a Virgilian forefather might hold a clue to the interpretation of an exile foretold through food. Long before his personal fate is made plain, the pilgrim stumbles rather incongruously upon the Harpies, who once threatened Aeneas and his men in the *Aeneid* and who now peck the rejected bodies of the suicides in *Inferno* 13. Their placement would seem to suggest that they are, as early commentators proposed, simply ministers of the suffering these souls deserve. The pilgrim describes them as a "tristo annuncio di futuro danno" (dire prophecy of their future woe; *Inf.* 13.12), ostensibly confirming this reading, though he hints at more with the intertext. Considering Dante's source more carefully, Stephany determines that its purpose must be otherwise, for Virgil's Harpies foretell a happy exile despite their cruel intentions.[6]

In book 3 of the *Aeneid*, the harpy Celaeno pronounces what appears to be a truly bleak prophecy: "You will go to Italy, and be free to enter her harbors: but you shall not surround with walls your promised city until dire hunger, and the wrong of striking at us, force you to gnaw with your teeth and devour your very tables!" (*Aen.* 3.253-57).[7] In the face of this pronouncement, and given the dire straits in which they find themselves at this point in their journey, Aeneas and his men begin to believe that they will reach Italy only as they wither and die from starvation. It is therefore not surprising that when Dante encounters the Harpies himself in *Inferno* 13 he interprets them as a reiteration of the withering and death he sees all around. But it would be a mistake on the part of the reader to accept this view, knowing that in book 7 of the *Aeneid*, the Trojans in fact arrive in Italy, where they eat ravenously after their long and harrowing journey. After they have consumed everything in sight, Ascanius pauses, then observes that they have eaten not only their food but the rough bread on which it was served, laughing that they have indeed eaten their "tables": "Soon, all thing else devoured, their hunger turned to taste the rough bread, which they attacked violently with tooth and nail, and consumed both round and square of that predestined leaven. 'Ha! we eat our tables even!' cried Iulus,

---

6   Stephany, "Dante's Harpies," pp. 37–44.

7   "Ibitis Italiam portusque intrare licebit sed non ante datam cingetis moenibus urbem quam vos dira fames notraeque iniuria caedis ambesas subigat malis absumere mensas." *Aeneid* 3.253–257, trans. Fitzgerald.

laughing" (*Aen.* 7.112–122).[8] The change from looming tragedy to future contentment is a conversion: eating their meal and bread alike, the Trojans take the literality of their prophecy—construed negatively by the wicked Harpies—and realize their happy fate with a comic metaphor, turning certain starvation into a celebratory feast.[9]

This conversion harkens back to the prophecy of exile that Cacciaguida projects first as a salty bite, and then reappraises in the light of the fullness of time. Just as Ascanius's joke allows Aeneas to grasp that the "dire prophecy of their future woe" was in reality a dim vision of their future success, so the pilgrim is reminded that his exile to a place with unfamiliar bread will be the first step toward finally succeeding in providing the bread of his words to those gathered at the table he first imagined in *Convivio*. Unlike the Harpies, Dante's beatified ancestor is capable of providing both the first reading and the gloss, and Cacciaguida tempers his revelation by telling the pilgrim that:

> "Coscïenza fusca
> o de la propria o de l'altrui vergogna
> pur sentirà la tua parola brusca.
> Ma nondimen, rimossa ogne menzogna,
> tutta tua visïon fa manifesta;
> e lascia pur grattar dov'è la rogna.
> Ché se la voce tua sarà molesta
> nel primo gusto, vital nodrimento
> lascerà poi, quando sarà digesta."
>
> *Par.* 17.124-132

(Then it replied, "A conscience dark, either with its own or with another's shame, will indeed feel your speech to be harsh. But none the less, all falsehood aside, make manifest all that you have seen; and then let them scratch where the itch is. For if at first taste your voice be grievous, yet shall it leave thereafter vital nourishment when digested.")

In the reference to the Eucharist that follows, the poet recalls the transubstantiated bread not in its role as a means of accessing divine knowledge but

---

8   "Consumptis hic forte aliis, ut vertere morsus exiguam in Cererem penuira adegit edendi, et violare manu malisque audacibus orbem fatalis crusti patulis nec parcere quadris: 'heus, etiam mensas consumimus' inqui Iulus nec plura, adludens." *Aeneid* 7.112–122.

9   Stephany, "Dante's Harpies," pp. 42–43.

rather as a shared meal that unites men on earth. Where once swords were used to wage bloody battles, now the pope cruelly denies the sacrament to political enemies, dividing the Christian community with the very meal with which it should be bound together:

> Già si solea con le spade far guerra;
>   ma or si fa togliendo or qui o quivi
>   lo pan che 'l pïo Padre a nessun serra.
> Ma tu che sol per cancellare scrivi,
>   pensa che Pietro e Paulo, che moriro
>   per la vigna che guasti, ancor son vivi.
>   *Par.* 18.127–129

(In the past they made war with swords, but now they do it by withholding, now here, now there, the bread the merciful Father locks away from no one. But you who write only to strike out, remember that Peter and Paul, who died for the vine you are laying waste, are still alive.)

The pope's perverted use of the bread and wine that represent the flesh and blood of Christ cannot undo the covenant they mark between God and the individual who receives him. What Cacciaguida describes as the pope's wrongdoing is his manipulation of the power of the Eucharistic bread to include or exclude, to arrogantly assume it is his right to delineate the boundaries of the Christian community, which is meant to be open to any who wish to partake of the bread. The poet's quick translation of Cacciaguida's revelation to the pilgrim disguises a more complex message behind the forewarning, and though there is no doubt he will consume a foreign bread, the poet knows he will have occasion to acquire a taste for it.

In the nearly complete view of the world that Dante has before him as the end of the poem approaches, it becomes clear that while his immediate future holds a salty bread, the poet knows it will nourish him in a way that allows him to in turn nourish others. Like the barley bread of his *Convivio*, the bread he will one day be forced to eat appears at first distasteful or unbecoming—something a Florentine of his historical moment, expecting the best white bread, would disdain—and indeed so too will the words he produces as a result of that sustenance. But Dante, who understands the vital power of distributing bread and consuming it together, does not shrink from what sustains him, knowing that a meal that fills many stomachs is more valuable than one for just a few.

The Weight of Love

After Cacciaguida has enlightened the pilgrim, Dante is lifted into the heaven of Saturn. Several readers have called this moment "the beginning of the end," and while that may seem an arbitrary distinction—or an attempt to create a teleology within a teleology—there is good reason to see the start of *Paradiso* 21 as the announcement of an approaching conclusion.[10] To begin, Dante is in something like a blind and deaf state at the outset, as the symphony that has accompanied him through the heavens now ceases to play and Beatrice denies him her smile, which will be too powerful for him here. Next, a ladder appears, providing the means for a more literal ascent than has been available up to this point. Finally, and least frequently considered, the heaven of Saturn is dedicated to the ancient god of generation, who consumes his children as a sign of the earth's creative potential and the passing of human generations, but whose consumption is also indiscriminate and heedless of those around him. It is the Saturnine cycle of eating and renewal that will form the pre-Christian point of contrast against which Dante begins his climb to commune at last, and completely, with God; moreover, it is the question of how a controlled appetite creates the foundation for a healthy human community that will propel Dante to that meeting.

Consumption and generative potential are, in fact, immediately invoked as the foundation for the poetry in *Paradiso* 21. The first thing the pilgrim encounters as he turns away from Beatrice—but before he meets his primary interlocutor—is a golden ladder upon which the souls of the beatified ascend and descend, fluttering up and down its rungs like so many small birds trying to warm their feathers in the cold morning air:

> vid'io uno scaleo eretto in suso
> tanto che nol seguiva la mia luce.
> Vidi anche per li gradi scender giuso
> tanti splendor ch'io pensai ch'ogne lume
> che par nel ciel quindi fosse diffuso
> E come, per lo natural costume,
> le pole insieme al cominciar del giorno
> si movono a scaldar le fredde piume,
> poi altre vanno via sanza ritorno,
> altre rivolgon sé onde son mosse,

10   See especially Barolini, *The Undivine Comedy*, p. 221.

e altre roteando fan soggiorno:
tal modo parve me che quivi fosse
   in quello sfavillar che 'nsieme venne,
   sì come in certo grado si percosse.
Par. 21.28–42

(I saw a ladder, the color of gold struck by the sun, erected upward so far that my light could not follow it. And I saw coming down by its degrees so many splendors that I thought every light that shows in the heavens must be poured out from there. As in their natural wont the magpies, when day begins, take wing together to warm their chilled feathers, then some go away without returning, others return whence they moved, still others stay to wheel above the spot: such seemed to be the manner there, in the flashings that came down together, as soon as they touched this or that degree.)

Commentators have traditionally seen a representation of the contemplative mind in this back-and-forth movement, following the explanation of Richard of St. Victor, or a mirror of religious life, following that of St. Bonaventure, a balance of the contemplative and the active in and out of the cloister. As this canto centers on the encounter with Pier Damiani, a monk who lived happily within his monastery but then followed the call to action to become a cardinal, diplomat, and renowned reformer, the wheeling birds seem to represent this fittingly. Certainly their motion captures the oscillation between contemplation and action; as Giuseppe Mazzotta has noted, Dante takes pains in *Paradiso* 21 to demonstrate that contemplation is never stasis, and that a tension between thought and act characterizes the ideal Christian existence.[11] Looking at the poetry itself, Teodolinda Barolini has further described this moment in the text as a literary "jump," an enjambment that stays attached to what was while pushing ahead to what must come next.[12]

But even as the movement of the birds and the language used to illustrate them may fit a predetermined scheme of Christian life, the specific type of bird chosen to represent the souls here has drawn curiosity. Though Dante has just received a speech from the eagle of justice, it is the *pola*, the jackdaw or magpie, that he selects as an analogue for the beatified in the seventh heaven. Peter Hawkins has suggested that the selection of this humble bird "reinforces the emphasis on humble simplicity celebrated throughout these cantos," in

11   Mazzotta, *Reading Dante*, pp. 233–234.
12   Barolini, *The Undivine Comedy*, pp. 222–223.

contrast with the proud and noble bird that occupied the preceding poetic and heavenly space.[13] As he gazes up at the the souls who wheel like jackdaws down the golden ladder that extends upward, the pilgrim sees a light separate itself, and he then meets Pier Damiani (though it will be serveral *terzine* before he is formally introduced). The monk known for straddling the space between quiet reflection and civic commitment describes his own humble lifestyle through his diet, drawing a vital line from humility to consumption practices to generative ability:

> e poi continüando disse: "Quivi
>   al servigio di Dio mi fe' sì fermo,
> che pur con cibi di liquor d'ulivi
>   lievemente passava caldi e geli,
>   contento ne' pensier contemplativi.
> Render solea quel chiostro a questi cieli
>   fertilemente; e ora è fatto vano,
>   sì che tosto convien che si riveli.
> In quel loco fu' io Pietro Damiano,
>   e Pietro Peccator fu' ne la casa
>   di Nostra Donna in sul lito adriano."
>   *Par.* 21.113–123

(Then, continuing, he said: "There I became so fixed in the service of God that with but the juice of olives I easily survived heats and frosts, content in my contemplative thoughts. That cloister used to produce fertile harvests for these heavens, but now it has become so empty that soon it must be revealed. In that place I was Peter Damiani, and I was Peter the Sinner in the house of our Lady on the Adriatic shore.")

Noting how in his early monastic life he survived both heat and cold by consuming only the "cibi di liquor d'ulivi," Damiani goes on to lament the behavior of the men who currently inhabit the roles defined by Saints Peter and Paul, now defined equally by their diet. In the case of the clergy, Damiani sees them acting in stark contrast to the humility and asceticism of their great predecessors, with their heaving frames that can barely stay atop a packhorse:

> Venne Cefàs e venne il gran vasello
>   de lo Spirito Santo, magri e scalzi

---

13   Hawkins, "Dante's Lesson of Silence: *Paradiso* 21," p. 43.

prendendo il cibo da qualunque ostello.
Or voglion quinci e quindi chi rincalzi
    li moderni pastori e chi li meni,
    tanto son gravi, e chi di rietro li alzi.
Cuopron d'i manti loro i palafreni,
    sì che due bestie van sott'una pelle:
    oh pazïenza che tanto sostieni!
Par. 21.127–135

(Simon came, and the great Vessel of the Holy Spirit came, thin and barefoot, taking their food in any hostel. Now the modern shepherds need someone on each side to hold them up and lead them, they are so fat, and someone to lift them up behind. They cover their palfreys with their mantles, so that two beasts go beneath one skin: Oh Patience that endures so much!)

These verses are hardly the first place Dante finds room for a jab at the clergy, but they are notable for presenting what Hawkins describes archly as "some of the broadest humor in the *Comedy*."[14] It is surprising to find a description like this in *Paradiso* 21; after all, Dante is so far from earth and from his earthly self that he will shortly be able to sustain the experience of Beatrice's full smile. The tangible materiality of food that adds weight to the body should be a distant memory: even if Dante wished to condemn the clergy for their inordinate appetite, this is an unlikely place for body-shaming. Most strikingly, Damiani's disgust for these "gravi moderni pastori" prompts the bewildering explosion of sound and light that concludes the twenty-first canto:

A questa voce vid'io più fiammelle
    di grado in grado scendere e girarsi
    e ogne giro le facea più belle.
Dintorno a questa vennero e fermarsi,
    e fero un grido di sì alto suono
    che non potrebbe qui assomigliarsi
né io lo 'ntesi, sì mi vinse il tuono.
Par. 21.136–142

(At this word I saw numerous bright flames come down from stair to stair and whirl, and every whirling made them lovelier. They gathered round

14   Hawkins, "Dante's Lesson of Silence: *Paradiso* 21," p. 44.

this one and stopped, and then uttered so loud a cry that nothing could resemble it down here, nor did I understand it, its thunder so overcame me.)

The pilgrim's confusion here is well-founded, though it is in response to the poet's choice: why does this quiet, restrained canto end with a violent bang, and why do the comically heavy bodies of the prelates elicit this reaction? What is it about the "pastori gravi" that troubles Pier Damiani (and thus Dante) so much, and what does the space between contemplation and action have to do with it? To suggest that these shepherds of the church paid too much attention to food and material goods is not quite adequate; as elsewhere in the poem, the layers of this gluttonous construct must be peeled back to contextualize a world in which gluttons were not necessarily betrayed by their body types. From Ciacco to Bonagiunta, Dante's overeaters have not proven to be "gravi" in the context of the poem.

As in the other moments in which Dante accuses people of being over-indulgent in their eating practices, the message in the last lines of *Paradiso* 21 is about something more—where one's mind should be focused instead, or what is lost when one's gaze is distracted by material goods. There is, however, a stricter tie here between gluttony and contemplation, and a nuance attached to the heavy body in particular as witnessed by the humble birds evoked in the canto's opening lines. The obvious contrast to the "pastori gravi" would be the man who turns away from other thoughts or desires and toward God in concentrated contemplation, as might be expected in this canto. But Dante does not do the expected; he instead provides Pier Damiani as a counterpoint, a monk who was expressly called *away* from contemplation (and his humble diet) *to* action. Like the bread that forms his prophecy of exile, the lines here require the reader to take a wider view of Dante's work in order to understand the connection between humility and the sustenance of the human community.

Paradiso 21 is not the first time Dante engages the image of humble birds wheeling over a virtuous city. In the fourth book of the *Convivio,* Dante exclaims that it is better to be a humble, low-flying bird than to soar over a vicious, failed city as a bird of prey:

> What wretches you are who govern now! and how wretched, too, are those who are governed! For neither through your own study nor through taking counsel of others does your activity as rulers operate in accordance with philosophical authority, so that the saying of the Preacher is applicable throughout the world: "Misfortune is yours, o country, whose king is a

child, and whose princes eat early in the morning!" And to no country can the words that follow be applied: "Blessed is the country whose king is noble, whose princes eat at the proper time, the amount needed, and not lustfully!" [...] Tell us how many times a day your counsellors call to your attention this end proper to human life! You would do better to fly low like swallows than to wheel on high like kites over things that are utterly base (*Conv.* 4.6.19-20).[15]

The angry accusation Dante flings here has often been misinterpreted, or even mistranslated, by readers who disregard the obscure mention of mealtimes and focus on the more general indications of noble or childlike behavior.[16] But the child king is threatened specifically by the princes who eat in the morning, a distinction that is made explicit in the original text Dante is citing from Ecclesiastes: "Vae tibi, terra, cujus rex puer est, et cujus principes mane comedunt. Beata terra cujus rex nobilis est, et cujus principes vescuntur in tempore suo, ad reficiendum, et non ad luxuriam" (Ecclesiastes 10:16-17). This distinction is not arbitrary for Dante. These titles presume an aristocratic conduct that aligns with their station and their breeding, but in the late medieval context, an early morning meal was reserved for those who engaged in physical labor: for those who performed tasks that used the energy from food, working from early in the morning until late in the afternoon. Princes who eat breakfast are, for Dante, a symbol of the abdication or rejection of duty, and like Forese's choice of grey partridge, their actions betray a profound misunderstanding of their role. Moreover, the early time of day suggests a private, individual meal, taken not at the primary mealtime shared with one's subjects, but in indulgent isolation like a child, without concern for the greater purpose of a shared meal: to reenact the social structure and secure the bonds of the community. The affinity for privacy, which would begin to change the setting for meals in the early

15 "Oh miseri che al presente reggete! e oh miserissimi che retti siete! che nulla filosofica autoritade si conguinge colli vostri reggimenti né per proprio studio né per consiglio: sì che a tutti si può dire quella parola dello Ecclesiaste: 'Guai a te, terra, lo cui re è fanciullo e li cui principi la domane mangiano!'; e a nulla terra si può dire quella che séguita: 'Beata la terra lo cui re è nobile e li cui principi si cibano nel suo tempo, a bisogno, e non a lussuria!' [...] guardate chi a lato vi siede per consiglio, e annumerate quante volte lo die questo fine dell'umana vita per li vostri consiglieri v'è additato! Meglio sarebbe a voi come rondine volare basso, che come nibbio altissime rote fare sopra le cose vilissime!" *Convivio* 4.6.19-20 (translation mine).

16 See Ryan's translation of these lines: "'Misfortune is yours, o country, whose king is a child, and whose princes' first thought is their own pleasure!' And to no country can the words that follow be applied: 'Blessed is the country whose king is noble, whose princes concern themselves with the needs of others and not with their own debauchery!'" In Dante, *The Banquet*, 4.6.19-20.

fifteenth century, had yet to emerge, and the overwhelming consensus in Dante's historical moment held that private dining diminished honor and bred contempt.[17]

The connection Dante draws in the *Convivio* between low-flying birds and the princes celebrated in Ecclesiastes for eating "a bisogno" (the right amount), is the one that also appears in *Paradiso* 21, though elaborated over the course of many more lines. While in his treatise Dante collapses this parallel into a brief and vehement invective, in *Paradiso* one must read through the end of the canto in order to see how the bird-like souls, fluttering up and down the ladder, relate to a controlled, considered diet. In the canto's final lines, Pier Damiani thunders so violently against the enormously fat clergy that it shakes Dante to his core. Reading these two elements as expressly linked (in the way they were first presented in the *Convivio*) draws the representation of contemplation into a debate about consumption politics and civic duty. In the same way that a line can be drawn from the starlings carried off by the wind in the cold season to Francesca's abandonment of obligation in *Inferno* 5, a double analogy between the birds' movement and human action is at play here. With an exemplar of the active life in the contemplative space of *Paradiso* 21, the poet presents the familiar struggle to be neither too abstinent nor too excessive in consumption: a search for the right balance between contemplation and action, for a body that is nourished adequately and properly with neither too much nor too little. Placing gluttony alongside contemplation and action provides a pattern for this back-and-forth motion, demonstrating the constant vigilance that is required to curb but not silence the appetite, and to remain thoughtful while accepting the need to act when appropriate.

The vision of gluttony that Dante has unfolded across the poem—a constant movement between too much and too little—is subtly reenacted in the movement on the ladder with which canto 21 begins. It is a daily struggle; it is introspective; it is a conscious attempt to use restraint and humility to grow and engage. The introduction of Pier Damiani, a monk who

---

17   See Montanari, *Gusti del medioevo*, pp. 53–54. The insistence on the head of household eating a single, substantial meal, usually at midday or late afternoon, in full view of the staff is repeated in many places as a tool of soft power: for example, the famous rules of Robert Grosseteste for the Countess of Lincoln, where he emphasizes that private dining brought "no honour to the Lord or Lady," and which Bridget Henisch contextualizes in *Fast and Feast: Food in Medieval Society*, p. 17, or Dante's own condemnation of Pope Martin IV's practice of eating his favorite eels in Vernaccia in *Purgatorio* 24, and which in his commentary Jacopo della Lana later expounded upon, noting that he did it alone in his private chambers after the main meal, discussed in Chapter 4.

wished to remain in contemplation but who accepted his appointment as cardinal and became an active reformer, reflects this further: he is a figure who has not cut himself off from civic participation, who leaves behind his meager diet sustained by the "pingue otium" of the cloister and confronts the real duties of community responsibility, feeding himself so he can feed others, fighting to bring the "vano chiostro" back to its past fertility. If we return to the *Convivio,* it becomes possible to see how Dante's thoughts on this began, and he warned his readers there against "child-like leaders" and those "princes who eat even in the morning," encouraging them to laud the "noble king" instead and the princes who eat "at the proper time, the amount needed, and not lustfully!" With these words, Dante imagines a mindful, farsighted leader, prepared to make sacrifices and put the good of the whole before the interests of the few. In *Paradiso* 21, he brings to life the promise of the abandoned philosophical treatise, reminding his readers that it is better to fly low like a humble bird than to soar higher, lest in slackening the rein they become too heavy to fly at all.

Dante's references to gluttony seem at times to come at cross-purposes in *Paradiso.* He frequently celebrates abundant nourishment and conviviality, and even encourages his reader to feed himself in *Paradiso* 10—"omai per te ti ciba"—but just as readily uses food to recall suffering or exclusion, as in the prophecy of his exile in *Paradiso* 17: "Tu proverai come sa di sale lo pane altrui." As David Gibbons has noted, this corresponds to Dante's metaphorics in *Paradiso* more broadly, and both gluttony and fatness swing between a positive and a negative semantic valence. In back-to-back examples in *Paradiso* 10, Thomas Aquinas speaks fondly of the Dominican flock that "si impingua" (fatten themselves) following their leader, and then in *Paradiso* 11 decries how some of that same flock have become "ghiotto" (greedy for food) in their distraction. Yet rather than a contradiction, this might be better interpreted as an articulation of the poet's own wavering conviction, his hope that his fellow citizens will someday fatten themselves not on the backs or meat of others, but in the well-provisioned city they have brought to life. Dante explores the potential for the relationship with food to either magnetize or destabilize not only from the beginning to the end of his *Comedy,* but indeed from his very first poetic experiments to the last lines he would ever compose. Over the course of the final canticle of his major work, he writes with faith that the community he imagined gathered around his table in his text will become a reality.

The beginning of the end marked by the exceptional conditions of *Paradiso* 21 is a confirmation that the next cantos will be filled with the incredible, the inaccessible, the impossible. But if the conceit of *Paradiso* is one of impossibility, as his readers enter the seventh heaven with the pilgrim the poet brings them back to the earthly concerns of time and space, something that can be grasped by anyone and everyone. The intertexts Dante provides in his own work create a closed universe, so that even as the pilgrim spins out into the heights of heaven his reader can turn back to the *Convivio* and feel tethered. Bringing gluttony into conversation with contemplation, Dante provides an accessible experience as a point of reference for the difficult or the ineffable.

Upon reaching the even more rarefied space of *Paradiso* 25, Dante once again pulls his reader down to earth, professing that the writing of his poem has literally emaciated him, "sì che m'ha fatto per molto anni macro" (so that for many years it has made me lean; *Par.* 25.3). That is, as his poem becomes fatter, the poet becomes thinner. The statement might seem to suggest that he has sacrificed himself for his work, and to be sure, when the pilgrim stumbles upon his teacher and father figure Brunetto Latini in *Inferno* 15, Latini assures Dante that his work will shine so brilliantly that "l'una parte e l'altra avranno fame / di te" (both sides will hunger for you; *Inf.* 15.71–72). Latini lauds the pilgrim for the insatiable hunger he arouses in his public, and he advises Dante to arm himself against those who would share his table. By writing himself into his text in this way, Dante is also giving a part of himself: the "agnello" (lamb) who battles the insatiable and incurable hunger of the "lupi che li danno guerra" (wolves that make war on it; *Par.* 25.5–6), and those who devour blindly like Ugolino, who will always read "sacra fames" as cursed hunger. In the blind prison of Hell, however, Latini has missed the message, and when Dante sees his ancestor Cacciaguida in heaven, he learns that it is not the hungry who come to his table that he should fear, but rather the over-fed.

Dante's last gesture blurs the line between real and metaphoric nourishment in a way that reinforces the characterization of his work as the foundation for the modern novel, proposed by many later literary critics.[18] Roland Barthes memorably insisted that before his postmodern death, the Author defined himself by being there "to *feed* the book, i.e., he lives before it, thinks, suffers, lives for it; he has the same relation of antecedence with his work that a father sustains with his child."[19] This is the definition that Dante established and enforced for the many generations to come before the Author's demise (or rebirth). Living before it, for it, and through it, Dante

18   Most notably, Lukács in *The Theory of the Novel.*
19   Barthes, *The Rustle of Language*, p. 52 (emphasis in the original).

left a human text that could be injured and die, but that could also grow and even generate new life. The remarkable parallel between his position on how to feed and sustain the human community and his presentation of his text continues. Indeed, Dante's authorial legacy has depended upon the approachability of the poem, grounded in its consumable and nourishing nature, in terms of its content and the means through which that content is presented alike. Alison Cornish concludes her discussion of the success of Dante's vernacular, and his cementing as the father of Italian literature, by undoing the anachronistic myth of Dante's prophecy of the success of the Italian language. She proposes, nonetheless, that the *Comedy* "is a poem rooted in the personal, historical flesh of a particular language, but is built to survive the inevitable obsolescence of that language—as indeed it has."[20] If through a real dinner table Dante demonstrated that the strongest bonds among humans are forged through conscientious consumption and the sharing of food, so too his magnum opus pushes back against the idea that the author must defend and fortify his work. Instead, he opens it up, beckoning his audience to take the sustenance of his words, and to fill their bellies at their discretion so that they might find what they need and use it to reproduce for others.

Works Cited

Alighieri, Dante. *The Banquet*. Translated by Christopher Ryan. Saratoga, CA: Amma Libri, 1989.

Alighieri, Dante. *The Divine Comedy of Dante Alighieri*. 3 vols. Translated and edited by Robert Durling and edited by Ronald Martinez. Oxford: Oxford University Press, 1996-2011.

Barolini, Teodolinda. *The Undivine Comedy: Detheologizing Dante*. Princeton: Princeton University Press, 1992.

Barthes, Roland. *The Rustle of Language*. Translated by Richard Howard. Berkeley: University of California Press, 1989.

Hawkins, Peter S. "Nightmare and Dream: The Earthly City in Dante's *Commedia*." In *Civitas: Religious Interpretations of the City*, edited by Peter S. Hawkins, 71–84. Atlanta: Scholars Press, 1986.

Hawkins, Peter S. "Dante's Lesson of Silence: *Paradiso* 21." *Lectura Dantis* 11 (1992): 42–51.

Henisch, Bridget. *Fast and Feast: Food in Medieval Society*. University Park: Pennsylvania State University Press, 1976.

20   Cornish, *Vernacular Translation in Dante's Italy*, p. 156.

Durling, Robert. "Deceit and Digestion in the Belly of Hell." In *Allegory and Representation: Selected Papers from the English Institute*, edited by Stephen Greenblatt, 61–93. Baltimore: Johns Hopkins University Press, 1981.

Kantorowicz, Ernst. *The King's Two Bodies: A Study in Mediaeval Political Theology*. Princeton: Princeton University Press, 1957.

Lukács, György. *The Theory of the Novel: A Historico-philosophical Essay on the Forms of Great Epic Literature*. Translated by Anna Bostock Berger. Cambridge, Mass.: MIT Press, 1971.

Mazzotta, Giuseppe. *Reading Dante*. New Haven: Yale University Press, 2013.

Montanari, Massimo. *Gusti del medioevo*. Rome: Laterza, 2012.

Pike, Burton. *The Image of the City in Modern Literature*. Princeton: Princeton University Press, 1981.

Schnapp, Jeffrey. "Introduction to *Purgatorio*." In *The Cambridge Companion to Dante*, edited by Rachel Jacoff, 2nd ed., 91–106. Cambridge: Cambridge University Press, 2007.

Stephany, William A. "Dante's Harpies: 'Tristo annunzio di futuro danno.'" In *The Poetry of Allusion: Virgil and Ovid in Dante's* Commedia. Edited by Rachel Jacoff and Jeffrey Schnapp, 37–44. Stanford: Stanford University Press, 1991.

Virgil. *Aeneid*. Translated by Robert Fitzgerald. New York: Random House, 1983.

Conclusion

> Quando avrà provato il pane salato che si mangia altrove,
> non si lagnerà più della minestra di casa sua.
> *I Malavoglia* 1.14[1]

In an uncanny response to Dante's vision of what gluttony might do to the human community and his poem alike, the Italian futurist F. T. Marinetti dedicated one of his many invectives against the Italian intellectual class of his time to a tirade against those who fancied themselves *dantisti*. The futurist exponent singled out twentieth-century commentators in particular for their regressive approach to the study of the poet, comparing their mindless feeding on Dante's corpus to maggots devouring a corpse:

> Who will deny that the Divine Comedy is today anything other than a filthy worm-ranch of commentators? To what end do they wander the battlefield of thought when the fight is over, to count the dead, examine the brutal wounds, collect the broken weapons and the abandoned insignia, under the heavy flight of knowing crows and the flapping of their paper wings?[2]

Marinetti's love for the medieval poet alongside his hatred for contemporary commentators is a typical expression of the futurist's complicated feelings about the past and passéism, and his graphic metaphor loses some of its shock value when compared to the dozens of manifestos of equal or greater

---

1   "When he has learned how salt the bread is that one eats elsewhere, he won't growl any longer about the minestra at home." Verga, *I Malavoglia*, p. 19; Mary A. Craig, trans., *The House By the Medlar Tree*, p. 7.

2   "Chi negherà che la Divina Commedia altro non sia oggi che un immondo verminaio di glossatori? A che pro avventurarsi sui campi di battaglia del pensiero quando la mischia è finita, per numerare i morti, studiare le belle ferite, raccogliere le armi infrante e i bottini abbandonati, sotto il volo pesante dei corvi dotti e il loro sbatacchiar d'ali cartacee?" Marinetti, "La Divina Commedia è un verminaio dei glossatori," p. 27.

Callegari, D., *Dante's Gluttons: Food and Society from the* Convivio *to the* Comedy.
Taylor & Francis Group, 2022
DOI 10.5117/9789463720427_CONCL

vulgarity. Marinetti is not often thought of as a serious reader of Dante—not least because of remarks like this—and yet the mindless feeding of maggots he describes would appear to indicate a surprising nuance in his reception of the *Comedy*, if only unconsciously. Just like the medieval poet, Marinetti knows that any table set with food, real or metaphoric, runs the risk of being set upon by parasites now that its author's body is devoid of life. Instead of building on the ground conquered by lost lives, scavenging readers pick through the remaining flesh for food and trophies and leave behind a sterile field of death for swooping crows. Their actions are those that Dante identifies in all of his gluttons: they consume voraciously and unthinkingly, and succeed only in becoming bloated and diluted, unmemorable and unrecognizable.

At the same time, Marinetti's very ability to make this accusation affirms the presence of the community Dante succeeded in creating through a gastronomic literary language that stood the test of time, speaking to those who read him centuries later. In fact, the poem's immediate resonance with audiences was accompanied by an explicit recognition of the framework rooted in food and foodways that Dante elaborated across his works. Already Petrarch, even as he sought to ignore the notion that Dante was inevitably omnipresent for the Italian author, reveals that Dante had effectively imprinted the image of himself at the head of the table, serving the food through which future generations of Italian literature would be born. Petrarch not only imagined himself to be sitting at a table with Dante, but went so far as to describe the interaction of the "three crowns" as such:

At a banquet I have seen someone seated in a place of insufficient honor suddenly rise to seek of his own accord the last place, on the pretext of humility, but it was really the urging of pride; I have seen another leave. Despite their seemingly mild manners, the cause of their behavior is either anger or pride, even though there is something gentle in it. They behave as though whoever does not get first place, which one person can have, and no more, could not deserve anything, or only last place, although there are degrees of glory as of merit [...] I understand that the old gentleman from Ravenna, a competent judge of such matters, always likes to assign you third place whenever the subject comes up. If this is too lowly, if I appear to block your way to first place, which I do not do, look, I gladly yield and leave second place to you; but if you spit at it, I am inclined to call you insufferable. In fact, if only those at the very top are illustrious, see how numerous are the ones in the dark, and how few are those reached by that light. You see, often second place is both safer and more advantageous. Ahead of you is someone to absorb envy's first blows, to show you the way at the risk of his own reputation, whose steps will teach you what to avoid and what to follow, someone to rouse you or shake off your numbness, someone for you to try to equal or to wish to surpass, so as not to see him always ahead of you.

Seniles 5.3[3]

Petrarch thus takes up Dante's request from *Paradiso* 10 directly—"Messo t'ho innanzi: omai per te ti ciba"—and recognizes the gesture of hospitality extended by his predecessor. Sitting down to the place set for him, he eats happily what is given willingly, receiving what he needs to be satisfied and to reproduce, in Dante's wake.

Boccaccio, too, picked up the thread, importing Dante's gluttons into the *Decameron*, and taking up the enigmatic figure of the glutton Ciacco from *Inferno* 6. If Ciacco remains shrouded in mystery for the reader of Dante, he gains a significant elaboration in Boccaccio's *Decameron*, where the author provides details about his life and the company he kept. In the eighth story of the ninth day, Ciacco is recalled as a gourmand without the money to support his gluttonous habits. He falls victim to a prank when he sees his would-be friend Biondello buying some excellent fish at the market, and believes he might have a chance to enjoy a specialty he would not have otherwise been able to afford. Insinuating himself into this sumptuous lunch, Ciacco finds that the expensive and rare lamprey he saw Biondello buying was only a lure, and that he has been tricked into eating a very humble meal of legumes and river fish. He later exacts his revenge on Biondello by enraging the wine salesman Filippo against him, who assaults Biondello upon seeing him. As Ciacco succinctly puts the lesson,

---

3   "Vidi ego, in convivio, aut confessu non sat honorifice locatum, subito surgere, extremunque ultro locum petere, humilitatis obtentu, sed superbiae impulsu, vide alium abire, et si hoc quiddam molle sit, vel ira, vel superbia, ita fiut hec quasi tui primus locus, qui unius, et non plurium esse potest, non obtigerit, non nisi aut nullo, dignus esse possit, aut ultimo, cum ut meritorum, sic et gloria gradus sint [...] Audio senem illum Ravenatem, rerum talium non ineptum iudicem, quotiens de his sermo est, semper tibi locum tertium assignare solitum. Si is sordet sique a primo obstare tibi videor, qui non obsto, ecce volens cedo locus tibi linquint secundus, hunc si respuis, nescio an ferendus fisque fin equidem soli primi clari sunt, que innumerabiles sint obscuri, quamque ad qucos ista lux redeat, advertere pronum vides, saepe cum tutior, tum altior secundus sit locus. Est qui primos invidiae ictus excipiat, qui tibi suae famae periculo viam signet, cuius vestigia intueare, quidve inns vites, et quid sequaris intelligas, qui te excitet, excutiatque torporem, quem aequare studeas, quem transire cupias, neu semper ante te videas, enitaris." Petrarch, *Letters of Old Age: Rerum senilium libri*, trans. Bernardo, Levin and Bernardo, vol. 1, p. 160.

"qualora tu mi vuogli cosí ben dare da mangiar come facesti, io darò a te cosí ben da bere come avesti" [since you wanted me to eat well, I wanted to be sure you drank equally well] (*Dec.* 9.8).[4] The gluttons of the bawdy and raucous world of the *Decameron* not only reveal Boccaccio's reliance on Dante's content, but also on his method, as Boccaccio pulls together the representative glutton Ciacco of *Inferno* 6, the fig of a punishment in exchange for a date of a sin that Fra'Alberigo suffers in *Inferno* 33, and the eels and wine of Martin IV in *Purgatorio* 24. He thus produces a vibrant new text that teaches a lesson through gluttony after consuming and digesting Dante's work.

These authors use Dante's work the way he intended—they see how food speaks, they engage with it; they are both influenced by the act of using food and by the contours Dante has given to the foods themselves. The ease with which those who came after him would employ this technique is a reminder that Dante's choice to invite his reading public to a table and speak to them by using this most basic form of communication as the cornerstone for his literary language truly created a new means of access, one that permitted the presence of a vast new audience while also laying the foundation for a new kind of authorship. As Albert Ascoli has asserted in his study of Dante and the construction of authority, the way to become an authority was to produce a text that "transcended the limitations of the inevitably fallible men who wrote them and to bear truths that exceeded the limitations of historical contingency—being valid in any time and any place."[5] The subtlety with which Dante performs the role of author while constructing it is one reason, Ascoli suggests, for which authority has been discussed so little with regard to Dante and his work. The ability to "naturalize" his authoritative position—make it appear "naturally supernatural"—enforces the radical change in who or what can be an author without giving reason for later readers to question or even consider the unlikelihood of his authority.[6] The relationship with food is the most natural and yet supernatural part of being human; Dante's ability to master and wield what is already present in nature is the ultimate sign of authority.

That the *Comedy* and its literary family continue to nourish a legacy of readership can only come from a space of vitality. The digestible nature of the work, which relies on the widely accessible, shared values of material food, while also being presented through a gesture of nourishment, allows

4   Branca, ed., *Decameron*, 9.8; Rebhorn, trans., *Decameron*, 9.8.
5   Ascoli, *Dante and the Making of a Modern Author*, p. 7.
6   Ibid., p. 13.

Dante to give his text the longevity he seeks. But beyond this, through food and its excessive or limited consumption, Dante finds the means to right a wrong that had detached him from the most human of experiences: citizenship. The salty bread of exile led him to understand how his individual suffering was also a symptom of a wrong that imperiled the very existence of citizenship and the human community at large. If there is irony to be seen in the fact that Dante goes to heaven and declares that he has not made the trip in order to learn anything about belonging to a community—"sì [...] e qui ragion non cheggio" (Yes [...] and here I ask for no proof; Par. 8.115–17)—there is nonetheless no rhetorical device or sleight of hand behind the poet Dante's suggestion that his readers follow him through Hell in order to come to the same conclusion. For Dante, community is not just worth living for; it is the only reason to live, and it is sustained or destroyed through the relationship with food, through feeding one another.

In the text he dedicates entirely to the presentation of his politics, *De Monarchia* [On Monarchy], Dante uses a metaphor based on gluttony to express the fundamental threat of the non-contributive member of a community. His natural desire and recognition of his duty to enrich the next generation will make him like a fruit tree, which flowers and fruits with each new season:[7]

> For all men whom the Higher Nature has endowed with a love of truth, this above all seems to be a matter of concern, that just as they have been enriched by the efforts of their forebears, so they too may work for future generations, in order that posterity may be enriched by their efforts. For the man who is steeped in the teaching which form our common heritage, yet has no interest in contributing something to the community, is failing in his duty: let him be in no doubt of that; for he is not "a tree planted by the rivers of water, that bringeth forth his fruit in due season" (Ps. 1:3), but rather a destructive whirlpool which forever swallows things down and never gives back what it has swallowed (*Mon.* 1.1).

---

7   "Omnium hominum quos ad amorem veritatis natura superior impressit hoc maxime interesse videtur: ut, quemadmodum de labore antiquorum ditati sunt, ita et ipsi posteris prolaborent, quatenus ab eis posteritas habeat quo ditetur. Longe nanque ab offitio se esse non dubitet qui, publicis documentis imbutus, ad rem publicam aliquid afferre non curat; non enim est lignum, quod secus decursus aquarum fructificat in tempore suo, sed potius perniciosa vorago semper ingurgitans et nunquam ingurgitata refundens." Original text and translation in Dante, *On Monarchy*, ed. and trans. Prue Shaw (Cambridge: Cambridge University Press, 1996), 00–00.

Where Dante has elsewhere been oblique, letting the presentation of food and eating practices lead his reader to the conclusions about the connection between an unrestrained appetite and the commitment to others, here instead he makes the leap quite plain: the person who has something to give but does not contribute to the community is a bottomless, insatiable pit—like the struggle against gluttony itself, the human *vorago* is a persistent adversary, swallowing and swallowing without ever pausing to think of how the next generation might be given what it needs to thrive. Indeed, perhaps the most telling of all of Dante's indictments of gluttony comes in his rewriting of the famous Epicurean motto, "Let us eat and drink for tomorrow we die" (manducemus et bibamus; cras enim moriemur). As George Corbett has highlighted, Dante transforms this in his *De vulgari eloquentia* into: "When the Florentines speak, they say things like 'Let's eat, as there's nothing else to do'" (locuntur Florentinie dicunt Manichiamo, introque che noi non facciamo altro; *De vulgari* 1.13.2).[8] On the contrary, as Dante reminds his reader, there is much to be done, and much to gain or lose through what and how we eat. The consumption of food is not a frivolity, but a crux of life in the most profound sense of the term, and gluttony, a danger to the individual body and soul and tantamount to the abdication of civic and spiritual responsibility, is a risk too great for a poet who knows the price of bread.

Works Cited

Alighieri, Dante. *De vulgari eloquentia*. Edited and translated by Steven Botterill. Cambridge: Cambridge University Press, 2009.

Alighieri, Dante. *The Divine Comedy of Dante Alighieri*. Edited and translated by Robert M. Durling, with introduction and notes by Ronald L. Martinez and Robert M. Durling. 3 vols. New York: Oxford University Press, 1996–2003.

Alighieri, Dante. *On Monarchy*. Edited and translated by Prue Shaw. Cambridge: Cambridge University Press, 1996.

Ascoli, Albert. *Dante and the Making of a Modern Author*. Cambridge: Cambridge University Press, 2008.

Boccaccio, Giovanni. *Decameron*. Edited by Vittore Branca. Turin: Einaudi, 2014.

Boccaccio, Giovanni. *Decameron*. Edited and translated by Wayne A. Rebhorn. New York: Norton, 2014.

---

8   Dante, *De vulgari eloquentia*, ed. and trans. Botterill.

Marinetti, F.T. "La Divina Commedia è un verminaio dei glossatori." In *Teoria e invenzione Futurista*, introduction and notes Luciano De Maria. Milan: Mondadori, 1968.

Petrarch, Francis. *Letters of Old Age: Rerum senilium libri*. Translated by Aldo S. Bernardo, Saul Levin, and Reta A. Bernardo. 2 vols. Baltimore: Johns Hopkins University Press, 1992.

Verga, Giovanni. *I Malavoglia*. Edited by Feruccio Cecco. Milan: Edizioni il Polifilo, 1995.

Verga, Giovanni. *The House By the Medlar Tree*. Translated by Mary A. Craig. New York: Harper, 1890.

Bibliography

Albala, Ken. *A Cultural History of Food in the Renaissance*. London: Bloomsbury, 2014.

Albala, Ken. *Eating Right in the Renaissance*. Berkeley: University of California Press, 2002.

Albertus Magnus. *Opera omnia*. Edited by Auguste Borgnet. 9 vols. Paris: Ludovicum Vives,

Alfie, Fabian. *Dante's* Tenzone *with Forese Donati: The Reprehension of Vice*. Toronto:University of Toronto Press, 2011.

Alighieri, Dante. *The Banquet*. Edited and translated by Christopher Ryan. Saratoga, CA: Anma, 1989.

Alighieri, Dante. *La Commedia secondo l'antico vulgata*. Edited by Giorgio Petrocchi. 4 vols. Milan: Mondadori, 1966–1967.

Alighieri, Dante. *Convivio*. Edited by Giorgio Inglese. Milan: Biblioteca Universale Rizzoli, 1993.

Alighieri, Dante. *The Divine Comedy of Dante Alighieri*. Edited and translated by Robert M. Durling, with introduction and notes by Ronald L. Martinez and Robert M. Durling. 3 vols. New York: Oxford University Press, 1996–2003.

Alighieri, Dante. *The Divine Comedy: 1. Inferno*. Translated, and with a commentary, by Charles S. Singleton. Princeton: Princeton University Press, 1970.

Alighieri, Dante. *De vulgari eloquentia*. Edited and translated by Steven Botterill. Cambridge: Cambridge University Press, 2009.

Ambrose. *De Helia et ieiunio*. Turnhout: Brepols, 2010.

Aquinas, Thomas. *On Evil*. Edited and introduction by Brian Davies. Translated by Richard Regan. Oxford: Oxford University Press, 2003.

Aquinas, Thomas. *Summa Theologiae*. Translated by Fathers of the English Domenican Province. 3 vols. New York: Benziger, 1948.

Aristotle. *De anima*. Edited by Christopher John Shields. Oxford: Oxford University Press, 2020.

Ascoli, Albert. *Dante and the Making of a Modern Author*. Cambridge: Cambridge University Press, 2008.

Ascoli, Albert. "Ponete mente almeno come io son bella: Prose and Poetry, 'pane' and 'vivanda,' Goodness and Beauty, in *Convivio* 1." In *Dante's* Convivio: *or How to Restart a Career in Exile*, edited by Franziska Meier, 115–143. Bern: Lang, 2018.

Augustine. *The City of God Against the Pagans*. 7 vols. Translated by George E. McCracken, et. al. Cambridge, Mass.: Harvard University Press, 1957–1972.

Augustine. *Confessions*. Translated by R. S. Pine-Coffin. New York: Penguin, 1961.

Augustine. *Enarrationes en Psalmos*. 3 vols. Turnhout: Brepols, 1956.

Augustine. *Sermons*. Translated by Edmund Hill, O.P. Hyde Park, NY: New City Press, 1990.

Baldelli, Ignazio. "Castrone." In *Enciclopedia Dantesca*, edited by Umberto Bosco. Rome: Istituto della Enciclopedia italiana, 1970–75.

Baraka, Amiri. *The System of Dante's Hell*. New York: Grove Press, 1963.

Barker, Francis, Peter Hulme, and Margaret Iversen, eds. *Cannibalism and the Colonial World*. Cambridge: Cambridge University Press, 1998.

Barolini, Teodolinda. *Dante and the Origins of Italian Literary Culture*. Fordham: Fordham University Press, 2006.

Barolini, Teodolinda. *Dante's Poets: Textuality and Truth in the Divine Comedy*. Princeton: Princeton University Press, 1984.

Barolini, Teodolinda. "From Editorial History to Hermeneutic Failure." In *Dante's Lyric Poetry: Poems of Youth and of the Vita Nuova*, edited by Teodolinda Barolini and translated by Richard Lansing, 3–28. Toronto: University of Toronto Press, 2014.

Barolini, Teodolinda. "'Only Historicize': History, Material Culture and the Future of Dante Studies." *Dante Studies* 127 (2009): 37–54.

Barolini, Teodolinda. "Sociology of the *Brigata*: Gendered Groups in Dante, Forese, Folgore, Boccaccio—From 'Guido, i' vorrei' to Grisela." *Italian Studies* 67, no. 1 (2012): 4–22.

Barolini, Teodolinda. *The Undivine Comedy: Detheologizing Dante*. Princeton: Princeton University Press, 1992.

Barthes, Roland. *The Rustle of Language*. Translated by Richard Howard. Berkeley: University of California Press, 1989.

Bartlett, Robert. *The Making of Europe: Conquest, Colonization, and Cultural Change, 950-1350*. Princeton, NJ: Princeton University Press, 1994.

Bianchi, Luca. "*Noli comedere panem philosophorum inutiliter*: Dante Alighieri and John of Jandun on Philosophical 'Bread.'" *Tijdschrift voor Filosofie* 75 (2013): 335–355.

Boccaccio, Giovanni. *Decameron*. Edited by Vittore Branca. Turin: Einaudi, 2014.

Boggioni, Valter and Giovanni Casalengo. *Dizionario storico del lessico erotico italiano: Metafore, eufemismi, oscenità, doppi sensi, parole dotte, parole basse in otto secoli di letterature italiana*. Milan: Longanesi, 1996.

Bosco, Umberto, ed. *Enciclopedia Dantesca*. 6 vols. Rome: Istituto della Enciclopedia italiana, 1970-75.

Borges Jorge Luis. *Selected Non-Fictions*. Edited by Eliot Weinberger. New York: Viking, 1999.

Boyde, Patrick. *Dante Philomythes and Philosopher: Man in the Cosmos*. Cambridge: Cambridge University Press, 1981.

Boyde, Patrick. *Perception and Passion in Dante's Comedy*. Cambridge: Cambridge University Press, 1993.

Brague, Remi. *The Legend of the Middle Ages: Philosophical Explorations of Medieval Christianity, Judaism, and Islam*. Translated by Lydia G. Cochrane. Chicago: University of Chicago Press, 2009.

Bynum, Caroline Walker. "Fast, Feast, Flesh: The Religious Significance of Food to Medieval Women." In *Food and Culture: A Reader*, edited by Carole Counihan and Penny Van Esterik, 138–158. New York: Routledge, 2008.

Bynum, Caroline Walker. *Holy Feast and Holy Fast: The Religious Significance of Food to Medieval Women*. Berkeley: University of California Press, 1987.

Bynum, Caroline Walker. *The Resurrection of the Body in Western Christianity, 200–1336*. New York: Columbia University Press, 1995.

Camporesi, Piero. *The Magic Harvest: Food, Folklore and Society*. Translated by Joan K. Hall. Cambridge: Polity Press, 1993.

Capatti, Alberto and Massimo Montanari. *La cucina italiana: Storia di una cultura*. Rome: Laterza, 1999.

Carruthers, Mary. *The Book of Memory*. Cambridge: Cambridge University Press, 1990.

Carruthers, Mary. *The Craft of Thought: Meditation Rhetoric, and the Making of Images 400-1200*. Cambridge: Cambridge University Press, 1998.

Cassian, John. *Conferences*. Edited and translated by Boniface Ramsey. Mahwah, NJ: Paulist Press, 1997.

Cherubini, Giovanni. *Agricoltura e società nel medioevo*. Florence: Sansoni, 1977.

Cherubini, Giovanni. *Città comunali di Toscana*. Bologna: CLUEB, 2003.

Cherubini, Giovanni. *Le città europee del medioevo*. Milan: Mondadori, 2009.

Cherubini, Giovanni. "The Peasant and Agriculture." In *Medieval Callings*, edited by Jacques Le Goff, 112–136. Chicago: University of Chicago Press, 1990.

Ciabattoni, Francesco. *Dante's Journey to Polyphony*. Toronto: University of Toronto Press, 2010.

Cook, William R. and Ronald B. Herzman. "Inferno XXXIII: The Past and Present in Dante's Imagery of Betrayal." *Italica* 56, No. 4 (Winter 1979): 377-383.

Cornish, Alison. "Music, Justice, and Violence in *Paradiso* 20." *Dante Studies* 134 (2016): 112–141.

Cornish, Alison. *Vernacular Translation in Dante's Italy: Illiterature Literature*. Cambridge: Cambridge University Press, 2011.

Courcelle, Pierre. *Late Latin Writers and their Greek Sources*. Translated by Harry E. Wedeck. Cambridge: Harvard University Press, 1969.

Curtius, Ernst Robert, *European Literature and the Latin Middle Ages*. Translated by Willard R. Trask. Princeton, NJ: Princeton University Press, 1953.

Dameron, George. "Feeding the Medieval Italian City-State: Grain, War, and Political Legitimacy in Tuscany, c. 1150–c. 1350." *Speculum* 92, no. 4 (October 2017): 976–1019.

Dartmouth Dante Project. "Comedia di Dante degli Allaghieri col Commento di Jacopo della Lana bolognese." Accessed July 7, 2021. https://dante.dartmouth.edu.

Dartmouth Dante Project. "Commento di Francesco da Buti sopra La Divina Commedia di Dante Allighieri." Accessed July 7, 2021. https://dante.dartmouth.edu.

Day, William. "Economy." In *Dante in Context*, edited by Zygmunt G. Baranski and Lino Pertile, 30–46. Cambridge: Cambridge University Press, 2015.

de Bury, Richard. *Philobiblon*. New York: P.C. Duschnes, 1945.

Di Pietro, Robert J. "Lectura Dantis: Inferno 33." *Lectura Dantis: A Forum for Dante Research and Interpretation* 1, no. 1 (1987): 73-84.

Dombroski, Robert. "The Grain of Hell: A Note on Retribution in *Inferno 6*." *Dante Studies* 88 (1970): 103–108.

Douglas, Mary. "Deciphering a Meal." *Daedalus* 101, no. 1 (Winter 1972): 61–81.

D'Ovidio, Francesco. *Nuovi studii danteschi: Ugolino, Pier della Vigna, i Simoniaci*. Milan: Hoepli, 1907.

Durling, Robert. "Deceit and Digestion in the Belly of Hell." In *Allegory and Representation: Selected Papers from the English Institute, 1979–1980,* edited by Stephen Greenblatt, 61–93. Baltimore: Johns Hopkins University Press, 1981.

Durling, Robert. "Body." In *The Dante Encyclopedia*, edited by Richard Lansing, 115–118. New York: Garland, 2000.

Durling, Robert. "The Body and the Flesh in the *Purgatorio*." In *Dante for the New Millennium*, edited by Teodolina Barolini and H. Wayne Storey, 183–191. Fordham: Fordham University Press, 2003.

Fiorilla, Maurizio. "Frate Alberigo e Branca Doria fra tradizioni antiche e riscritture moderne." In *Lectura Dantis Interamnensis*, edited by Giancarlo Rati, 155-177. Rome: Bulzoni, 2010.

Fisher, M. F. K. *An Alphabet for Gourmets*. New York: North Point Press, 1949.

Flandrin, Jean-Louis, and Odile Redon. "Les livres de cuisine italiens des XIVe et et XVe siècles." *Archeologia medievale* 8 (1981): 393–408

Flandrin, Jean-Louis and Massimo Montanari, eds. *Storia dell'alimentazione*. Rome: Laterza, 1996.

Foster, Kenelm and Patrick Boyde, eds. and trans. *Dante's Lyric Poetry*, 2 vols. Oxford: Clarendon Press, 1967.

Freccero, John. *The Poetics of Conversion*. Edited and with an introduction by Rachel Jacoff. Cambridge: Harvard University Press, 1986.

Freedman, Paul, ed. *Food: A History of Taste*. Berkeley: University of California Press, 2007.

Freedman, Paul. *Out of the East: Spices and the Medieval Imagination* (New Haven: Yale University Press, 2008.

Freedman, Paul. "Spices and Late-Medieval European Ideas of Scarcity and Value." *Speculum* 80, no. 4 (Oct. 2005): 1209–227.

Frosini, Giovanna. *Il cibo e i signori: La mensa dei priori di Firenze nel quinto decennio del sec. XIV.* Florence: Accademia della Crusca, 1993.

Giagnacovo, Maria. "Due 'alimentazioni' del basso Medioevo: la tavola dei mercanti e la tavola dei ceti subalterni." *Alimentazione e nutrizione secc. XIII-XVIII*, edited by Silvia Cavaciocchi, 821–830. Florence: Le Monnier, 1997.

Giagnacovo, Maria. *Mercanti a tavola: prezzi e consumi alimentari dell'azienda Datini di Pisa.* Florence: Opus, 2002.

Gibbons, David. "Alimentary Metaphors in Dante's *Paradiso.*" *The Modern Language Review* 96, no. 3 (2001): 693–706.

Gilson, Etienne. *Dante et la philosophie.* Paris: Vrin, 1972.

Gilson, Simon. "The Anatomy and Physiology of the Human Body in the *Commedia.*" In *Dante and the Human Body: Eight Essays,* edited by John C. Barnes and Jennifer Petrie, 43–60. Dublin: Four Courts Press, 2007.

Gilson, Simon A. "Medieval Magical Lore and Dante's *Commedia*: Divination and Demonic Agency." *Dante Studies* 119 (2001): 27-66.

Goodson, Caroline, Carol Symes, and Anne Lester, eds. *Cities, Texts and Social Networks, 400–1500: Experiences and Perceptions of Medieval Urban Space.* New York: Routledge, 2010.

Goody, Jack. *Cooking, Cuisine and Class: A Study in Comparative Sociology.* Cambridge: Cambridge University Press, 1982.

Gorni, Guglielmo. *Il nodo della lingua e il verbo d'amore: Studi su Dante e altri duecentisti.* Florence: Olschki, 1981.

Gowers, Emily. *The Loaded Table: Representations of Food in Roman Literature.* Oxford: Oxford University Press, 1997.

Grafton, Anthony, Glenn W. Most, and Salvatore Settis, eds. *The Classical Tradition.* Cambridge: Harvard University Press, 2010.

Gragnolati, Manuele. *Experiencing the Afterlife: Soul and Body in Dante and Medieval Culture.* South Bend: University of Notre Dame Press, 2005.

Gragnolati, Manuele. "From Plurality to (Near) Unicity of Forms: Embryology in *Purgatorio* 25." In *Dante for the New Millenium.* Edited by Wayne Storey and Teodolinda Barolini, 192-210. New York: Fordham University Press, 2003.

Gragnolati, Manuele. "Gluttony and the Anthropology of Pain in Dante's *Inferno* and *Purgatorio.*" In *History in the Comic Mode: Medieval Communities and the Matter of Person,* edited by Rachel Fulton Brown and Bruce Holsinger, 238–250. New York: Columbia University Press, 2015.

Grieco, Allen J. *Food, Social Politics and the Order of Nature in Renaissance Italy.* Cambridge, Mass.: Harvard University Press, 2019.

Grieco, Allen J. "From Roosters to Cocks: Italian Renaissance Fowl and Sexuality." In *Erotic Cultures of Renaissance Italy,* edited by Sara F. Matthews-Grieco, 110–122. Surrey: Ashgate, 2010.

Grieco, Allen J. "Menu, Banchetti e Tavole Imbandite in Toscana." In *Et coquatur ponendo: cultura della cucina e della tavola in Europa tra medioevo e eta moderna*, eds. Orazio Bagnasco, et. al., 373–379. Prato: Istituto internazionale di storia economica 'Francesco Datini,' 1996.

Grieco, Allen J. "The Social Politics of Pre-Linnaean Botanical Classification." *I Tatti Studies: Essays in the Renaissance* 4 (1991): 131–149.

Grosz, Elizabeth. *Volatile Bodies: Towards a Corporeal Feminism* London: Routledge, 1994.

Guest, Kristen, ed. *Eating Their Words: Cannibalism and the Boundaries of Cultural Identity*. Albany: State University of New York Press, 2001.

Grumett, David and Rachel Muers. *Theology on the Menu: Asceticism, Meat and Christian Diet*. London: Routledge, 2010.

Hanska, Jussi. "'Volebam tamen ut nomen michi esset Dyonisius': Fra Salimbene, Wine and Well-Being." In *Mental (Dis)Order in Later Medieval Europe*. Edited by Sari Katajala-Peltomaa and Susanna Niiranen, 128-150. Leiden: Brill, 2014.

Hawkins, Peter S. "Nightmare and Dream: The Earthly City in Dante's *Commedia*." In *Civitas: Religious Interpretations of the City*, edited by Peter S. Hawkins, 71–84. Atlanta: Scholars Press, 1986.

Hawkins, Peter S. "Dante's Lesson of Silence: *Paradiso* 21." *Lectura Dantis* 11 (1992): 42–51.

Henderson, John. *Piety and Charity in Late Medieval Florence*. Chicago: University of Chicago Press, 1994.

Henisch, Bridget. *Fast and Feast: Food in Medieval Society*. University Park: The Pennsylvania State University, 1976.

Herlihy, David. *Pisa in the Early Renaissance: A Study in Urban Growth*. New Haven: Yale University Press, 1958

Herlihy, David. *Medieval Households*. Cambridge, Mass.: Harvard University Press, 1985.

Herlihy, David. "Medieval Demography." In *Dictionary of the Middle Ages*, vol. 4, edited by Joseph R. Strayer, 136–48. New York: Scribner, 1989.

Herzman, Ronald. "Cannibalism and Communion in *Inferno* XXXIII." *Dante Studies* 98 (1980): 53-78.

Hill, Susan. *Eating to Excess: The Meaning of Gluttony and the Fat Body in the Ancient World*. Oxford: Praegar, 2011.

Hoffman, Richard C. *An Environmental History of Medieval Europe*. Cambridge: Cambridge University Press, 2014.

Holloway, Julia Bolton. *Twice-Told Tales: Brunetto Latini and Dante Alighieri*. New York: Peter Lang, 1993.

Hugh of St. Victor. *De Tribus Maximis Circumstantiis Gestorum*. Edited by William M. Green. *Speculum* 18, no. 4 (1943): 484–493.

Hulme, Peter. "Introduction: The Cannibal Scene." In *Cannibalism and the Colonial World,* edited by Francis Barker, Peter Hulme, and Margaret Iversen, 1-38. Cambridge: Cambridge University Press, 1998.

Ito, Marie D'Aguanno. "Orsanmichele – The Florentine Grain Market: Trade and Worship in the Later Middle Ages," Ph.D. diss, The Catholic University of America, January 2014.

Jerome. *Select Letters.* Translated by F. A. Wright. Cambridge, Mass.: Harvard University Press, 1933.

Jordan, William Chester. *The Great Famine: Northern Europe in the Early Fourteenth Century.* Princeton: Princeton University Press, 1996.

Kantorowicz, Ernst. *The King's Two Bodies: A Study in Mediaeval Political Theology.* Princeton: Princeton University Press, 1957.

Keen, Catherine. *Dante and the City.* Gloucestershire: Tempus, 2003.

Lancerio, Sante. *I vini d'Italia giudicati da papa Paolo III Farnese e dal suo bottigliere Sante Lancerio.* Livorno: Bastogi, 1890. Reprinted with an introduction by Arturo Celentano. Capri (Naples): La Conchiglia, 2004.

La Roncière, Charles M. de. *Florence: centre economique regional au XIVe siecele: le marche des denrees de premiere necessite a Florence et dans sa campagne et les conditions de la vie des salaries, 1320–1380.* 3 vols. Aix-en-Provence: S.O.D.E.B., 1976.

La Roncière, Charles M. de. *Prix et salaires à Florence au XIVe siècle (1280–1380).* Rome: École Française de Rome, 1982.

Laurioux, Bruno. *Le moyen âge à table.* Paris: Biro, 1989.

Laurioux, Bruno. "I libri di cucina italiani alla fine del Medioevo: un nuovo bilancio." *Archivio Storico Italiano* 154, no. 1 (Jan-March 1996): 33–58.

Laurioux, Bruno, ed. *Scrivere il Medioevo: lo spazio, la santità, il cibo, un libro dedicato ad Odile Redon.* Rome: Viella, 2001.

Laurioux, Bruno. "Table et hiérarchie social à la fin du moyen âge." In *Du manuscrit à la table: essais sur la cuisine au moyen âge et répertoire des manuscrits médiévaux contenant des recettes culinaries,* edited by Carole Lambert, 87–108. Montreal: Université de Montréal, 1992.

Le Goff, Jacques. *La civilisation de l'occident médiéval.* Paris: Arthaud, 1964.

Le Goff, Jacques, ed. *Dizionario dell'occidente medievale.* 2 vols. Turin: Einaudi, 2011.

Lincoln, Bruce. *Discourse and the Construction of Society: Comparative Studies of Myth, Ritual, and Classification.* Oxford: Oxford University Press, 2014.

Lovejoy, Arthur O. *The Great Chain of Being.* Cambridge: Harvard University Press, 1936.

Lubac, Henri de. *Medieval Exegesis: The Four Senses of Scripture.* 3 vols. Translated by E.M. Macierowski. Grand Rapids, MI: Eerdsman Publishing, 2000.

Lukács, György. *The Theory of the Novel: A Historico-philosophical Essay on the Forms of Great Epic Literature.* Translated by Anna Bostock Berger. Cambridge, Mass.: MIT Press, 1971.

Malgarini, Patrizia Bertini. "Il linguaggio medico e anatomico nelle opere di Dante." *Studi Danteschi* 61 (1989): 1–108.

Marchesi, Simone. "'Epicuri de grege porcus': Ciacco Epicurus and Isidore of Seville." *Dante Studies* 117 (1999): 117–131.

Martellotti, Anna. *I ricettari di Federico II. Dal* Meridionale *al* Liber de coquina. Florence: Olschki, 2005.

Martin, A. Lynn. "The Baptism of Wine." *Gastronomica* 3, no. 4 (Fall 2003): 21–30.

Martinez, Ronald L. "Dante 'buon sartore' (*Paradiso* 32.140): Textile Arts, Rhetoric, and Metapoetics at the End of the Commedia." *Dante Studies* 136 (2018): 22–61.

Martinez, Ronald L. "Dante's Jeremiads: The Fall of Jerusalem and the Burden of the Pharisees, the Capetians, and Florence." In *Dante for the New Millennium*, edited by Teodolinda Barolini and Wayne H. Storey, 301–319. New York: Fordham University Press, 2003.

Mazzotta, Giuseppe. "Dante's Poetics of Births and Foundations." *Dante Studies* 127 (2009): 129–146.

Mazzotta, Giuseppe. *Reading Dante*. New Haven: Yale University Press, 2013.

Miller, William Ian. "Gluttony." *Representations* 60 (Autumn 1997): 92–112.

Montanari, Massimo. *L'alimentazione contadina nell'alto Medioevo*. Naples: Liguori, 1979.

Montanari, Massimo. *Alimentazione e cultura nel medioevo*. Rome: Laterza, 1988.

Montanari, Massimo. *Campagne medievali: Struttura produttive, rapporti di lavoro, sistemi alimentari*. Turin: Einaudi, 1984.

Montanari, Massino. *La fame e l'abbondanza*. Rome: Laterza, 2006.

Montanari, Massimo. *Gusti del medioevo*. Rome: Laterza, 2012.

Montanari, Massimo. *Medieval Tastes: Food, Cooking, and the Table*. Translated by Beth Archer Brombert. New York: Columbia University Press, 2015.

Nardi, Bruno. *Dante e la cultura medievale: nuovi saggi di filosofia dantesca*. Rome: Laterza, 1949.

Nardi, Bruno. *Nel mondo di Dante*. Rome: Edizioni di Storia e Letteratura, 1944.

Nardi, Bruno. *Studi di filosofia medievale*. Rome: Edizioni di Storia e Letteratura, 1960.

Najemy, John. *A History of Florence, 1200–1575*. Oxford: Blackwell, 2008.

Nicoud, Marilyn. "Food Consumption, a Health Risk? Norms and Medical Practice in the Middle Ages." *Appetite* 51 (July 2008): 7-9.

Nicoud, Marilyn. "Nutrirsi secondo i medici nell'età antica e medievale." In *Nutrire il corpo, nutrire l'anima nel Medioevo*, edited by Chiara Crisciana and Onorato Grassi, 41–68. Pisa: Edizioni ETS, 2017.

Nicoud, Marilyn. *Les régimes de santé au Moyen Âge: Naissance et diffusion d'une écriture médicale*, 2 vols. Rome: Ecole française de Rome, 2007.

Noakes, Susan. "Virility, Nobility, and Banking: The Crossing of Discourses in the *Tenzone* with Forese." In *Dante for the New Millennium*, edited by Teodolinda Barolini and H. Wayne Storey, 241–258. New York: Fordham University Press, 2003.

Nutton, Vivian. "Dante, Medicine and the Invisible Body." In *Dante and the Human Body: Eight Essays,* edited by John C. Barnes and Jennifer Petrie, 11–42. Dublin: Four Courts Press, 2007.

O'Brien, William J. "The 'Bread of Angels' in *Paradiso* II: A Liturgical Note." *Dante Studies* 97 (1979): 97–106.

Ó Gráda, Cormac. *Famine: A Short History*. Princeton: Princeton University Press, 2009.

Olson, Kristina. "Uncovering the Historical Body of Florence: Dante, Forese Donati, and Sumptuary Legislation." *Italian Culture* 33, no. 1 (March 2015): 1–15.

Olson, Kristina. "Shoes, Gowns and Turncoats: Reconsidering Cacciguida's History of Florentine Fashion and Politics." *Dante Studies* 134 (2016): 26–47.

Origo, Iris. *The Merchant of Prato: Francesco di Marco Datini, 1335-1410.* Jaffrey, NH: Nonpareil, 1986. First published 1917.

Palma, Pina. *Savoring Power, Consuming the Times: The Metaphors of Food in Medieval and Renaissance Italian Literature*. South Bend, IN: University of Notre Dame Press, 2013.

Pease, Arthur Stanley. "Medical Allusions in the Works of St. Jerome." *Harvard Studies in Classical Philology* 25 (1914): 73-86.

Pertile, Lino. "Ciacco, Brunetto and the Voice of God." In *Legato con amore: Essay in Honor of John A. Scott*, 157–174. Florence: L.S. Olschki, 2013.

Pertile, Lino. "Il nodo di Bonagiunta, le penne di Dante e il Dolce Stil Novo." *Lettere italiane* 46 (1994): 44–75.

Peter of Poitiers. *Sententiae Petri Pictaviensis*. Edited by Marthe Dulong and Philip S. Moore. Notre Dame: University of Notre Dame Press, 1943–50.

Petrarch, Francis. *Letters of Old Age: Rerum senilium libri*. Translated by Aldo S. Bernardo, Saul Levin, and Reta A. Bernardo. 2 vols. Baltimore: Johns Hopkins University Press, 1992.

Pietrobono, Luigi. *Dal centro al cerchio: la struttura morale della Commedia*. Turin: Società editrice internazionale, 1956.

Pike, Burton. *The Image of the City in Modern Literature*. Princeton: Princeton University Press, 1981.

Pinto, Giuliano. *Il libro del biadaiolo. Carestie e Annona a Firenze dalla metà del '200 al 1318*. Florence: Olschki, 1978.

Pinto, Giuliano. *Toscana medievale: paesaggi e realtà sociali*. Florence: Le Lettere, 1993.

Plato. *Timaeus, Critias, Cleitophon, Menexenus, Epistles*, edited and translated by R. G. Bury. Cambridge, Mass.: Loeb Classical Library, 1960

Purdy Moudarres, Christiana. "Bodily Starvation and the Ravaging of the Will: A Reading of *Inferno* 32–33." *Viator* 47, no. 1 (2016): 205–228

Purdy Moudarres, Christiana. *Table Talk: Perspectives on Food in Medieval Italian Literature.* Newcastle upon Tyne: Cambridge Scholars Publishing, 2010.

Quellier, Florent. *Gola: Storia di un peccato capitale.* Translated by Vito Carrassi. Bari: Edizioni Dedalo, 2012.

Reeds, Karen. "Albert on the Natural Philosophy of Plant Life." In *Albertus Magnus and the Sciences: Commemorative Essays 1980,* edited by James Weisheipl, 341-354. Toronto: Pontifical Institute of Medieval Studies, 1980.

Reynolds, Philip Lyndon. *Food and the Body: Some Peculiar Questions in High Medieval Theology.* Leiden: Brill, 1999.

Rousselle, Aline. "Abstinence et continence dans les monastères de Gaule méridion-ale à la fin de l'antiquité et au dèbut du moyen âge: Etude d'un regime alimentaire et da sa fonction." In *Hommages à André Dupont (1897-1972): Etudes médiévale languedociennes par ses anciens collègues, élèves et ami,* 239-54. Montpellier: Fédération Historique du Languedoc Mediterranéen et du Rousillon, Université Paul-Valery, 1974.

Scully, Terrence. *The Art of Cookery in the Middle Ages.* Woodbridge, UK: Boydell, 1995.

Seneca. *Epistolae morales ad Lucilium.* Translated by Richard M. Gummere. 10 vols. Cambridge, Mass.: Loeb Classical Library, 1920.

Sercambi, Giovanni. *Il novelliere.* Edited by Luciano Rossi. Rome: Salerno Editrice, 1974.

Shaw, Teresa M. *The Burden of the Flesh: Fasting and Sexuality in Early Christianity.* Minneapolis: Augsburg Fortress, 1998.

Shapiro, Marianne. *Dante and the Knot of Body and Soul.* New York: St. Martin's Press, 1998.

Shoaf, R. Allen. "Delivering Dante: Representations of Reproduction in the *Commedia*." *MLN* 127, no. S1 (January 2012): S81-90.

Schnapp, Jeffrey. "Introduction to *Purgatorio*." In *The Cambridge Companion to Dante,* edited by Rachel Jacoff, 2nd ed., 91–106. Cambridge: Cambridge University Press, 2007.

Siraisi, Nancy. *Taddeo Alderotti and his Pupils: Two Generations of Italian Medical Learning.* Princeton: Princeton University Press, 1981.

Siraisi, Nancy. *Medieval & Early Renaissance Medicine: An Introduction to Knowledge and Practice.* Chicago: University of Chicago Press, 1990.

Squatriti, Paolo. *Water and Society in Early Medieval Italy.* Cambridge: Cambridge University Press, 1998.

Steinberg, Justin. *Dante and the Limits of the Law.* Chicago: University of Chicago Press, 2013.

Stephany, William A. "Dante's Harpies: 'Tristo annunzio di futuro danno.'" In *The Poetry of Allusion: Virgil and Ovid in Dante's* Commedia. Edited by Rachel Jacoff and Jeffrey Schnapp, 37–44. Stanford: Stanford University Press, 1991.

Strong, Roy. *Feast: A History of Grand Eating.* London: Jonathan Cape, 2002.

Toussaint-Samat, Maguelonne. *A History of Food.* Translated by Anthea Bell. London: Wiley-Blackwell, 2009.

Treherne, Matthew. "Liturgical Personhood: Creation, Penitence, and Praise in the *Commedia.*" In *Dante's* Commedia: *Theology as Poetry,* edited by Vittorio Montemaggi and Matthew Treherne, 131-160. South Bend: University of Notre Dame Press, 2010.

Triolo, Alfred. "Inferno 33: Fra Alberigo in Context." *L'Alighieri* 11 (1970): 39-70.

Tucci, Hannelore Zug. "La caccia, da bene comune a privilegio." In *Storia d'Italia: Annali,* vol. 6, edited by Ruggiero Romano and Ugo Tucci, 397–445. Turin: Einaudi, 1983.

Verga, Giovanni. *I Malavoglia.* Edited by Feruccio Cecco. Milan: Edizioni il Polifilo, 1995.

Verga, Giovanni. *The House By the Medlar Tree.* Translated by Mary A. Craig. New York: Harper, 1890.

Villa, Claudia. "Rileggere gli archetipi: la dismisura di Ugolino." In *Leggere Dante,* edited by Lucia Battaglia Ricci, 113-129. Ravenna: Longo, 2003.

Villa, Claudia. "'Unicuique suum': Observations on Dante as a Reader of Classical Authors." In *Italy and the Classical Tradition: Language, Thought, and Poetry, 1300-1600.* Edited by Carlo Caruso and Andrew Laird. London: Bloomsbury, 2013.

Virgil. *Aeneid.* Translated by Robert Fitzgerald. New York: Random House, 1983.

Webb, Heather. "Dante's Stone Cold Rhymes." *Dante Studies* 121 (2003): 149–168.

Weisheipl, James. ed. *Albertus Magnus and the Sciences: Commemorative Essays 1980.* Toronto: Pontifical Institute of Medieval Studies, 1980.

William of Conches. *Glossae super Boethium.* Turnhout: Brepols, 2010.

Williams, A. N. "The Theology of the *Comedy.*" In *The Cambridge Companion to Dante,* 2nd ed., edited by Rachel Jacoff, 201-217. Cambridge: Cambridge University Press, 2007.

Yowell, Donna. "Ugolino della Gherardesca." In *The Dante Encyclopedia,* edited by Richard Lansing, 1586-1591. New York: Routledge, 2010.

Zama, Piero. *I Manfredi, signori di Faenza.* Faenza: Fratelli Lega, 1954.

Index

For Product Safety Concerns and Information please contact our EU
representative GPSR@taylorandfrancis.com
Taylor & Francis Verlag GmbH, Kaufingerstraße 24, 80331 München, Germany